Norfolk Recorders present

Norfolk Allotments

the plot so far

Research and writing:
Dinah Thompson

Survey:
Christopher Hulse
Julie Hulse

*Legal framework, research
and technical support:*
Bob Wilkinson
Judy Wilkinson

Illustrations:
Marian O'Hare

Published by Norfolk Recorders © 2007

Designed by Graham Land Creative Services, 01953 603200

 Printed by Norwich Colour Print, Drayton, Norfolk
on Cyclus Offset 140gsm recycled paper

resources for the community
care for the environment

This book is available for reproduction or reuse

ISBN 978-0-9555924-0-9

Norfolk Recorders thank the Local Heritage Initiative for its contribution to the
Norfolk allotments project with money provided by the National Lottery

Local Heritage *initiative*

Cover illustrations:
Front: Mousehold Allotments looking towards Norwich Cathedral © Judy Wilkinson
Back: Sheringham Allotments from the North Norfolk coastal path © Bob Wilkinson

contents

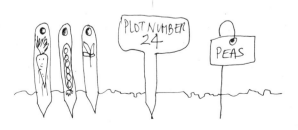

contents *continued*

*With thanks to Uncle Leslie
and codgers like him, old and new,
for the inspiration.*

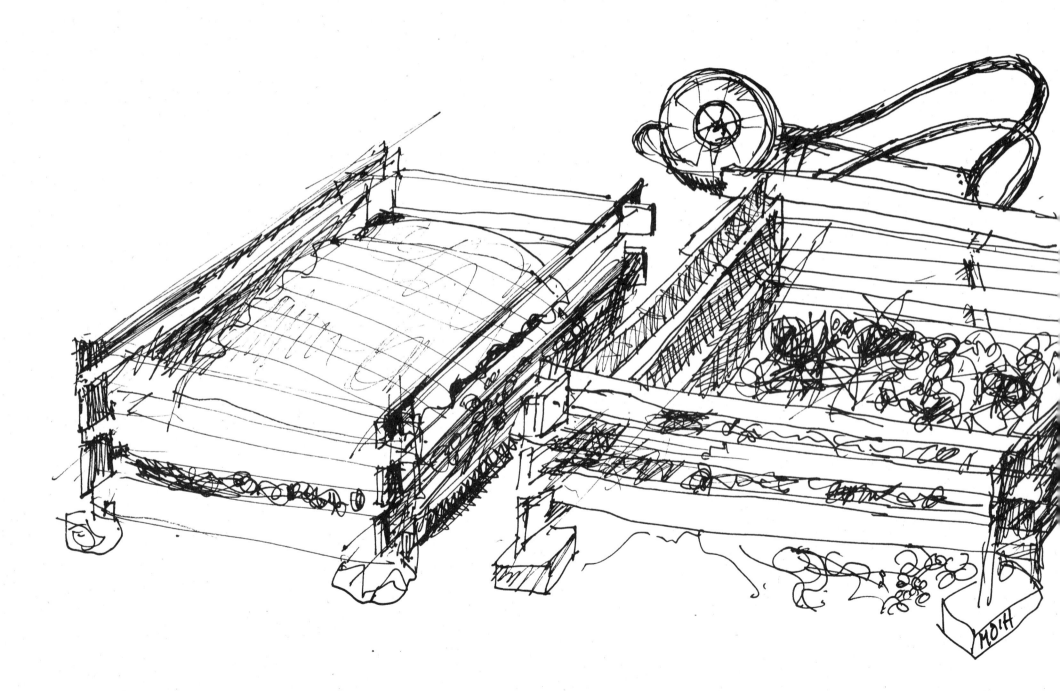

notes

abbreviations

In the text, names in bold print, like **Castle Acre**, **Cley-next-the-Sea** and so on, have a case-study. The symbol [] by the name of a case-study indicates that there are photographs of the site, collected by the Norfolk Recorders.

Words in bold italic print, like ***dole***, ***enclosure***, ***spong***, have a glossary entry.

Measurements given in the text have not been standardized. They are as found in written sources or maps or as provided by answers to the Survey questionnaires. For example, in nineteenth century materials which include Zachary Clark and Arthur Young's books, in reports to the Poor Law commissioners, and in parish allotments' registers areas are given as 'A R P', standing for 'acres rods poles(or perches)'.
On twentieth century Ordnance Survey maps areas are shown as acres to (usually) three decimal places. Current usage is for hectares to three decimal places. Sorry.

References in the text can be decoded by reference to the 'references and bibliography' section of the book; names that appear in capitals in the text have a reference. The bibliography, still rather small for this subject, is those books shown highlighted.

Where the reference is to material collected in the course of Norfolk Recorders' researches, it is given simply as 'Survey' in the main text.

ARI	Allotments Regeneration Initiative
DofE	Department of Environment
DETR	Department of the Evironment, Transport and the Regions
DEFRA	Department of the Environment, Farming and RegionalAffairs
CAEC	County Agriculture Emergency Committee
FACHRS	Family and Community Historical Research Society
GRLM	Gressenhall Rural Life Museum
LFS	Labourers' Friend Society
MAF	Ministry of Agriculture and Fisheries
MAFF	Ministry of Agriculture, Fisheries and Food
NAGT	National Allotment Gardens Trust
NALU	Norfolk Agricultural Labourers' Union
NAS	National Allotments Society
NRO	Norfolk Records Office
NSALG	National Society of Allotment and Leisure Gardeners
RHS	Royal Horticultural Society
SBCP	Society for the Betterment of the Conditions of the Poor
WarAgs	County Agriculture Emergency Committee

Thanks to the many people of Norfolk who helped the project with information and guidance and to historians and archivists amongst whom the Family and Community Historical Research Society played an important part. Thanks especially to Dr Sara Birtles for her support and generosity with materials and time.

1 | allotment origins and land ownership

*Among material resources, the greatest, unquestionably,
is the land. Study how a society uses its land, and you
can come to pretty reliable conclusions as to what its
future will be.*

Small is Beautiful (1973)
E F Schumacher

What we now know as allotments can be thought of as having two
identities. There are the familiar spaces of hand-worked and carefully-
tended vegetables, fruit and flowers, perhaps with a shed and a
compost heap, perhaps some trees, even a scarecrow or more likely
these days glittering cds strung across precious seedlings or fruiting
bushes. Allotment sites also have an existence in law, or more
accurately laws because there are several of them, to the irritation of
tenants, allotment associations and local authorities who find
themselves calling upon scattered pieces of legislation when they
establish and maintain allotment sites or waving disputed clauses when
sites are being 'moved' or eliminated. So the history of allotments is
about two sorts of things that coalesced. Going back as far as you like
into english history there were parcels of land that would be
recognizable today as allotments but the instantiation of allotments in
law is a fairly recent event, a recognition of more than just the idea of
allotments but encapsulating the whole definition of property in an
emerging capitalist economy, of compromises and concessions, even of
a firmer grasp on british society of democracy.

Given that allotments' place in modern landscape, modern culture is
due to recent legal clarifications, it is hindsight that sees them in the
distant past. Probably the first british example of small bounded fields,
an essential element of the idea of an allotment, is found in the West
Country where vestiges of small fields marked by stone walls dating
from the Iron Age circa 100 *bce* can be seen on Dartmoor and Bodmin
Moor. Roman rulers with their genius for administration took the
principle a stage further by introducing a scheme for renting small plots

of land to needy retired army veterans from 123 *bce*, extended to England including Norfolk at what is now Norwich after the invasion in 43 *ce*. This aspect of the roman legacy did not survive after their departure nearly four hundred years later (Poole/5, pp16–7).

Prevailing opinion has them appear first in mediaeval England and there were two routes through which allotments can be traced. The first of these is the use of strips in farming (from which the Norfolk village names of Northrepps and Southrepps come), a mechanism that allocated land between competing claims and which gave farmers both subsistence and income. The limits of the strip were marked by a **dole**, either a landmark like a tree or by a stone for a boundary and these same marks indicated proprietorship as well: the dole showed the allocation of each farmer. One-acre strips can be seen still in the allotments of a number of Norfolk parishes (Lingwood, **Terrington-St-Clement**) and residual evidence of strip allotments marked by ditches is visible on the marshy land of Lolly Moor at **Westfield**.

Another reason for linking allotments to the mediaeval subsistence economy is that reliance on **commons** and **wastes** was a part of it and when **enclosure** began to encroach upon these open spaces local people had to establish their right to use the commons in order to be repaid with an allotment of land elsewhere. Commons were a significant part of the economy, enabling peasant farmers to use traditional skills towards their subsistence. 'In no part of England were common rights more important than in the Fenland', wrote H C Darby who describes the interdependence of Fenland villages (**Terrington-St-Clement** again) through intercommoning. Upland commons and water-meadows would have been used for grazing and the lowland parts supplied hay, fuel and timber, while fowl and fish were taken from the marshy and riverine sectors.

The idea of letting a small piece of land for private and personal use was an early one and, ironically, was enabled by enclosure: only when an institution or individual had sole title to land could they dispose of a chunk of it for rental. Enclosure of land to obtain sole use emerged as an official practice as early as the tenth century when the first Abbot of Ely, Brithnoth (970–81) laid claim to open land by creating boundaries

using ditches and hedges which would have had the further function of draining the land and making it fit for crop production. The farmer and cottager committed their fair share of sequestrations, too. Manorial court records and records of Quarter Sessions attest to seizure of land by ploughing beyond the strip, or by increasing a holding by taking a slice of highway, footpath or green lane. The Church owned land, may have had it awarded following the Norman Conquest or acquired it through bequest, purchase or enclosure, but farmed it independently of the laity. Norwich Cathedral accounts show that the gardens were a vital component of life within the precinct: 'wedged in amongst this motley array of buildings were gardens of all shapes, sizes and functions…' and letting between officials of the Cathedral was commonplace (Noble, p4). The natural historian, philosopher and physician to Queen Elizabeth I, Sir Thomas Browne, was granted a lease from the Dean and Chapter of 'a little meadowe in the precinct…during his naturell life' from 1669: 'In a meadow I use in this citty, besett about with sallowes, I have observed there to growe upon their bare heads builders, corants, gooseberries, *cynocrambe*, raspberries, barberries, bittersweet, elder, hawthorne'. The meadow was on the south side of a causeway leading to the ferry, presumably Pull's Ferry, which connected Cathedral land to the county beyond. Later the meadow accommodated houses and a vegetable garden for the Dean of Norwich, and then allotments for residents of the Close (Shaw, pp12–13). Although there is no direct line of succession, the Cathedral precinct has a walled garden plot to this day. Church officials were amongst the first to promote garden allotments in Norfolk, and still do.

Between strip farming and the emergence of garden allotments at the end of the eighteenth century there were economic and social developments and disjunctions which meant that garden allotments were introduced into a very different environment. Property and land ownership instead of rights, the exchange of contract in lieu of custom and practice – cash and rental – became the framework in which the need and desire and sometimes the demand for land to provide subsistence had to operate. There were also continuities, including the insistence on rights, and finally on the cusp of the twentieth century rights were given by law, not by word or understanding.

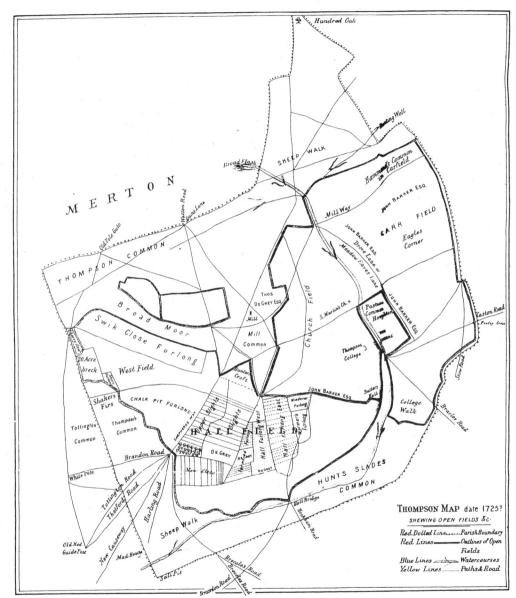

Figure 1.1: Map of the parish of Thompson, thought to be dated 1725. Central fields are marked in strips. (Thanks to the Stevenson Library, Norwich School)

Strip-farming persisted in Norfolk at least until the end of the eighteenth century, later than in other parts of the country where parliamentary enclosure had added legal status to allotments on top of their existence in the landscape, mostly as **poor's** and **fuel allotments**. Enclosure became a sore that chafed when events reduced further the meagre conditions of life of the poor labourer and artisans dependent upon them, invoking protest and even riot. The link between allotment and poverty persisted for hundreds of years, can even be glimpsed in the twentieth century, and provoked many instances of new law and many legal formulations designed to preserve the march of enclosure while redressing the balance of general rights to land for the commonalty. In 1235 came the earliest piece of legislation that addressed commons' rights. This was the Statute of Merton which allowed lords of the manor to appropriate entire commons as far as the wastes provided that sufficient grazing was left for any freeholders who claimed rights of pasturing. Eventually it was ignored and in 1489 the Husbandry Act, otherwise known as the Act Against the Pulling Down of Towns, required that any person owning twenty acres must maintain houses and buildings upon the ground and land necessary for maintaining and upholding tillage and husbandry. It was intended to protect the small farmer from the predations of the landowners on whose land he farmed. It was a failure. Sir Thomas More wrote a vivid critique of the process of enclosure in his book of 1516, *Utopia*:

> 'So what happens? Each greedy individual preys on his native land like a malignant growth, absorbing field after field, and enclosing thousands of acres with a single fence. Result – hundreds of farmers are evicted.'

More goes on to describe in withering detail the state of trade and growth of property, preoccupations that increasingly defined the nation's life and culture.

A connection between the poor and gardens was made through the medium of hospitals and almshouses. In Norfolk notable hospitals date back to 1553, the first year of Edward VI's reign, with the building of the Great Hospital in Bishopgate, Norwich. Trinity Hospital at Castle Rising was founded in 1616 by Henry Earl of Northampton and endowed with £100 per year for its maintenance. He intended it 'for the support of thirteen poor spinsters and widows aged fifty and over: six should be from Castle Rising, four of Roydon and two of North Wootton'. There were apartments for a governess, a common hall and a chapel, and "a garden surrounded by a wall and divided into portions for the almspeople; and another garden on the north-west divided in the same manner" (White's *Trade Directory 1845*, p590). Similarly King's Lynn Hospital of St Mary Magdalen, Gaywood was rebuilt to consist of twelve tenements and a chapel creating a quadrangle with a grass plot in the centre and small gardens around the exterior. Lynn also had various almshouses, including Framingham's Hospital in Broad Street completed by 1704 and comprising a small chapel and twelve single-roomed dwellings forming a square, with a small piece of garden attached to each.

At the same time as the ordinary man found himself shunted to the margins of society another process was occurring which would contribute to the mix from which allotments evolved. The european climate became as unsettled as its intellectual life, with the shift into the Little Ice Age from the 1530s. This was a period of some three hundred years during which weather fluctuated between extremes: it was not unremittingly bad but the bad patches were very bad indeed – the Thames famously froze over in 1564, six times between 1607 and 1749 and ten times from 1708 to 1814 – which led to dearth and disease.

Disparities in wealth between rich and poor led to disaffection across the country. Norfolk brewed its own mixture of rebellion. In 1549 Robert Kett at the head of ten thousand men marched on Norwich and encamped just outside the city precinct for seven weeks. Whatever the exact provocation, local enclosure was the visible part of the mix of reasons, exacerbating if not being sufficient cause for the perceived injustice which clearly was felt by many thousands of ordinary folk. In 1589 Elizabeth I created an early version of the poor laws in the form of an Act which established a right arising from a need for land, recognizing that if land was entirely withheld from the poor then abject poverty and social ill would follow. It required cottages (with certain stated exceptions) to have 'four acres of land attached' – the allotment

– 'and a cow', deemed to be necessary to keep a cottager and his family in subsistence.

As enclosure and improvement of the land to make it fit for farming continued inexorably, more great estates came into being and new game laws restricted the poor man's diet still further. One of the factors delaying the process in Norfolk was the General Drainage Act 1600 which permitted landowners to quash local rights to commons if they impeded drainage schemes: ambitious projects transformed the western fenland and eastern seaboard of Norfolk making available yet more land for cultivation. The mid-seventeenth century saw the Great Fen Drainage and grain production increased massively, today provides 48% of Britain's arable land, but the price of corn was still subservient to weather patterns and rose, doubled even, in dearth years. *Ad hoc* enclosure by agreement or sequestration persisted through the early modern period and by 1700 barely one third of the land of England and Wales remained open. The picture across the country was not uniform, with open field systems chiefly remaining in the arable midlands and to a lesser extent in East Anglia and enclosure, not surprisingly where animals wandered, throughout Wales and East Anglia and south-east England. Unenclosed commons survived in low-lying wetland areas like the silt fens of Norfolk, the Waveney River Valley and the Broads, which were used for fishing and fowling, for peat fuel and for harvesting reeds and rushes. East Ruston in the Broads still has a large area of common land, some of it marshy or even under water. As ever, landscape dictated agricultural practice.

In the general melee that was the English Civil War (1648–54) protest groups were formed. Two of these are credited with being precursor allotment claimants. The **Diggers'** assertion of independence in 1649 stemmed as much from their claim to equality, as to a claim to land but the connection with land – almost a sort of communism – was inextricable. It represented any number of contemporary declarations of freedoms-to-be, of which the **Levellers'** was another one. Following the Reformation, religious dissenters had clumped into recognizable groups who sought freedom to practice in the way they thought fit and protected from malign influences on land that was theirs. The term 'puritan' became a term of abuse in elizabethan and jacobean England.

Puritans felt under threat from James I whose reform of the church was half-hearted, perhaps tokenist, and the first of the Puritans sailed on the *Mayflower* to Cape Cod, New England in 1620. George Fox began preaching in 1641 and founded the **Quaker** movement, part of whose credo protested self-sufficiency. Quakerism arrived in Norfolk in 1648; records of their meetings and maps of their lands (without enabling an exact date to be ascribed but at least by the nineteenth century) show portions of land marked out for 'allotments'. The royalist Thomas Hobbes' *Leviathan (1651)* justified property rights, or 'propriety', as a riposte to the anarchism of dissenting groups who wanted land as much for somewhere to express their beliefs as for survival.

DIGGERS

The occupation of commons by squatters, resulting in its eventual sequestration, was an ancient practice. It was carried to its extreme by the Diggers who went further than Levellers than just pulling down fences enclosing former commons: on 1 june 1649 Gerard Winstanley, a failed merchant from Wigan but then living in Walton-on-Thames in Surrey, led a small band of agricultural labourers and poor artisans to St George's Hill. This was enclosed land, formerly commons, and their aim was to found an independent community, made self-sufficient through their capacity to 'dig' their own food. This was the first of hundreds of communities formed on the basis of agrarian communism, notably in Kent, Essex and Gloucestershire. 'At first such groups were dismissed as idealist revolutionaries. Local farmers detested the Diggers except at Wellingborough where they were given seed by them. Local labourers and users of the commons were furious that their land had been commandeered. In 1650 Winstanley's band was charged with "affray and unlawful congress". None of the groups survived' (Poole/7 p22). To introduce egalitarian ideals and in such a public way and to tie them to the landscape, to enclosure and the commons was the first time that such a concrete form of political radicalism had emerged in England. Winstanley took his text from the Bible. He died a Quaker, a natural home since the newly-founded Society of Friends included the creation of independent communities amongst their achievements.

LEVELLERS

At the time of the Civil War (1642–9) in England the Levellers were a radical group that wished to see the rights of english people (at least, male property-owning english people) taken further by demanding religious liberty and civil enfranchisement. Discontent with pay and conditions in the New Model Army encouraged Leveller claims to spread from civilians to the army in early 1647. Senior officers re-established control swiftly, stamping on pro-Leveller mutineers in the winter of 1647–8. In civilian life between 1645 and 1653 both men and women were active: in 1649 Leveller women claimed 'a proportionable share in the freedoms of this commonwealth and the right to defend them independently' (Capp p123). The term 'leveller' persisted as a label for those who pulled down fences built to enclose commons: in 1765 the *Gentleman's Magazine* records a riot of some forty men of Banbury who demolished a newly-erected fence on the estate at Warkworth. On being told of this at dinner a company of gentlemen abandoned their port, mounted their horses and rode off to rout the 'levellers'.

QUAKERS/1

The Society of Friends, known familiarly as the Quakers, came into being in the 1640s and was established in Norfolk by 1654. Each establishment, consisting mostly of meeting houses and their attached lands and burial grounds, was expected to be financially self-sufficient and to make a financial return to the Quarterly Meeting, the area centre. Of the twenty-three meeting houses that existed at one time, two of them appear from their records to have incorporated allotments. The Meeting House for Tasburgh and Hempnall had lands which, from their Minute Books, were let to raise income, partly to cover their own costs and partly to alleviate the 'sufferings' of their members. For the destitute of the seventeenth and eighteenth centuries membership of the Society of Friends was a recourse because they looked after their own. Tasburgh was enclosed in 1813 and awards were made in 1818 for which Tithe Apportionment maps exist. Friends' Meeting House and lands Title Deeds, well before enclosure and the term 'allotment' to signify recognition of commons rights, show the existence of a "burial ground, pightle and allotment of 1 rod 24 poles in Tasburgh and Hempnall 1707–1902. In 1707 Robert Jarmy purchased the premises (except for the allotment) from John Sporle. In 1708 he assigned them to a group of Trustees". Other than this intriguing reference, there are no documents in the Norwich Archive Centre to enlighten us about this use of the term 'allotments' and the records for the other meeting houses in Norfolk make no allusion to them.

The move to land ownership that had gripped Britain and its people increasingly through the sixteenth century became an obsession in the seventeenth and eighteenth centuries. A rising population benefited from new technologies which made the commons potentially productive where before they had not been economically viable, creating more work for the labourer. Concomitantly the property debate gained impetus: it became linked not just, as it had in Hobbes' mind, to the basis for power but to economic beliefs and entities – capitalism and cash – which were so to rule William Cobbet's thinking at the end of the eighteenth century. The notion of property was debated in pamphlets and books. John Locke's towering work *Treatises of Government* (1690) examined Hobbes' thesis and found it wanting in respect of the basis and purpose of property rights. For Locke the awarding of rights in property is not an incidental aspect of authority. It is its sole purpose:

> 'The great and chief end of men uniting in commonwealths and putting themselves under government is the preservation of their property' (*Treatises*, Ch IX, para 124).

But his account of the institution of property – how ownership is arrived at – is casual: 'Though before it was the common right of everyone' (Section 29), a man has a right to the sole possession of everything he is able to remove from the common pool, provided that he has 'mixed his labour with it' (Ch V, para 26). For example, a man gathering acorns or collecting turfs has a right to them and to the 'turfs my servant has cut'.

To reach the idea of enclosure Locke tells a theoretical history that begins with a 'state of nature' and manoeuvres via bartering, money, commerce and capitalism to the exchange of land with a compact or agreement, regulated by government and law: this mechanism is the 'way how a man may, rightfully and without injury, possess more than he himself can make use of…without encroachment on the right of others' (Section 51). Locke is strictly against engrossment: what is owned may not exceed what someone 'can make use of to any advantage of life before it spoils…whatever is beyond this is more than his share and belongs to others' (Section 31). This does not meet the case of non-perishables, nor of land itself but land is claimed through investment in the earth: 'As much land as a man tills, plants, improves, cultivates and can use the product of, so much is his property. He by his labour does, as it were, enclose it from the common' (Section 32). Provided there is enough left for others to use, he 'does as good as take nothing at all' (Section 33). What is not improved is 'waste' (Section 41) and hence neither usable nor desirable.

Improvement through a community of ideas seized the new industrial areas – innovations in science and technology were proliferated through correspondence and meetings much as they had been at the start of the scientific revolution in the sixteenth and seventeenth centuries. Appropriation of land was the economic aspect of a movement that had political roots: investment in scientific invention created an expertise that eventually filtered into agricultural method and technology, making commons lucrative and hence desirable. It was appropriate that the year 1662 in which the Royal Society received its Charter was also that in which Thomas Fuller published *The Worthies of England*, the earliest gazetteer recording county by county the agricultural produce of each – its crops, its animal breeds, its cheeses, its timbers. Fuller's was the first report of a series that were produced by famous men and provide such a rich vision of rural life. He extolled the virtues of what would become known as **spade husbandry**, a very old-fashioned technology given a new spin. The practice was adopted with enthusiasm by wealthy landowners for their walled gardens along with exotic plants and innovative techniques that were brought by the Dutch (glass houses, crinkle-crankle and heated walls) in order to impress the neighbours and guests: at Holkham Hall, seat of the Earls of Leicester and home to many nineteenth century innovations, pineapples from their own gardens were served at Christmas. Eventually, a century later, spade husbandry would be recommended for use by farmers wishing to employ more labourers instead of the plough, and would become a condition of holding a garden allotment.

The benefits of the garden allotment emerged in the industrial north. In the new factory settlements built by Richard Arkwright at Cromford, Joseph Derby (1769) and Jedediah Strutt at Belper (from the 1770s with Arkwright) workers were housed and partly fed from their allotments, a device which helped to alleviate the severe national shortage of cash required to pay their wages. An advertisement produced in 1793 by the Society of Agriculture at Manchester, whose subscribers included Robert Peel, James Watt, Samuel Oldknow, and **Arthur Young** offered 'prizes for planting the greatest number of poplars, hoeing the greatest number of turnips, for discovering the best methods of destroying rats and cockchafers, preserving cabbages and keeping rivers within bounds'(Unwin, pp213–4).

Garden allotments, so called, do not appear in Norfolk until a few decades later although something similar was noted in **Zachary Clark**'s 1811 gazeteer *An Account of the different Charities belonging to the Poor of the County of Norfolk*. Clark based his compendium on *terriers* which he researched painstakingly himself, parish by parish, until he discovered the 1786 Returns resulting from Gilbert's Act. He describes 'small pieces of land' and 'small rents' and 'separate tenants', showing that the idea of the poor benefiting from charitable gifts, some of which he dated back to the elizabethan era, had either been introduced or maintained. Where Clark records the number of poor beneficiaries the plots vary in size from, say, one-third to half-an-acre through one acre in several cases to as much as five acres. Whatever their function, the principal that amongst parish responsibilities was that of providing small amounts of land to the poor for rents was well-established by the time of the Returns. Clark shows that scarcely a parish in Norfolk was without its charities, and some had several. A few of many examples are Feltwell where Clough's Charity by a Deed of 1737 left six acres for six poor families; Haddiscoe's benefactor was Thomas Strange who in 1556 willed twelve acres to be divided into twenty pieces; and Larling where 1 acre 2 roods in Larling Field was divided into three pieces. Many of these lands reappear in the Brougham *Report* of 1843, with their use for and by the poor intact and some of them, at least, are noted to have been cultivated.

ZACHARY CLARK (17?–1815)
A citizen of Downham Market in Norfolk, he lived in the White House, Ryston End which is now part of Downham High School. He was a member of the Society of Friends and well-known as a philanthropist who, on his death in august 1815 was much mourned by the numerous poor and indigent folk who had benefited by his charitable gifts.

AN

ACCOUNT

OF THE DIFFERENT

CHARITIES

BELONGING TO

THE POOR

OF THE

COUNTY of NORFOLK,

ABRIDGED FROM THE RETURNS

UNDER

GILBERT'S ACT,

TO THE HOUSE OF COMMONS IN 1786;

AND FROM

THE TERRIERS

IN THE OFFICE OF THE

LORD BISHOP OF NORWICH.

─────────

BY ZACHARY CLARK.

─────────

BURY ST. EDMUND'S:
PRINTED BY GEDGE AND BARKER;
FOR LONGMAN, HURST, REES, ORME, AND BROWN,
PATERNOSTER-ROW, LONDON.

1811.

Thomas Fuller's 1662 gazetteer of England was the progenitor of Daniel Defoe's touring companion, in which he advocated measures for alleviating the impoverishment of the agricultural labourer, and of Nathaniel Kent's 1775 survey of English agriculture, *Hints to Gentlemen of Landed Property* in which he urged the division of waste land for the poor or at least the provision of good gardens. Arthur Young of Suffolk became famous for his tours of England. Just as the Royal Society was the embodiment of the empiricist spirit and as Oldknow and others experimented with breeds and farming methods, Young travelled and observed and witnessed. In 1772 *The Farmer's Tour through the East of England* took in Norfolk and in 1804 as President of the Board of Agriculture he authored the Report entitled *General View of the Agriculture of the County of Norfolk drawn up for the consideration of the Board of Agriculture and internal improvement*. The final word of this expansive title was, for Young, the final word and the watchword of the modern agriculture of his day and he extols examples of good practice from Bentinck's embankment of the Fens to the Reverend Priest's barrow for dropping wheat – which attempted to replace *dibbling* – to the many practices and innovations in managing the soil, ploughing and planting, breeding and feeding animals.

ARTHUR YOUNG
Inspired by Thomas Fuller and Daniel Defoe, Young made a tour of England in 1771, publishing his *Observations on the present state of waste lands in Great Britain* in 1775 in which he argued that government should purchase all waste land offered for sale and resell it in lots of 20–30 acres, letting those purchasers with eight to ten or more children have their lots free of charge. From 1784, Young spoke to the farming community (with a circulation of three thousand, it was to a select few) in his journal *Annals of Agriculture*: an 1801 edition noted, 'a very few of the poor who occupy a garden of a rood of land received relief from the parish rates' (Volume XXXVI p377). In 1800 his pamphlet *The question of scarcity* advocated cow pastures and in 1801 he published *Inquiry into the propriety of applying wastes to the better maintenance and support of the poor*. As a farmer committed to observation and enquiry he was 'the foremost authority of his day' (Crouch and Ward, p44). Of Norfolk he said, 'half the county of Norfolk within the memory of man yielded nothing but sheep feed but by the end of the century it was covered by fine barley, rye and wheat' (Porter p205). By the 1820s, having lived to witness the terrible outcome of the Napoleonic Wars and changes in agricultural practice, he renounced his former support for enclosures.

Rural settings for allotments in Norfolk

Wells East

Wells West

Trowse, Block Hill

Dereham, Cemetery Road

Dereham, Cherry Lane

East Runton

Castle Acre, School Gardens

Castle Acre, School Gardens

Upper Sheringham

The garden plot of Norwich Cathedral represents continuity with Norfolk's mediaeval past.

Lingwood retains one-acre strips for its plots.

Young's report post-dated the General Inclosure Act 1801 which contained clauses relating to allotments. As he travelled he examined in detail the land enclosed by parliamentary act, parish by parish, and considered whether or not the poor had suffered as a result. His measurement of changes in their condition was the number of burials compared with births for periods before and after enclosure but where possible he also detailed any local provision for those who had lost rights on enclosed common land. Provision on loss of commons rights took different forms and was dependent not only on the rights previously held but also upon whether proof could be provided and even upon the standard of proof demanded. In a few cases allotments were made with consideration for the needs of the commoners and even with generosity as in Cawston where Colonel Bulwer provided 1300 acres of common and warren, the latter subject to sheep-walk. Bulwer 'arranged the divisions in such a manner that the roads open into all the pieces…By means of small allotments let by him to the poor, cows will increase as they exceed the rights that were actually exercised' (Young, pp93–4).

It need not be thought that, even though enclosure by Act demanded that portions of land be allocated to legitimate claimants, it brought about a redistribution of land but Young was able to name parishes where communities had benefited:

▧ At Hethersett, enclosed in 1798, 'there were fifty or sixty small allotments', (p119);

▧ At Heacham, enclosed 1780, along with other measures 'there [were] from 12–15 little and comfortable proprietors and renters of small plots from two to ten acres; who have cows and some corn and what they like to cultivate. A remarkable instance and I cordially wish it was universal' (p125);

▧ At Langley, enclosed 1800, 'Mr Burton [the Commissioner] pointed out many cottages with good gardens annexed and various small grass fields enclosed to all who kept cows; Sir T Beachamp's orders being at all times to furnish land to such as were able to get a cow. They have each a piece near the river, assigned for mowing fodder for their cows – too much cannot be said in favour of that system' (p134);

▧ Winfarthing, enclosed 1781, made 'many allotments to little people; and they are well content; and have kept them: they have much hemp, wheat etc and well-managed' (p180).

To add to this picture the Survey returns state that a number of early allotments were created by enclosure act, as shown by Table 1. Whether or not they were for cultivation at the enclosure cannot be said with certainty; some were described in those terms by later sources. These were not garden allotments in the modern sense but sometimes, as Young and Clark indicate, the poor were the direct beneficiaries of allotments and sometimes the allotments were poor's allotments. Sometimes, as at **Salthouse**, the picture is blurred still further by the creation at enclosure of garden allotments that are rented

Table 1: allotment lands created by enclosure, date given, and used for cultivation, at least in part.

1780	*Heacham	
1781	*Winfarthing	
1803	Lingwood	one-acre strips
1802	West Bradenham	charity lands, formerly fuel allotment of which part let from 1804
1804	Holme Hale	former fuel allotment
1810	**Westfield**	former fuel allotment, O/S map 1906 shows garden allotments
1811	Great Witchingham	
1813	Guist	
1815	**Toftwood**	
1847	Yaxham	
1850	Runhall	charitable trust created post-1882
1852	Bramerton	
1853	**Salthouse**	allotments 1853
1857/60	**Costessey**	allotments 1860
1868	Swaffham	allotments 1868
Late 19th century	South Creake	

*based on Young's account, the rest from the Survey which confirmed their existence at the time of the Survey. Later sources – Brougham, trade directories – confirm land usage as garden allotments at least by mid-19th century unless otherwise stated.

which benefit the not-rich where the income goes to the poor – it seems to be a matter of defining poverty, as much as the notion of an allotment. The picture is of *ad hoc* provision with great variety of kind and use but extensive coverage.

Most enclosures leading to 'small occupiers' or 'small proprietors' or 'small pieces of land' or 'small rents' described by Zachary Clark or Arthur Young referred to fuel allotments or cow pastures. Clark makes no mention of cultivation, Young only twice. Scepticism about proto-

allotments aside, the record shows that rights and even custom was sometimes viewed as the basis for a claim in land under early parliamentary enclosure. Young cited many examples where enclosure in Norfolk had increased the wellbeing of the labourer and some where it had not. Where they had been compensated with small parcels of land, Young claimed, the improvement in their own condition was unquestionable.

what is an allotment?

There is more than one meaning to the term 'allotment'. Over the centuries allotments may have been *poor's allotments*, *fuel allotments* or garden allotments and sometimes one has been converted into the other. There are also plots described as *potato grounds* or *potato lots*, and *cow pastures* which mostly predate allotments. *Smallholdings* were formerly called allotments and not distinguished from garden allotments, since both were cultivated by *spade husbandry*. The provision by landowners of a *cottage* with land attached could also be referred to as an allotment.

During the period of *enclosure* the poor were often given some compensation by the creation of allotments, including fuel allotments which were intended to supply fuel for the poor, often in lieu of the former practice of collecting turves from the waste areas of the manor (again, Lolly Moor provides an example – see **Westfield**). Such provision was not merely an act of charity but a way of avoiding local unrest from the poor at the loss of their rights to use common land. At Stokesby in Norfolk in 1720, for example

The poor inhabitants finding that no allotment was set out for their benefit under the Inclosure Act...proceeded in a riotous manner and insisted upon having some allotment given to them (Williamson, Vol 1).

Although enclosures sometimes left allotments for the poor which allowed them to graze cows and cultivate, as Arthur Young's 1804 report on Norfolk shows, poor's allotments were encouraged by the 1819 Poor Law Amendment, or Select Vestries, Act. The link with enclosures died with the Allotments Extension Act of 1882 when allotments could be made by representations to parish councillors by agricultural labourers and paupers. Finally the 1908 Allotments and Smallholdings Act consolidated early legislation and made allotments the duty of parish and town councils if six or more people of any background wanted them.

The broadest definition of an allotment is probably that it is a small cultivated plot but that is probably not too useful as there have been cultivated plots for as long as there has been agriculture. Since the early nineteenth century allotments were secured by rental. A more precise definition adds that the land should not be attached to a house but rather in a field divided into similar plots, and yet other descriptions insist that the produce be for the sustenance of the labourer and family and that it should only be cultivated during leisure hours.

An allotment garden is defined in the Allotments Act 1922 as 'an allotment not exceeding 40 poles (or 1 000 square metres) which is wholly or mainly cultivated by the occupier for the production of fruit and vegetables for consumption by himself and his family'. The later Act of 1925 spoke of 'an allotment garden or any parcel of land not more than five acres in extent [reverting to the confusion about allotments and smallholdings] cultivated as a garden farm or partly as a garden farm and partly as a farm'.

There is merit in all these definitions and they reflect the different social and political, interests of their time but what they all have in common is the deep need of people to have a small area of land that they can call their own and, whether it is for economic survival or as a leisure activity, to be in some way connected to the soil and to produce at least some of their own food.

For the purposes of this book 'allotment' will usually apply to a piece of land let by a council or other public, private institution or individual for the spare time cultivation of, chiefly, vegetables, fruit, flowers and animals but this does not exclude all the other forms of allotment which are part of this rich history.

2 | riot and reward

Swamps of wild rush-beds and sloughs' squashy traces,
Grounds of rough fallows with thistle and weed,
Flats and low vallies of Kingcups and daisies,
Sweetest of subjects are ye for my reed,
Ye commons left free in the rude rags of nature,
Ye brown heaths beclothed in furze as ye be,
My wild eye in rapture adores every feature,
Ye are dear as this heart in my bosom to me.

Common Land *from* The Village Minstrel (1821)
John Clare

1793 was the year in which the Society of Agriculture was formed in Manchester, signalling the application of expert minds to agricultural improvement; and in which Arthur Young, a member, became President of the Board of Agriculture to add authority to his assessment of the state of agriculture in England; and when the first of the Napoleonic Wars (to 1815), which would have such a devastating impact on the market in corn, the Norfolk labourers' staple, was fought; and the date on which future commentators would reflect as the point at which the capitalist model overtook agricultural practice, changing forever the relationship between the labourer and his master.

Outside the estate walls neither Locke's optimism nor Fuller's confidence were fulfilled: through the seventeenth century, as we have seen, exceptionally poor climate had caused a series of poor harvests and between 1693–99 the price of bread doubled. The rate of population rise declined from the 1660s to 1750 but by then the population was so high that underemployment was endemic and in Norfolk one-eighth of men were unemployed: between 1718 and 1759 rents on the Holkham Estate rose by 44 per cent; in 1796 Nathaniel Kent's *Survey of Norfolk Agriculture* showed that wages rose by 25 per cent as compared with a 60 per cent rise in the cost of living. Even then Norfolk was a net exporter of grain and sent out of county more than did the rest of the United Kingdom combined. The dearth years of 1709, 1727, 1756, 1766, 1795 and 1800 saw riots.

Citizen unrest at home was matched by rebellion abroad. In 1776 the American War of Independence was supported by a son of Norfolk,

Thomas Paine. Paine's writing in pamphlets and books wove together the threads of democracy and independence with a concept of property and with rights in land. 1789 saw the start of the French Revolution and the Reign of Terror; if nothing else, these events struck fear into the hearts of landowners in England and food riots at home, apart from the damage that they immediately caused, were viewed as a sign of a revolution to come.

THOMAS PAINE (1737–1809)

Thomas Paine was born in Thetford, the son of a Quaker farmer. He was a pamphleteer who espoused independence from colonial rule as an expression of man's democratic right. He was as much feared for sedition as revered for defining and promoting natural rights. Paine went to America in 1774 and supported the independence movement: he wrote for the *Pennsylvania Magazine* from january 1775, advocating the 'modern' world by comparison with the Old European model; and he published *Common Sense*, also in 1775, to rally the american independence movement. Famously, Paine's later works are regarded as the blueprint on which the founding fathers worked to produce the american constitution. His support for the French Revolution (1789) led to his removal to France (1792–1802) where he lived during the Reign of Terror. But it was the publication of Edmund Burke's *Reflections* in 1790 which provoked him to formulate his theory of the *Rights of Man*, in two volumes published in 1791 and 1792 respectively, which argues for the framework and mechanism of representative government. The successive overthrowing of american and french feudal systems generated a foment of fear and panic in english landowning class writing, as well as a fever of debate on the principles of government. Paine's last major publication was *Agrarian Justice* (1797) in which he proposed the redistribution of wealth through taxation and allowances – the first benefit, rather than charitable, system of welfare; one based on equitable rules; one which gives practical expression to justice for all. The philosophical basis of the text addresses another concept that was key to eighteenth century social development – that of property. It was the land-grab through enclosure acts that prompted discussion of the basis of property rights. For Paine 'it is the value of the improvement only, and not the earth itself, that is individual property'. Hence the poor are poor because landless. Earlier he had disparaged '... the custom of attaching *Rights* to place, or in other words to inanimate matter, instead of the *person* independently of the place, which is too absurd to make any part of a rational argument'. Hence, too, the landless are due compensation. No wonder he struck terror into the hearts of both Houses of Parliament!

An attempt was made to address the problem of rising poverty and its expense through legislation which referred the problem to local communities. Between 1782 and 1786 Gilbert's Act made provision for groups of parishes to form unions so that they could share the cost of poor relief through poorhouses, which were established for looking after only the old, the sick and the infirm. Able-bodied paupers were explicitly excluded from poorhouses. Instead they were either to be provided with outdoor relief (that is, they were supported in their own homes) or employed near their own homes.

Adam Smith's *Wealth of Nations* (1776) was part of the public dialogue on capitalism and property that so exercised the eighteenth century. Smith's doctrine, still respected, was that of economic *laissez-faire*: his legacy was the breaking of the linkage with the language of rights and creation of the marketplace as a frame of reference; it was the function of the government to protect property from 'the indignation of the poor...It is only under the shelter of the civil magistrate that the owner of that valuable property, which is acquired by the labour of many years or perhaps successive generations, can sleep a single night in security'. It should be noted that in the eighteenth century the person of the magistrate and of the owner of valuable property were one and the same.

Paine's riposte *Agrarian Justice* (1797), used that same language of wealth to remind Smith that in the case of government-sponsored *laissez-faire* justice would be measured as taxes, redistribution of wealth to guarantee welfare for all. As if to reinforce awareness of the need for some measure to address the problem of the poor, which by the end of the eighteenth century was a pressing one, Thomas Malthus cried 'doom!' in his *Essay on the Principle of Population as it affects the future Improvement of Society* (1798) in which he argued that the population and its demand for food will always outstrip the availability of food: '...the power of the population is indefinitely greater than the power in the Earth to produce subsistence for man...the race of man cannot escape from...[this law]...and its effects are...misery and vice. The former, misery, is an absolutely necessary consequence of it. Vice is a highly probable consequence and we therefore see it abundantly prevail'.

The prospect of an exponentially increasing number of claimants to the poor rate alarmed amongst others **Lord Suffield of Gunton Park** who was persuaded of this argument, as were many others, and both it and the visible discontented crowd which it described satisfied him, but not the majority, that a remedy must be found.

William Cobbett, whose *Rural Rides* (1830) had convinced him long before Friedrich Engels penned the definitive counter-argument to Malthus' Dismal Theorem, that land was far more productive than was being allowed, disagreed with Lord Suffield on this, as on other issues: 'The state of this valley seems to illustrate the infamous and really diabolical assertion of MALTHUS, which is, that the humankind have a NATURAL TENDENCY, to increase beyond the means of sustenance for them.. Hence, all the schemes of this and other Scotch writers for what they call checking population. Hence, all the beastly, the nasty, the abominable writings put forth to teach labouring people how to avoid having children'. Amongst the beastly consequences of a naïve acceptance of Malthus' doctrine was the segregation of the sexes in English workhouses under the Poor Law Amendment Act of 1834 (Williams, p521). He continued, 'Now, look at this valley of Avon. Here the people raise nearly twenty times as much food and clothing as they consume. They raise five times as much, even according to my scale of living. They have been doing so for many, many years. They have been doing it for several generations. Where, then, is their NATURAL TENDENCY to increase beyond the means of sustenance for them? Beyond, indeed the means of that sustenance which a system like this will leave them?'.

Cobbett agreed that it was '…Far beyond the means that the taxing and monopolizing system will leave in their hands: that is very true; for it leave them nothing but the scale of the poor-book: they must cease to breed at all, or they must exceed this mark; but the earth, give them their fair share of its products, will always give sustenance in sufficiency to those who apply to it by skilful and diligent labour…'((Cobbett, p317).

WILLIAM COBBETT (1762–1835)

William Cobbett was a Radical and royalist and the editorial pen behind the journal *Political Register* (published 1817–1826). His many other writings include *Cottage Economy* (1822), the *English Gardener* (1829) and *Rural Rides* (1823 and 1830), a record of his travels alone on horseback through the southern countries of agricultural England. A farmer himself, his knowing eye observed the life and economy of the agricultural labourer and his pen recorded their wisdom, while expressing in the liveliest of language his opinions on national events, policies, people, economic trends and injustices. His sympathies lay with those who added wealth to the land, rather than just taking from it. In 1822 he wrote:

'…if any attempt be made to repeal the *Corn Bill*, the main body of the farmers will be crushed into total ruin…I know, that, even with present prices, and with *honest labourers fed worse than felons*, it is *rub-and-go* with nineteen-twentieths of the farmers; …with the thousands of industrious and care-taking creatures reduced to beggary by bank-paper; with panic upon panic, plunging thousands upon thousands into despair: …will they again advise their Royal Master to tell the parliament and world that this country is 'in a state of *unequalled prosperity*', and that this prosperity 'must be *permanent*, because *all* the great interests are *flourishing*'? Let them! That will not alter the result. I had been for several weeks, saying, that the *seeming prosperity* was *fallacious*; that the cause of it must lead to *ultimate* and shocking ruin; that it could not last, because it arose from causes so manifestly *fictitious*; that, in short, it was the fair-looking, but poisonous, fruit of a *miserable expedient*. I had been saying this for several weeks, when, out came the *King's Speech* and gave me and my doctrines the *lie direct*, as to every point. Well: now, then, we shall *soon see*' (Cobbett, pp287–9).

And they did, as the riots of that year testify.

On the life of the poor agricultural labourer in the difficult 1830s he wrote, 'What injustice, what a hellish system it must be, to make those who raise it skin and bone and nakedness, while the food and drink and wool are almost all carried away to be heaped on the fund-holders, pensioners, soldiers, dead-weight, and the other swarms of tax-eaters! If such an operation do not need putting an end to, then the devil himself is a saint' (Cobbett, p22).

In his sympathy for the impoverished agricultural worker Cobbett surveyed some of the many remedies proffered to reduce the distress of the poor: he thought potatoes, grown by some on potato plots, were a vile import of the Irish labourer and not fit food for Englishmen; and he dismissed the measures of home colonies and emigration which his contact with the labouring poor seemed to indicate was another term for transportation:

'The survey of this Valley is, I think, the finest answer in the world to the 'EMIGRATION COMMITTEE' fellows...I remember that, last winter, a young woman complained to one of the Police Justices, that the *Overseers* of some parish were going *to transport her orphan brother to Canada*, because he became chargeable to their parish! I remember also that the Justice said that the intention of the Overseers was *'premature'*, for that 'the BILL *had not yet passed'*! This was rather an ugly story; and I do think, that we shall find, that there have been, and are, some pretty propositions before this 'COMMITTEE'. (Cobbett, p319).

Cobbett's desire and ability to interpret the evidence before him was not shared by his exact contemporary in Norfolk, Lord Suffield of Gunton Park, who was swayed by Malthusian hysteria but he was in agreement on the subject of garden allotments, and advocated their provision for the agricultural labourer, but differed from him about who should provide the land: Lord Suffield argued that the parish should provide the land. Cobbett owned a small freehold property in Norfolk and although he entered into a private agreement with his own workers, providing gardens for them, Cobbett laid the responsibility for relinquishing land at the door of estate owners.

Changes in the structure and practice of agriculture were an extension of the new capitalism and industrialization that had created the large towns of the midlands and north of England. Specifically, an engineer named James Meikle of Dunbar invented a threshing machine at around 1784. Threshing was carried out in the winter months and was a vital support for labouring families who found themselves unemployed once harvest was completed and, in imitation of the manufacturing cities, working for piece-rate. Just as in 1811 Luddites had broken up the new industrial machines, agricultural workers protested against their greater insecurity and poverty by disabling threshing machines.

Meanwhile wages for the labourer continued to decline to near starvation levels throughout the first half of the nineteenth century, especially in Norfolk: in 1787 the agricultural authority William Marshall had recorded: '...a Norfolk labourer will do as much for one shilling as two men in many other places will do for eighteen pence

each', a view reinforced in 1804 by Arthur Young in his *Annals of Agriculture*: '...the circumstances in rural economy which for many years distinguished Norfolk in a remarkable manner was the cheapness wherewith the farmer carried out his business'. Labour was not only cheap but '...had greater activity and a spirit of exertion' (quoted in Susanna Wade-Martins, *Changing Agriculture*, p63).

And more, farmers were under pressure to pay higher taxes and duties in order to meet the huge cost of the Napoleonic War and they were not inclined or able to ameliorate conditions for their workers. In 1801 a Board of Agriculture Enquiry recognized that farmhands 'living-in' had declined and that farmers hired by the year less than previously; men were hired for the job. A witness observed 'you cease to feed your men when it is hardest for them to feed themselves'. Those not hired by the year were on piece-rate, plus gifts in kind such as reduced prices for corn and meals after harvest. Underemployment during the winter months especially, when traditional hand-threshing had maintained most families, was endemic.

Throughout the Napoleonic Wars Norfolk saw unrivalled levels of enclosure (Figure 2.1). John Howlett in *An Enquiry into the Influence which Enclosures have had upon the Population of England* (1806) derided 'those who think enclosure of commons and waste good if it is divided into small allotments for the poor' and believed wholeheartedly in enclosure and improvement. Problems persisted throughout the War and beyond until by 1831 the Census registered the proportion of men in rural parishes out of work as one-eighth and the ratio of casual (including women and children) to regular workers as 3:2. At **Castle Acre** there was an open settlement of surplus labour, camped on the common beyond the town boundary, controlled by gang-masters which fed shortages in neighbouring landlord-controlled farms (Susanna Wade-Martins op cit p66).

The plight of the poor moved some gentlemen to act for them. The Society for Bettering the Conditions and Increasing the Comforts of the Poor (SBCP), with the King as its patron, had been founded in 1796 by philanthropic and influential reformers that included clergymen, the slavery abolitionist William Wilberforce and a pioneer promoter of

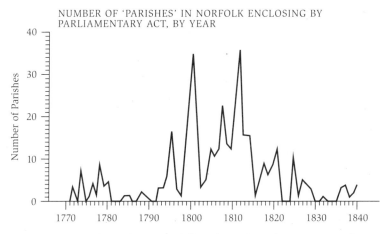

NUMBER OF 'PARISHES' IN NORFOLK ENCLOSING BY
PARLIAMENTARY ACT, BY YEAR

Figure 2.1: Number of 'Parishes' in Norfolk enclosing by Parliamentary Act, by year
Sources: Norfolk Record Office, Norwich, List of Inclosure Awards, Map and Acts;
W. E. Tate, A Domesday of English Enclosure Acts and Awards ed. M. E. Turner
(Reading, 1978), p178–90. Thanks to Dr. Sara Birtles for permission to reproduce
the figure.

garden allotment schemes, Sir Thomas Bernard. The latter wrote that 'a cottager with property, however small – a cow, a pig or even a garden – had an interest in his country and in the good order of society' (Burchardt, p20). The letting of land to the labourer for cow pasture or spade husbandry was the SBCP's clarion call during its active life, into the first decade of the nineteenth century.

The final months of the Napoleonic Wars in 1815 saw great hardship in Norfolk. The winter of 1815–16 was harsh and a dearth year; by the spring of 1816 corn was scarce and had risen in price.

Farmers, some of whom had withheld wheat in anticipation of a price rise, had not increased wages to ease labourers' difficulties. There ensued the 'bread or blood' riots in East Anglia, named after the cry of the crowd whose main objective was to deter farmers and landowners from replacing their winter labour with threshing-machines. A wrecking took place at Great Hockham, resulting in four of the ringleaders of a

VOLCANIC EVENTS/1

I had a dream, which was not all a dream.
The bright sun was extinguish'd, and the stars
Did wander darkling in the eternal space,
Rayless, and pathless, and the icy earth
Swung blind and blackening in the moonless air;
Morn came and went – and came, and brought no day,
And men forgot their passions in the dread
Of this their desolation; and all hearts
Were chill'd into a selfish prayer for light:
And they did live by watchfires – and the thrones,
The palaces of crowned kings – the huts,
The habitations of all things which dwell,
Were burnt for beacons; cities were consumed,
And men were gather'd round their blazing homes
To look once more into each other's face.

Darkness
Lord Byron (1816)

In april 1815 the volcano of Tambora in Indonesia erupted, sending a vast quantity of ash (2400×10^{11}kg), aerosols (150×10^{9}kg) and gases into the upper atmosphere (Colling, p124, Table 4.3). The spin of the globe carried the debris around the globe. At eight degrees south of the equator, the eruption products were close to the northerly circulatory systems and were carried up to the european landmass where they persisted as a layer intercepting the warmth and light of the sun's rays for the next eighteen months. As anyone knows who has experienced a full eclipse of the sun, the removal of solar radiation has an instantaneous and dramatic effect on the temperature on the ground. Not only would the summer have felt miserably cold, the year was an exceptionally wet one, with 200 mm, or roughly 25%, of precipitation more than was usual for that period. 1816 became known as the 'year without a summer' with an average temperature for the summer months of 13.4°C and for the year as a whole of 7.9°C, again a low average even for those inclement times. It was inevitable that crops would not have been able to grow in the dark and wet conditions and 1816 was a year of dearth (Hulme and Barrow, p 272 and p403ff).

mob of about one hundred men being convicted of riotous assembly and two of these spending a year in Norwich Castle Gaol.

In april 1816 protest was made through arson and machine-breaking; demonstrations became hostile gatherings so that riots were seen at Bury St Edmunds on 14 may, at nearby Brandon in Suffolk on 16 may, at Feltwell on 18 may and at Downham Market on 20 and 21 may. Starting at Southery and picking up reinforcements at Denver, a crowd of some hundreds marched on Downham to petition magistrates. Looting of bread shops occurred. A delegation met the magistrates; their demands were for more employment, a wage of two shillings a day and cheaper food. But when after deliberation the magistrates addressed the crowd a further demand, the release of a poacher, was made. Ordinary folk had been used to catching a pigeon or a rabbit on the commons and the criminalization of these acts was a sticking-point. The mood became more hostile and stones were thrown, when the magistrates made their escape. The crowd took over the town, ransacking and looting food and flour. At about five o'clock in the afternoon the yeomanry were brought in to control the crowd, the Riot Act was read and the men eventually dispersed.

The following day, 21 may, men from Southery and Hilgay marched again to Downham, demanding of the magistrates that they release those arrested for rioting the previous day; the magistrates acceded and the men left peaceably. One of the magistrates rode that same day to London to inform a Government Minister of the demonstration and requested that sufficient troops be made available to quell the rioters.

As the week progressed uprisings occurred in the same area at Littleport and Ely, but as it became clear to the crowd that the improvements to which the magistrates had agreed were not going to materialize, there was further unrest in Downham which was rapidly quashed by the Upwell yeomanry with those formerly put into gaol re-arrested. 'Of those rioters who faced trial several were sentenced to death but in all but two cases the death penalty was commuted to transportation, either for a specified period or for life. The two exceptions, Thomas Thody and Daniel Harwood, were hanged at Norwich on 31 august 1816 before a large crowd, in which the presence of sympathisers was significant.' Another chronicler records, '...Thody, after first displaying great fortitude, "sank under the agony of grief and terror, at the recollection of his wife and children, and the horror of immediate death"'(Nesta Evans p69).

The consequences of the riots in Norfolk and the nation were mainly talk but some of that talk and a little action revolved around allotments. The action was instigated by the Reverend Ambrose Goode of **Terrington-St-Clement** who acted benevolently for his parish in a number of respects and the impact of a miserable climatic phase and of fiscal impositions on staples would have been motivation enough. The record does not speak about the thinking of the landowners who donated land, which included the Bentinck family, and it may just be coincidence that Terrington-St-Clement is in the same part of Norfolk as experienced disturbance. But it was in 1816 that the Reverend Goode gave up his tithes, a condition of some clergy later for their support of the Tithe Commutation Act 1836 (FHCRS Newsletter/1 p6), and the churchwardens hired a sizeable 22 acres of land from the Bentincks in order to create allotments, to the alleviation of famine and dependence of the labouring and poor people on the parish. The *Norfolk Chronicle* for december 1821 reported that 'An experiment has been tried for the bettering of the conditions of the labourers in agriculture and for reducing the poor rates in the parish of Terrington by the apportionment of parcels of land from one to five roods which have been found after three years of trial to be productive of the happiest effect'. The Survey has been unable to find other allotment sites created as a resolution of the 1816 strife but from the date of the *Chronicle's* report, 1821 to 1826 the Survey finds a further four new sites (of which three, Burnham Thorpe, Kimberley and Weasenham Hall (Burchardt, Table 2, p36) were on estates lands: Coke of Holkham the first of these, Townshend of Raynham the latter two.

In the same year the Labourers' Friend Society (a branch of which founded the **West Winch** allotments in 1844) was formed 'to show the utility and national advantage of allotting land for cottage industry' (Barnett, p167). With seventeen branches in the southern counties and one in the midlands, it appears to have been the precursor of *farmers' and agricultural associations* for promoting best practice. Following the 1816 uprising a Select Committee on the Poor Laws was convened, resulting in a recommendation that parishes be entitled to let allotments. This found its way into the Select Vestries Act, also known as the Poor Law Amendment Act, of 1819. Its primary aim was to improve the powers of parochial government and so stem the flood of applicants for poor rate. The unemployed went 'on the parish' if they were fortunate enough to be granted money to help support their family but money was granted by application, just what the trustees of the poor considered to be enough, and was not guaranteed. The Select Committee having witnessed a number of successful instances of allotment provision, the allotment clauses of the Act gave parishes powers to take in hand parish land, or purchase or hire other land, in order to provide employment for the poor and to give parishes permission to let parish land for allotments. There is little evidence of parishes in Norfolk having seized this initiative.

Farmers in Norfolk were as exercised by the level of poor rates stemming from the Poor Laws as was the rest of the country and a county debate was convened. During the period of the Napoleonic Wars when there were no imports the price of corn had risen to unprecedented levels: from a norm of 50 shillings per quarter in 1792 it had reached 155 shillings per quarter in 1812, a year of dearth. But the price of corn post-War seldom achieved that level and the Prime Minister, Sir Robert Peel's proposal through the 1815 Corn Law was that corn be imported on payment of a duty which reduced as the price of corn rose, to maintain a stable price at home through dearth years. This measure would hit hardest the labourer, while penalising imports in times of plenty and thus protect the farmer.

Adam Smith's dictums had guaranteed that *laissez-faire* economics were universally held by politicians and their farming constituents of whatever political colour or status through succeeding generations. Despite the artificial conditions of the War the wealth accrued throughout the period must have seemed to provide incontrovertible evidence for the tenets of free trade. Much of that wealth was used to pursue the enclosure and improvement of land. The cost of enclosure, of pursuing a Parliamentary Act, and subsequently of securing boundaries, drainage and fertilization of the land far outweighed the profits accrued from that land in the short and even medium term; but while prices of corn were high the enterprise was deemed profitable.

In the post-War period, when imports of corn resumed and prices fell, farmers and landowners began to feel the pinch. Financial squeeze was increased by residually high rents on farming land which, having risen during the profitable War years, remained high as their 20–30 years' leases ran out; and by governmental measures taken to return Britain, having incurred £200 million of debt, to peacetime governance. Income tax was abolished in 1816, leaving duties which hit the farmer most to cover the colossal war debt. Further, tithes continued to represent a cost that could be ill-afforded by the farmer in hard times. And the poor rates, since 1795 when wages had failed to rise as sharply as prices, were allocated as subsidies in proportion to the number of adults and children in the workers' family; with the rate being further adjusted for the price of bread. This Speenhamland System as it was known had produced extreme hikes in the poor rates, up to as much as eightfold the 1795 rate. It was the cause of additional discomfort in the farming community. The pinch felt by farmers was passed on to the labourers in the form of low wages.

Thomas Coke, Lord Leicester of Holkham, convened a county meeting to discuss these complexities. It was attended 'numerously' and was 'one of the most stormy ever held in Norfolk', according to Lord Suffield's biographer. Lord Suffield addressed the meeting at length, as was his wont, offering 'only two remedies for the local difficulty: one an increase in the price of corn and the other the removal of causes' – by which he meant a reduction of tariffs – 'preventing the farmer from obtaining a remunerating price for his produce'. He moved a further resolution for the meeting, one 'praying for reform', the introduction of limited enfranchisement, an issue of hot national debate and one linked to the balance of power in Parliament and hence bearing on the immediate problems. Amongst parliamentarians this was considered to be inflammatory; most would have preferred to dissociate economics and power and hope that the problems in the countryside could be solved without relinquishing a single shred of control. Locally, apparently, the speech 'was received throughout with the most flattering attention and with loud tokens of general approbation'.

Through the 1820s the price of corn declined overall from its wartime high, although there were political crises as it rose in the dearth years from 1822 to 1827. The farmers' grievances were addressed through reduction of rents by landowners in general nearly to the 1792 level; but labourers, as we have seen, were dealt with harshly.

February 1822, another year of dearth, was the next to see rioting by agricultural workers in Norfolk. The Editor of the *Norwich Mercury* was Richard Mackenzie Bacon, a Quaker and correspondent of Lord Suffield; he commented, 'the distresses of the farmer are fast falling on the labourer. No wonder that there should be engendered discontent and every kind of bad feeling'. As before the threshing machine was the focus of dissatisfaction. A crowd hauled one such a mile or so from Shimpling into Burston, leaving it undamaged on the Green. At about this same time unemployed labourers in Winfarthing moved a machine to Southanger, whose poor moved it on to Westbrook Green in Diss, some three miles further south. No mean feat. It must have sent out a powerful message as it stood, stranded in that public and common space (Diss, p70).

On saturday 16 february 1822 it was reported that 'a great number assembled at Diss and manifested great disposition to riot and mischief'. The ringleaders of the Diss disturbance originated from Shimpling and were bailed to appear at the next sitting of the Quarter Sessions at Norwich; but the level of unrest in the city was such that the hearing had to be postponed until more militia could be drafted in to support the local troops.

These warnings were unheeded and when James Sparham, a Burston farmer attempted to move a thresher from Burston to Shimpling a hostile crowd of fifty men first blocked the road and then unhitched the horses and set about the machine with hatchets, hooks and pickaxes, hacking it to destruction while James Sparham made a note of the ringleaders in his pocketbook. When six of the rioters were summoned to appear before the Justice of the Peace at the King's Head in Diss they were escorted by a mob of two hundred, the whole of Shimpling protesting against detention of those arrested. The Riot Act was read and the six were bailed until the next Quarter Sessions when two were

sentenced to twelve months' imprisonment in Aylsham Bridewell: 'Robert Chatten was named as the ringleader and, although the judge recommended him for merciful consideration on account of his youth, he was sentenced to twelve months imprisonment in Aylsham Bridewell, fined £5 and bound over in the sums of £100 himself, with two additional sureties of £50 to keep the peace for two years. James Goddard, too, came in for a harsh sentence, mainly because he had to be restrained from "committing an act of outrage on the person of the Magistrate acting in suppression of the Riot". James Sparham spoke up for the other four who were treated more leniently. James Caley, who received the lightest sentence, had "behaved in an exemplary manner. He has shown much contrition for his offence and expressed his full conviction of error by having been employed for working a machine since the riot"' (Cattermole pp14–5).

Severe sentences failed to suppress the grievance felt in south Norfolk and on 28 february men from Winfarthing, Bressingham and Shelfanger wrecked two machines. Seven men were named in the warrant issued to the Petty Constables of Winfarthing. Before they had to act on the warrant, ' the civil power availed itself of the assistance of the military'. The 16th Lancers broke their return journey from Norwich to Romford at Diss and, at dawn on 18 march, arrested the offenders and brought them to Diss to appear before the Justices. They were bailed to appear at the Quarter Sessions. The three ringleaders, one from each of the villages that contributed to the incident, were gaoled in the Norwich Castle Gaol for eighteen months in one case and twelve months in the two others. Apparently the riot was confined to the area around Diss at this time.

In the absence of parliamentary reform which might have enabled pressure to be applied to the roots of agricultural distress, a measure advocated by Lord Suffield, various remedies to alleviate it were proposed. The essayist Robert Carlyle took seriously the discontent of the labouring class and thought the call of the governing class for the working class not to breed so fast was unrealistic. Instead he proposed planned emigration to Canada and South Africa (America no longer being available) which were thought to be suitably in John Locke's original 'state of nature' that would permit land-grab by the english destitute. In 1829 William Allen's pamphlet *Colonies at Home*, recommended and circulated by Lord Suffield amongst receptive parliamentary colleagues, put forward the idea of settling the impoverished of the parish on wasteland with a house and seven acres. Lord Suffield argued that the cost of this, and of creating a commitment to the offspring of the poor as the Poor Law provided, was not financially feasible. Rather he favoured the provision '...for the man himself about half an acre, perhaps a quarter-acre of garden ground...' and as far as his sons went, 'I will apprentice these boys out to trades as soon as they become of sufficient age and at a great expense in the first instance rid myself of the burden forever'. Quaker records for this period show that apprenticeship schemes were favoured also by them. This was not, Lord Suffield admitted, a '...scheme of universal philanthropy...[but]...what I conceive to be most advantageous to my own interest'; and 'he who calculates upon the general adoption of a scheme upon other grounds must make up his mind to disappointment' (4 december 1829). Lord Suffield's biographer records: 'It is one of the most curious facts in the history of the effects of the Poor Laws that Lord Suffield offered [one of his labourers] one thousand pounds to abandon his claims on the parish and emigrate to Van Diemen's Land and that the offer was absolutely *refused*. He would allow no-one of his large family to make a settlement off the Gunton property'.

Yet another ruse, promoted by Lord Suffield, was that of spade husbandry (insisted upon by the rich landowner who saw the benefit of such industry in his own walled kitchen gardens) which could make the labouring man's garden productive for the family. In the context of alleviating the burden of poor rate spade husbandry was confined to the application of the technique to land inaccessible to or unworkable by the plough: because of the greater productivity of land worked by hand the farmer gained in profit at least what he spent in wages through the greater number of labourers that he employed and through the reduction of poor rates on the parish. Ingenious schemes all.

None of them quite met the case. As expedients to loosen the grip of costs on the landowner, farmer and parson they might have served but they scarcely addressed the problems of lack of food, low wages and underemployment and nor did they take the wishes, still less the demands, of the clamouring labourer and artisan into account.

LORD SUFFIELD OF GUNTON PARK
Based on Memoir of Lord Suffield
by his friend and correspondent, Richard Mackenzie Bacon

The allotments at Terrington-St-Clement were not the only provision of cultivable land for labourers in Norfolk in the early part of the nineteenth century: Lord Suffield of Gunton Park put forward arguments for instituting them in the parishes of his estate in march 1830 by reference to a successful experiment that had taken place thirty-six years earlier, in an unnamed neighbouring parish.

Edward Harbord, Third Baron Suffield (1781–1835) inherited the title and estate including Gunton Park on the death of his brother in september 1821. In the north-east of the county, its parishes stretched from the coast and as far south as North Walsham. Formerly he had attempted to enter public life by standing as a member of Parliament, first for Yarmouth and later for Norwich, but failed; and finally became MP for Norwich in 1820. Lord Suffield, in his own words, 'did not belong to any political party', by which he 'meant *faction*, understanding *faction* to be founded upon men, party upon principle.' He commented, 'The struggle of the first was for power, of the second for a system of measures '.

Lord Suffield's correspondence shows that he counted neighbours Coke of Holkham and Bulwer of Heydon amongst his friends and colleagues in the House of Lords which, by virtue of the baronetcy, was to be one of two arenas for public debate to which he addressed himself and through which he promoted his ideals; the other was the magistracy of Norfolk.

Lord Suffield inherited the baronetcy at a time of agricultural unrest: his gloomy view of a precarious situation had been expressed in a letter to his correspondent and biographer Richard MacKenzie Bacon, in 1820:
> 'Nothing I think can be more certain than that a revolution must ensue if the present Ministers continue in office but, with you, I think the frightful part of the equation follows: will a change of Ministers prevent revolution? I fear this now admits of doubt. If alive on the 23rd of January, I shall be in London ...'.

On becoming Third Baron, Lord Suffield did two unusual things: the first was to address a letter to all his agents and tenants, telling them that he was to break the custom of requiring those under his patronage to vote as he dictated. Instead he required his men to vote according to their consciences. He also observed that the encouragement of hares for sport on his land was a plague to his tenants whose crops were at their mercy: he ordered a cull of thousands of hares and offered them to any of his workers who cared to claim them. As fast as they could collect and dispose of them, tenants returned for more so that the hares were distributed, and probably sold or bartered, to many who were not entitled. At this time Lord Suffield's philanthropy was as great as his naivety.

These acts signal two of Lord Suffield's drives during his tenure which stem from a fundamental conscientiousness as to his duty by virtue of his position in life. Far from being an absentee landowner, he spent much of his time at Gunton and saw it as his responsibility, more than to provide for it and maintain it, to improve it. That meant making a profit, firstly, and then investing the profit in the house and the estate lands. But these improvements extended to the meaning given to the changes in agricultural practice that were being initiated throughout Norfolk by Coke and others: with enthusiasm he introduced the new technology on his estate in 1822 in the forms of machinery, one to break stones and to break and grind bones which was positioned on the canal at Antingham so that barges could transport the calcareous material for marling the fields; the other a sawmill, which exists and works still.

In his enthusiasm for the new machinery can be seen the source of a conflict which was continually to be played out in Norfolk during Lord Suffield's baronetcy: by effecting his duty to his estates, as he saw it, he sometimes undermined his desire and his capacity to help the needy tenants and labourers under his charge. Lord Suffield was persuaded that machines which carried out such hard labour would benefit his workers, not put them out of a job. As the visible and tangible source of grievance the new machinery eventually became the focus of riot on the estate. Lord Suffield was outspoken in defence of agricultural interest throughout his career in the Lords; he died on his estate, from a riding accident, in 1835. He settled the estate on his son in 1834, on the day of his coming to majority, with great celebration:

'A spacious square in front of the house was roped out, and three tables with seats, forming three sides of a square, were erected and covered with a plenteous dinner of beef, veal, mutton and plum puddings. Barrels of ale were placed in the centre. To this rustic feast were invited the labourers of sixteen parishes in which Lord Suffield's property lies. The first party that arrived came in waggons from Frettenham, attended by a band of music and they gave three hearty cheers on entering the park, which were joyously re-echoed by the spectators. The nearer neighbours marched up, headed by the principal tenants, and about one o'clock four hundred were comfortably seated. A more agreeable sight cannot be imagined. The men were all neatly clothed and looked like labourers of the most respectable class. These persons were the cottage tenants of his Lordship, and each of them had a garden allotment of from half an acre to two acres, and a habitation of at least three chambers. Nothing could be more cheerful and orderly ...'.

The 1830 agricultural riots have reached the history books as the 'Swing Riots', so-called because notices of threat signed by an alleged Captain Swing – the name is believed to derive from the swinging stick of the flail used in threshing, though the association with the gibbet connotes a more sinister implication – were pinned anonymously to the doors of those who had offended the labouring peasantry. The riots were rife in much of southern England and trouble was visited upon more parishes in Norfolk than in other counties.

This was rural protest. Aside from breaking up machinery, especially threshing-machines, and arson, meetings to demand higher wages and lower tithes took place: 'Lord Suffield was in London at the time but he was summoned by his steward, Mr Smith, who apprised his Lordship of the intention of the mob to proceed to Gunton and destroy a saw-mill which had been erected near the entrance of the Park, and was moved by water…They were at the moment of writing in the act of endeavouring to persuade and terrify Archdeacon Glover, of Southrepps, into a reduction of his tithes'. Gunton Park then employed 177 labourers, on a yearly tariff.

The troubles persisted from 22 november 1830 with offences committed every night until 30 november (even sundays were not sacred, it appears) right across the county and then intermittently through december, january and february 1831 and finally as late as april 1831. No sector of Norfolk was untouched by protest and discord, with incidents occurring in over 150 parishes, towns and villages and arrests in fifty cases, which tended to be concentrated in the central strip of Norfolk and in Broadland. Centres where there was severe trouble elsewhere included the north-west corner (adjoining the l'Estrange estate and the Holkham and Raynham estates) and in Fenland (FACHRS/2, Appendix I and II, pp261–94).

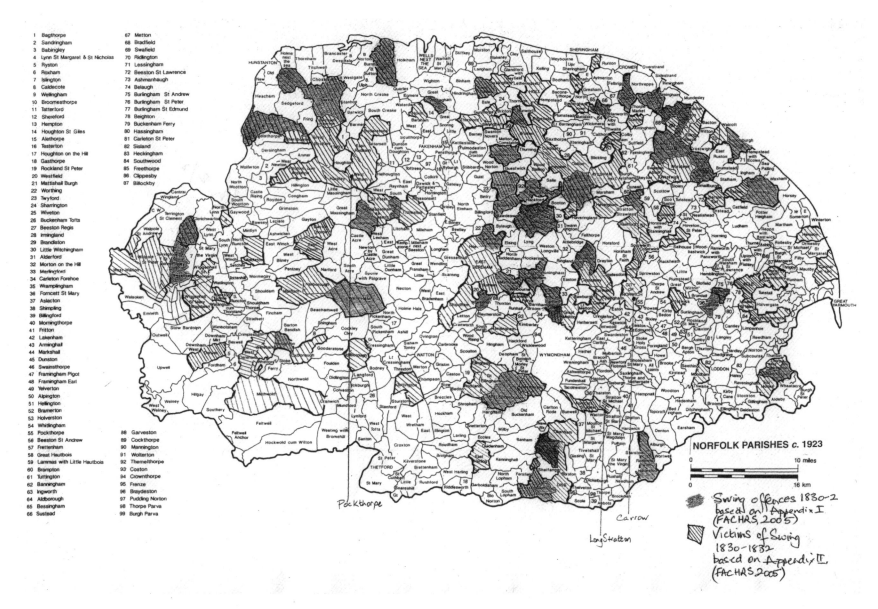

1 Bagthorpe
2 Sandringham
3 Babingley
4 Lynn St Margaret & St Nicholas
5 Ryston
6 Roxham
7 Islington
8 Caldecote
9 Wellingham
10 Broomesthorpe
11 Tatterford
12 Shereford
13 Hempton
14 Houghton St Giles
15 Alethorpe
16 Testerton
17 Houghton on the Hill
18 Gasthorpe
19 Rockland St Peter
20 Westfield
21 Mattishall Burgh
22 Worthing
23 Twyford
24 Sharrington
25 Wiveton
26 Buckenham Tofts
27 Beeston Regis
28 Irmingland
29 Brandiston
30 Little Witchingham
31 Alderford
32 Morton on the Hill
33 Merlingford
34 Carleton Forehoe
35 Wramplingham
36 Forncett St Mary
37 Aslacton
38 Shimpling
39 Billingford
40 Morningthorpe
41 Fritton
42 Lakenham
43 Arminghall
44 Markshall
45 Dunston
46 Swainsthorpe
47 Framingham Pigot
48 Framingham Earl
49 Yelverton
50 Alpington
51 Hellington
52 Bramerton
53 Holverston
54 Whitlingham
55 Pockthorpe
56 Beeston St Andrew
57 Frettenham
58 Great Hautbois
59 Lammas with Little Hautbois
60 Brampton
61 Tuttington
62 Banningham
63 Ingworth
64 Aldborough
65 Bessingham
66 Sustead

67 Metton
68 Bradfield
69 Swafield
70 Ridlington
71 Lessingham
72 Beeston St Lawrence
73 Ashmanhaugh
74 Belaugh
75 Burlingham St Andrew
76 Burlingham St Peter
77 Burlingham St Edmund
78 Beighton
79 Buckenham Ferry
80 Hassingham
81 Carleton St Peter
82 Sisland
83 Heckingham
84 Southwood
85 Freethorpe
86 Clippesby
87 Billockby

88 Garveston
89 Cockthorpe
90 Mannington
91 Wolterton
92 Themelthorpe
93 Coston
94 Crownthorpe
95 Frenze
96 Braydeston
97 Pudding Norton
98 Thorpe Parva
99 Burgh Parva

NORFOLK PARISHES c. 1923

Swing offences 1830-2 based on Appendix I (FACHRS, 2005)

Victims of Swing 1830-1832 based on Appendix II. (FACHRS, 2005)

Figure 2.2: Swing Riots in Norfolk 1830 (based on FACHRS 2005, Appendix I and Appendix II).

A focal point was North Walsham, the population centre and market town adjacent to Lord Suffield's estate, Gunton Park. Action initially took the form of arson and machine-breaking. Lord Suffield, Bulwer at Heydon and Thomas Coke at Holkham (whose extensive lands included a pocket at Sparham, next to Lyng where the papermill frequented by the diarist Parson Woodforde had worked; and at Weasenham) were all improvers and had introduced machines. Riots occurred in **Reepham** on 26 november 1830 and in later incidents the Heydon village fire engine was immobilized. By december 1830 local landowners and farmers agreed a minimum wage and the local use of threshing machines was banned. In North Walsham magistrates had supported labourers by printing a notice urging farmers to dismantle machinery and increase wages both. Farmers turned the wrath of the labourers towards the clergy by agreeing to wage increases provided that their costs, the tithe, was reduced and so the labourers transferred their effort to the local parson. The rare combination of farmer and labourer sometimes accomplished tithe reduction but it was a temporary alliance only. The Select Committee on Agriculture reported in 1833 that ill-will between the two groups had increased since the arson attacks (Susanna Wade-Martins/4, p126).

Insurgency spread south to Norwich and beyond, through Attleborough to the area around Diss and into Suffolk. Holders of land at Cranworth were subjected to machine-breaking but these were the most southerly to experience that effect. By the time the rebellion reached the southern and western parishes wage riots and tithe meetings were the order of the day, perhaps because the 1816 and 1822 riots had quashed any enthusiasm for introducing machinery in those areas, and these occurred as far west as Terrington-St-Clement – the Reverend Goode is given as a victim of insurgency there, despite his good offices in the 1816 troubles (FACHRS/2, p286) – on the north coast around Cromer and Sheringham and in some of the south-eastern parishes. This time the demand was for higher wages, the other plank of the labourers' platform (Rudé, p152).

On 23 january 1830 a third County Meeting was held, petitioning still for a reduction in the taxes on malt. But it was at the Quarter Sessions in march 1830 that Lord Suffield used his position as Chairman to address the Grand Jury of yeomanry, returning to the subject of rent reduction. Admitting that rents did contribute to the price of corn, they were not the sole nor main contributor: since 1792, the pre-War point of reference to which farmers were clamouring for a return, Lord Suffield said, 'tithe has increased, taxes have been augmented to an amount I will not venture to state and poor's rate has in some cases tripled'. Lord Suffield detailed the miserable consequences of the Poor Law:

> 'It is remarkable that in the same ratio in which the rate has increased the condition of the poor has become worse...If the labourer strive hard and earn much the gratuity from the parish is small; if he be idle and earn little his gratuity is large. Now I will ask, can human ingenuity devise a more effectual scheme for the *prevention of industry?*'

Lord Suffield evidenced the absence of increase in the poor rate where the poor had small portions of land attached to their cottages. He added that where the parish paid a reasonable wage to those cultivating on the parish acres they would reduce underemployment and create competition with farmers, who would be forced to find a fair wage. Since the poor rate had to make up the deficit between wage and the set rate, this would end the effective subsidy to the mean farmer and ensure that he paid properly for his workers' services. He argued that there was a remedy in law in the 1819 Select Vestries Act/Poor Law Amendment Act (59 Geo III) which empowered parishes to take 20 acres for cultivation: also, there were measures which allowed the idle poor to 'be set to labour as to the tread-wheel', while for the industrious inhabitant the land may 'by him or her be occupied and cultivated on his or her own account, and for his or her own benefit, at reasonable rent and...terms'. But 'labour without participation in its fruits will never inculcate a love of industry'. He concluded triumphantly,

> 'Apply the first to the idle, the last to the industrious and I am persuaded we should soon lose sight and feeling of the poor's rate and our peasantry would become, what we all desire to see them, *useful, moral and happy*'.

He added,

> 'As a matter of policy, had I no other motive, I shall extend this beneficial system as speedily and widely as possible on my own property. Last week I was much occupied in making such allotments'.

He was not alone. The Survey has identified seven parishes each in 1830 and 1831 in which allotment sites were created, the greatest number for any single year recorded. In 1832 the Survey identifies but one, but in 1833 the figure was five (of the total, sixteen are found in Archer, p62). The north and west of the county was dominated by the large estate-owners including Coke of Holkham who maintained more than forty-three thousand acres so it is not surprising that it was from these lands that parcels were found to dedicate to allotments (Susanna Wade-Martin/2, Figure 15, p13).

Following the troubles of 1830 many were the voices raised in recognition of the labourers' need. By this time the Reverend Steven de Mainbray had no hesitation in connecting enclosure with rural poverty and the increase in poor relief in his writing of 1831 *The Poor Man's Best Friend; or, Land to Cultivate for his Own Benefit:* cottagers were 'reduced to wage labourers' since they had no land left attached to their cottages and he advocated giving the four acres of the original Act of Elizabeth I. In the same year William Allen had *A Plan for Benefiting the Agricultural Labourers,* also arguing that they be given 'a cottage and land'. This proposal was endorsed by Thomas Postans who in his *Letter to Sir Thomas Baring* of 1831 deplored the consequences of enclosure and proposed that labourers have available a cottage on farm land, 'and the erection of cottages on waste lands, with an allotment of the soil'. In a less specific vein, Montague Gore wrote an open *Letter to Landed Proprietors* entitled *Allotments of land:* 'The first great advantage of this plan appears to one to consist in its certain tendency to diminish the amount of poor's rates. It is the poor's rate which is the curse that at present preys on the vitals of agricultural prosperity; which diminishes the landlord's rent and debases the character of the peasant. But give the labourer half an acre of land and allow him reasonable wages and you will find your own incomes freed from a

burthensome charge and the parish pauper converted into an industrious peasant'.

Between 1795 and 1835 some 184 pamphlets had been produced which lauded the benefits of allotments. In the period 1830–3 alone 62 pamphlets were printed (Barnett p175). Allotments gradually replaced other proposals, such as home colonization, spade husbandry, cow pastures and potato grounds for repairing the condition of the agricultural labourer and for those whose minds were bent to the problem the issue of rural poverty became inextricably meshed with individual rights to land.

Lord Suffield continued to press for the abandonment of poor rate in favour of allotments of land granted and ultimately rented to labourers in a 'charge' which he printed and sent to influential parliamentary figures, among them his neighbour Lord Walpole, the Member of Parliament John Fleming and Lord Dacre. The last of these was an active participant in the Sturges Bourne Parliamentary Committee which strongly supported the garden allotments scheme.

On 11 november 1830 the Earl of Winchilsea's Agricultural Employment Bill was introduced which promoted the adoption of a 'labour rate' to alleviate distress; Lord Suffield spoke in favour of allotments as a measure for minimizing the poor rate. The Bill was not pursued, but by the end of the month a similar Bill was introduced in the Commons, by Lord Nugent; voices in support of allotments were heard, including those of J I Briscoe, MP for Surrey and prominent in the Labourers' Friend Society, the leading organisation advocating allotment provision. Lord Nugent, himself a member of LFS and allotment supporter, despite the clauses in the 1819 Poor Law Amendment Act addressing land rental, believed that additional legislation would be required in order to enable parishes to create allotments for all: this was provided by Acts of 1831 and 1832.

At the end of the year, on 12 december 1830, Lord Suffield was able to write: 'Tranquility now being restored, all the farmers are of course reducing their wages to that miserable rate that led to the recent disturbances and, as I expected, those who raised the wages to the highest pitch under extreme alarm, and perhaps a little consciousness of injustice towards the labourer, are among the first to return to the former rate of payment'.

Winter 1831–2 saw some further trouble in north-east Norfolk, in Happisburgh especially where six people fell victim to Captain Swing. Unrest spilled into the summer: in Witchingham a Robert Guymer was arrested in april, to be followed by ten more Witchingham men on 29 may; North Walsham saw one arrest in may and in the same month Winfarthing notched up seven victims; seven were arrested in Stody on 2 july 1832; there was a further arrest in Swaffham in October 1832, to close the series (FACHRS op cit). The parishes of Briston and Edgefield, adjacent to the Stody estate, were 'an extreme example...a sorely disturbed parish experiencing five arson attacks in 1832–3 and an extremely high unemployment rate' (Archer, p23).

The reasons for the uprisings and outcry were no longer directly tied to the seizure of commons and wastes used by poor people; of the 153 places in Norfolk where incidents took place five had been enclosed before 1793 and a mere 22 were enclosed from 1793–1815 (*Atlas*, pp24–5 and Figure 1, from Birtles/2 p151). 'One of the few instances of violent opposition to enclosure in East Anglia was at North and South Lopham (enclosed 1812 and 1815) where, as it happens, two hundred acres had been allocated to the poor (the present town lands and fuel allotment in the fen)...[when]..."William Mason, Thomas Brook, Edmund Chilley and Ann Rush were indicted for wilfully and maliciously damaging a fence, the property of Charles Green, made under the Lopham Inclosure Act, which offence is made felony...The prisoner Mason addressed the Court as champion of the rights of the poor, whose property he said the commons were. The judge stated distinctly to the prisoners and to the jury that the poor had no such right...Mason was sentenced to twelve and the others to three months' imprisonment" (Tate, pp214–5).

The areas in which trouble was rife were those that experienced population increase through the first half of the nineteenth century (*Atlas*, pp132–3) so that competition for work would have been still keener. The major estate-owners of the county experienced trouble on their holdings, as we have seen, but not on every piece of it, suggesting that when feelings overran it was due to some more local experience, which the Swing letters make explicit: the introduction of machinery, pitiful wages and swingeing tithes. The men and their families could not live on what was paid.

It would appear, if any conclusion can be drawn at all, that allotments did not become the whole even if they were part of a solution to rural poverty; or perhaps the idea had not been introduced on a sufficiently large scale. Every site required the sacrifice of real estate, and landowners – estate holders, parishes, the clergy – squabbled about whose responsibility it was. Some were reluctant to sacrifice the land: if it was profitable then the profits should be those of the landowner and if it was waste then it was not profitable for landowner, tenant or labourer. Farmers took advantage of the poor masses in keeping wages low. And the clergy resented the pressure to lower tithes. In the end it was the argument for keeping down the poor rate which swayed the Trustees of the poor and in 1834 the Poor Law Commissioners.

Fenland Terrington-St. Clement, still with a single one-acre plot, was the first certain garden allotment site in Norfolk, created in 1816.

Amongst the oldest allotments in Norfolk, Litcham was created at enclosure.

The acre garden plot next to St. James's Church, Castle Acre is let from the Holkham Estate.

Church lands have been let for garden allotments in Norfolk from the mid-nineteenth century. These are next to St. Nicholas' Church, Dereham.

3 | farmers fall out

Places were changed – a tree gone here, a bough there, bringing in a long ray of light where no light was before – a road was trimmed and narrowed, and the green straggling pathway by its side enclosed and cultivated. A great improvement it was called; but Margaret sighed over the old picturesqueness, the old gloom, and the grassy wayside of former days.

North and South (1854)

Elizabeth Gaskell

In the sense that local tenants produced crops on a portion of land for their own benefit, the Survey has identified 56 new allotment sites in Norfolk for the period 1816–1860:

Table 3.1: Norfolk allotment sites (based on Survey):

Period	to 1816	1816–1830	1831–1840	1841–1850	1851–1860
	7	11^	19^	13	12*

^ *of the thirty identifications 1816–1840, 24 are in Archer/3 p24.*
* *of the twelve parishes for which the record indicates that they gained allotments between 1851–1860 seven may have been founded earlier; the record represents the earliest ascription but does not reveal the founding date based, as it is, on White's Trade Directories of 1845 and 1854.*

Archer identified a burst of allotment provision between 1831–3 (Archer/2, p24). Even on Lord Suffield's estate at Gunton allotments were not widespread until the 1830s: a resident of Gunton, a Mr Smith, gave evidence to the Poor Law Commissioners on the Employment of Women and Children for their 1843 Report, saying that

'…the system…has been made general here in the last ten years. There were allotments before that, but only a few; we found that they worked so well, that they made the tenants so much more thrifty than those without them, that the late Lord Suffield made it general'.

After 1860, beginning a period of benevolent climate, the rate of acquisition drops dramatically to two in the following decade, but the significant finding of the figures is that it did not slow between 1830 and 1860.

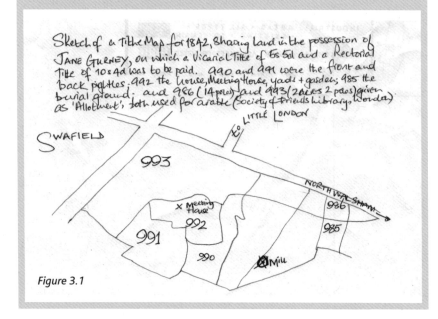

Figure 3.1

In this period rural protest remained a recurring feature of Norfolk life, through the depredations of continuing poor climate and resultant dearth years. In his 1844 *Report on Agriculture in Norfolk* which was awarded first prize by the Royal Society of Agriculture Richard Noverre Bacon, the Earl of Leicester's Estate Manager, provided a Table of labourers' wages relative to wheat prices for the years 1804–1843 inclusive (p144). Despite substantial fluctuations in wheat values, wages barely reflect those movements. The farmer could not expect that there would be an increase in price of his product over the long term but neither could the labourer, whose wage of nine shillings per week in 1843 was lower than the mean and in the lowest quartile for the period reviewed. The only sign of improvement in his position, if it can be called that, was an overall decrease in difference between the price of wheat and the weekly wage. Bacon concluded,

> "It ought, however, in justice to be stated that in almost all the enquiries which have been made upon this point we have invariably found the rate of wages higher in proportion when the price of corn was low than when high prices have been obtained" (p143).

In other words, the farmer was keeping his profits when wages rose above the barest subsistence.

The single biggest change to the status of the agricultural labourer over the prior forty years identified by Bacon was severance from the 'mutual respect and attachment' engendered by the inclusion of the labourer in the farm household, and reduction to the weekly or piece-rate. To this uncertainty could be added the resulting market-place in housing and the depredations of unemployment and underemployment, leading to the inevitable 'retrograding…[of their] moral and physical condition … until at one period a complete disorganization of the rural districts in Norfolk was threatened' (p142) by the 'destruction of machinery and similar violences' (p149), by which Bacon meant the Swing Riots of 1830.

After the 1830 troubles the clergy and landowners mended the relationship with the worker by offering better conditions of work, which included year-long contracts and allotments in some cases. Farmers remained set against allotments and the 1834 Poor Law Commissioners recorded a number of witnesses speaking to that effect:

'In the minds of many occupiers there exists considerable prejudice on this subject…they are afraid of making labourers independent and some look with an evil eye to a supposed diminution of their profits by introducing a new class of producers.'

And, again:

'The farmers object very generally to the introduction of allotments. They are jealous of such deductions from their holdings; they have to go further for manure; and they object to the increasing independence of the labourers.'

Bacon reported that, following the severest troubles, the labourer and occupier had both 'become aware of their mutual dependence', resulting in improvements to the conduct of the labourer who has become 'more steady, diligent and obliging' (Bacon p156). He went on to describe the provision in north Norfolk 'following Legislation' – he does not specify what – of accommodation and support and yearly wages for labourers of different states. He continued,

'…the system of Cottage Allotments … has also been found a great inducement to industry and sobriety; the public-house has been forsaken for the garden and the home of the labourer has become more happy' (Bacon p157).

Labourers were further persuaded of the benefits of 'industry, attachment and morality' by the formation of Associations for the Reward of Industry of deserving Labourers and their Children, and of Horticultural Societies which rewarded the responsive (Bacon p158). The aim of improvement was applied to the allotment-holder as well. Created in 1833, the Agreement for **Litcham** allotments establishes that they were to go to 'poor parishioners who are selected as likely to make good use of them', those of 'industrious habits and good character'. To those who 'cultivate their land in the cleanest and most fruitful manner' there should be a 'further premium or reward', following inspection by the Minister and Churchwardens. This conception of allotments as reward for good behaviour was a precursor to the establishment of competitions held within **agricultural associations**.

Following the Swing Riots there was a flurry of activity in Parliament to alleviate the distress of the poor and to concede some recognition of the stake of workers in the land. Where the poor still had access to the commons the poor rates were usually lower than where they had lost such rights (Susanna Wade-Martins/4 p82) and the same was alleged of allotment schemes. The belief grew throughout the nineteenth century – it was argued in Parliament – that parishes with allotments had not been subject to riot and would not be, **Terrington-St-Clement** notwithstanding. With the Inclosure of Wastes Act 1831, allowing parishes with the permission of the Lord of the Manor to use or rent up to fifty acres of commons or wastes for providing employment or letting to the poor; and the Crown Lands Inclosure Act 1831 which enabled parishes to do the same with forest or wastes belonging to the Crown, when they should apply for permission to the Treasury, the nobility were seen to be relinquishing land to the poorest. These two Acts were consolidated by the Fuel Allotments Act 1832, by which it was suggested that parishes let unproductive fuel allotments in small portions to the poor, thus giving parishes the powers of creating allotments in the modern sense of the word.

Government expected parishes to introduce allotment schemes as a matter of course and the 1832–4 Poor Law Commissioners' Enquiry heard evidence as to their efficacy: as at Terrington-St-Clement, Cranworth was a parish in which allotments had been offered by the local clergyman, the Reverend Philip Gurdon, to alleviate extremities of need:

'There cannot, I think, exist a doubt of the general benefit arising from the allotment system…[I know]…of no plan that I could have adopted that could possibly have so materially improved the welfare and respectability of my parishioners' (Burchardt, p191).

He was one of many attesting to the benefits of allotments to the tenant and parish, both, and to the demand for them. The traditional association between clergy and gardens and their promotion of allotments through allotment societies persisted throughout the nineteenth century (Buchan pp888–893).

Although in the smallest group by far, allotments on church land persisted over time. On the other hand, farmers in East Anglia were more set against allotments than in other regions and were more likely than previously to be targeted in the decades 1840–70. Some farmers released land for **potato grounds**, a temporary expedient, but most remained obdurate in their opposition to allotments. By 1833 when the Parliamentary Enquiry into the State of Agriculture reported some farmers were tired of 'the struggle of keeping profits up by beating down wages…[it] is so painful that men are indisposed to embark on it'. Another farmer regretted 'the nuisance of having a quantity of unemployed people teasing for allowances and threatening'. One remedy was to delay mechanization; and in view of the low wages of the area there cannot have been an incentive to convert to machines. Some farmers took further advantage of the plight of the agricultural labourer by using the gangmasters, an expedient at its height after 1834 and the introduction of the New Poor Law, to recruit labour that did not have secure employment and which was forced to congregate in speculatively-built cottages or in camps on the outskirts of parishes, as at Castle Acre, which were not part of estates (Riches, p144).

Researches record that Norfolk had 34 allotment sites, representing less than one quarter of all its parishes (Table 3.2, shows 31 which the Survey found).

In 1834 came the Poor Law Amendment Act, the New Poor Law as it has come to be known, which prohibited Guardians of the poor to pay for outdoor relief any longer. The Boards of Guardians and Unions created by the Act administered a harsh regime in which conditions inside the workhouse were to be less attractive than impoverishment on the outside, with man and wife – Malthus' population vector in mind – separated.

Shortly after the new law was put into practice in Grimston, for example, in december 1835 of those 23 who applied for relief only seven were granted it and by january 1836 when there were 103

Table 3.2: allotment sites in Norfolk to 1834

1779 Inclosure Award	^ Grimston
1802	Bressingham
1803 Inclosure Award	^ Lingwood
1810 Inclosure Award	^ Westfield
1813	^ Guist
1815 Inclosure Award	^ Toftwood
1816	^ Terrington-St-Clement
1820 (not later than)	^ Foulsham
1822	^ Burnham Thorpe
	^ Kimberley
1826	Weasenham
1830	Cranworth
	* Great Witchingham
	Heydon
	Ovington
	Plumstead (prob N Norfolk)
	Postwick
	Reepham
1831	Brockdish
	North Elmham
	Quidenham
	Roydon
	Shotesham
	Sutton
	Thorpe Abbots
1832	* Pulham St Mary Magdalen
1833	Briston
	Edgefield
	Frettenham
	Gunton
	^ Litcham

^ source the Survey
* source *White's Trade Directory* 1854
  Other identifications are found in Archer/3, p24.

requests 66 were refused. On 5 february 1836 the Guardians' meeting was interrupted by rough music and had to be abandoned (Lee, pp49–62). The Commissioners' recommendations were based on the premise that employment would be available to all able-bodied; if able-bodied and unemployed, then idle; if idle, undeserving.

A kinder solution was administered at Dickleburgh. In 1834 the Weekly Book is

'…full of references to payments to parish paupers for work done on the green…the poor enclosure stands on an island of arable within a pasture on the Tithe Map of 1840…and the Trustees of the Poor as its owners. This suggests that the land was used as garden allotments'.

Land was sold off in 1853 to meet the costs of enclosure. After that the poor had access to garden allotments provided 'outside the terms of the enclosure' (Birtles/1 p91).

The demand for allotments can only have been reinforced when the 1834 Act was used to screw down wages to a further low point. Bacon shows that they recovered again in accordance with wheat prices but returned once more to the nine shillings per week low by 1843; the Survey indicates that between 1834 and 1840 the provision of new allotments appears to have all-but ceased and only picked up after 1843. With the exception of Lingwood parishes in which the workhouse stood appear not to have introduced allotments, suggesting that neither farmers, landowners nor the clergy as Trustees of the Boards of Guardians saw the need for an alternative to the problems of unemployment.

In 1838 John Yelloly FRS wrote that caution must be applied in allocating allotments:

'Some degree of prejudice against…the allotment system, which is viewed by many with disapprobation and distrust…for an allotment of ground may…imply such a portion as is sufficient to occupy a person's whole time in cultivating it, or what may be merely enough to fill up his leisure hours. In the former case a man quits the position of a labourer; in the latter, the care of his garden does not interfere with his regular employment as a husbandman, and with his permanent and paramount duties as a servant'.

But he was aware of a beneficial scheme introduced by John Mitchell of Wattelfield, near Wymondham who rented to his labourers not only a cottage with a quarter-acre garden attached, but also a two-acre plot, provided that the latter was cultivated by spade or fork, so-called spade husbandry:

'It is clear, however, that only a small portion of this ground can be managed by themselves as the men have usually full work under Mr Mitchell, which is necessarily required to be the prime object of their attention; but they find it worth their while to pay such labourers as may happen at particular times to be out of employ fair wages for working their ground; they often contrive to throw in a little labour of their own at mealtime or in the morning or evening…I saw very luxurient crops of wheat, barley and beans on their little allotments'(pp15–6).

Yelloly knew of other examples: Mr Gedney of Redenhall, near Harleston who had increased the acreage under allotments from eighteen to fifty acres the previous year; Lord Braybrooke in Essex; Sir Edward Kerrison in Suffolk and also in Bungay where the 'inhabitants have in the past two to three years had 68 allotments of a quarter-acre each, used by mechanics and working people'. **Norwich** had garden allotments in 1840 (Archer, p24), location unknown.

Another review in 1844 by James Henry Kent of Suffolk addressed two letters to the Duke of Grafton, passing *Remarks on the injuriousness of the Consolidation of Small Farms and the benefits of Small Occupations and Allotments; with some observations on the past and present state of the Agricultural Labourers.* Kent's analysis is interesting for the points where he and Bacon agree on the history of agricultural unrest and where there is disagreement; specifically, in detailing the 1843–4 rebellions, not mentioned at all by Bacon. Bacon's optimistic gloss did not anticipate the period of 'arson and agricultural depression' in the winter of 1843–4 and again through 1849–51 (following potato blight 1845–9) which persisted to the mid-1850s. Apparently farmers recognized the risk in converting to machinery as late as 1861 when George Gray, an 'engine driver' from Mundesley, died at the age of 35, having caught pneumonia while 'watching over' a threshing machine (letter from Richard Watts 17 november 2006). Perhaps those with whom Bacon was in contact were immune to the worst attacks since the latter series of troubles targeted farmers, rather than landowners and clergy, who had been the objects of ire by the 1816–32 series (Archer/2 pp21–36). Bacon attests to the 'new paternalism' evoked in landowners like his own master. This may explain the surprising words of the great sceptic, Cobbett, who wrote in 1822,

> 'Here at Holt as everywhere else I hear every creature speak loudly in praise of Mr Coke. It is well-known to my readers that I think nothing of him as a *public* man...but it would be base of me not to say that I hear from men of all parties, and sensible men too, expressions made use of towards him that affectionate children use towards the best of parents. I have not met a single exception.'(p34).

But in 1843 little in the attitude of the farmer had changed (Mozelle, pp493–4).

Kent's appeals to the Duke of Grafton speak of the urgency of events as late as 1840 whereas Bacon refers only to the troubles of 1830. Having reviewed the plight of the agricultural labourer since the onset of the Napoleonic Wars in 1793, Kent rounds on the New Poor Law of 1834:

> 'During the seven years ending 1842 no less than 10 869 individuals have been committed to Gaol from the Workhouses of England and Wales for breaches of the regulations in those places...crime has increased fifty per cent within the seven years ending 1842' (p51).

Further, incidents of incendiarism

> '...had not been of such frequent occurrence...as it has been in the county of Suffolk and the adjoining counties in the years 1843 and 1844, during twelve months of which time there have been upwards of two hundred incendiary fires, or one every forty-eight hours' (p31).

James Kent then detailed the benefit of allotments by the example of his own parish of Stanton where 44 acres of land were divided into plots of half an acre for the married men, whose families worked the land, and a quarter of an acre for the single men; and through general remarks eulogizing both spade husbandry and the allotment system.

In 1843 Sir Henry Brougham reported on the workings of the New Poor Law and told in wonderful detail what provisions existed in each Norfolk parish for supporting the poor; insofar as he described each charitable benefit his work mirrors that of Zachary Clark in 1811. He named a number of towns and parishes in which land was used to provide plots for the poor but either a poor wage or the workhouse was the norm.

The 1843 Select Committee on the Labouring Poor (Allotments of Land), whose backbone was Members of the Labourers' Friend Society, in 1843 conducted an investigation into the '...results of the Allotment System and into the propriety of setting apart a portion of all waste lands which shall be inclosed by Act of Parliament...' (pii) and repeated the assertion of the 1834 Committee that allotments were beneficial both to lessor and tenant.

The preamble to their Report explains that after the Swing troubles and the creation of allotments by landowners throughout southern England, LFS had been formed from within the gentry with the aim of disseminating through their magazine information about the benefits of the system. **West Winch** acquired both parish and glebe allotments in October 1844 through the formation of a branch of the LFS, whose inspiration was 'the Christian and active benevolence' of the Right Honorable the Lord W H H Cholmondley of Houghton Hall and Lord of

Table 3.3

Report on the County of Norfolk by Sir Henry Brougham (1843), showing parish' charitable and statutory measures for alleviating the distress of the poor – small pieces of land allocated to local people – where his notes clarify their usage. (NB: unless other evidence corroborates the ascription, these parishes have not been included in the Survey tally.)

Attleborough	57A 2R 0P	An allotment for 'certain poor...cut for fuel and cultivated'
Bressingham	24A 3R 35P	'Fuel allotment...held in plots by poor parishioners'
Briston	'Small pieces...	Town Land'
Feltwell St Mary & St Nicholas	4A 2R 19P	Clough's Charity 'divided amongst six labourers'
Hemsby	10R 0R 22P	Poor's Lands 'part-let to poor in lots at low rents'
Hingham	2A 2R 8P	Payne's Charity 'let to poor in lots'
	8A 0R0P	Church Estate 'part let to poor in lots'
Holme Hale	21A 3R 33P	Fuel allotment 'let to 30 poor at 5s.an acre'
Topcroft	1A 2R 0P	Allotment
Walpole-St-Andrew	85A 0R 27P	Dole lands and houses for the 'industrious poor not receiving relief. Part of lands (45 acres) divided in plots and let to poor at certain rents. Since 1829 no rents paid' [Coincidence or not, current O/S maps show the land around Wisbech littered with allotments.]

the Manor of West Winch. The purpose of the West Winch Society was 'hiring land and letting it out to the poor, on the *allotment system*' and the Rules and Regulations of the Society established the means to and extent of benevolence.

Evidence was taken from members of the LFS and supporters of allotment schemes but also from MP William Miles who believed that allocating the fifty acres allowed by the Fuel Allotments Act of 1832 was 'legalized robbery' unless those with an interest in the land were recompensed through savings brought about by a General Inclosure Act, which would relieve them of the financial burden of prosecuting a private Act of Parliament. A General Inclosure Act was indeed the recommendation of the Select Committee. It also specified the quarter-acre limit of the plot so that it would be 'no bigger than can be cultivated in leisure hours' and only by spade husbandry, not plough; that they 'should be near the labourers' dwelling'; that they 'should not charge excessive rent'; and that 'tithes, rates and taxes should be paid by the owner, not occupier'. It concluded:

'The allotment system...appears to be the natural remedy for one of the detrimental changes in the condition of the labouring classes of this country, which the lapse of years has wrought, by gradually shutting them out from all personal and direct interest in the produce of the soil, and throwing them for subsistence wholly and exclusively upon wages...the increased value which the passing a General Inclosure Act would confer on the property possessed by individuals in common lands renders it equitable for Parliament to make provision in such an Act for the benefit of the industrious poor and the rate-payers; more especially as the enclosure of most common land deprives some poor persons of advantages which they would otherwise enjoy, either by sufferance, by payment, or by rights which have been extinguished...the tenancy of land under the garden allotment system is a powerful means of bettering the condition of those classes who depend for livelihood upon their manual labour'.

Bills were put before the House in riot years 1843 and 1844. The debate was prolonged. The issue of allotments as Lord Suffield had foreshadowed had implications for democracy and rights. Through the Bill the allocation of land for gardens was linked with the fight for preservation of recreational common land and some factions within Parliament accepted one or other of these proposals but not necessarily both. The Radicals led by Arthur Roebuck, a member of the Utilitarian Society formed by the philosophers and humanitarians Jeremy Bentham and John Stuart Mill, supported recreational land but not garden allotments. Mill, dryly logical in the face of the emotion of the crowd, argued that allotments were a device to 'make people grow their own poor rates'. The process of enclosure in Norfolk was nearing the end of its natural life so, despite the Act giving powers to Enclosure Commissioners to authorize enclosures *only on condition* that land be set aside for garden allotments, there is no evidence from the Survey of an accelerated allocation of allotment land in parishes after its passing. Further, much later on, in 1868 at Swaffham and 1870 at Fakenham, when the populace was facing enclosure of the commons, it had to protest in order to secure allotments.

But there was general acceptance that severance of the poor from rights to land needed to be curbed and the Bill became Act in 1845. The General Enclosure Act gave the appearance of being a landmark in restoring some level of security to the labourer and in *requiring* that provision be made for the landless poor in the form of **field gardens**, limited to a quarter acre, on the enclosure of commons and wastes; for placing the responsibility for doing so formally in the hands of the parish trustees; and for creating designated Allotment Wardens from the ranks of the churchwardens and 'other elected persons'.

Enclosure eventually came to a close in the decade 1865–75. From the 1840s fen drainage schemes, using wind and steam pumps – the latter a sign that mechanization was finally becoming established – enabled yet more land to be taken into production. This was a period of grand estates and farming improvements including those like the Earl of Leicester's Holkham Estate plans for estate buildings, field layouts and crop rotation systems that marked a golden age of farming. Land acquisition meant more work, albeit in many cases of a piecemeal kind which left the labourer without guarantee of employment in the long term.

It would be surprising if allotment schemes were the mechanism that solved the problem of unrest in all localities and where the picture of relationships was more complex still, as at Syderstone, their introduction fomented civil strife when the allotment scheme that benefited one set of labourers was seen by a rival group as favouritism, setting up those labelled deserving as a target for the unrewarded (Archer/2 p30).

But rather than accept the fate of the workhouse emigration to the mill towns of the north via the Grand Union Canal, work guaranteed, was a scheme offered to the rural unemployed and two thousand men, women and children eligible to work in factories from Norfolk and Suffolk had elected to take that option in the 1830s. Some emigrated to Canada and America (the latter no longer off-limits).

Eventually allotments gradually replaced other means to repairing the condition of the agricultural labourer. The total number of schemes overall even to 1850 was but a small proportion of the 722 parishes existing in Norfolk then but allotments represented a gentler solution until the railways came to Norfolk in the 1850s, offering both employment and allotments.

4 | unions and urbanization

It was now the season for planting and sowing; many gardens and allotments of the villagers had already received their spring tillage; but the garden and the allotment of the Durbeyfields were behindhand. She found, to her dismay, that this was owing to their having eaten all the seed potatoes – that last lapse of the improvident. At the earliest moment she obtained what others she could procure, and in a few days her father was well enough to see to the garden...while she herself undertook the allotment-plot which they rented in a field a couple of hundred yards out of the village...The plot of ground was in a high, dry, open enclosure, where there were forty or fifty such pieces and where labour was at its briskest when the hired labour of the day had ended. Digging began usually at six o'clock and extended indefinitely into the dusk or moonlight. Just now heaps of dead weeds and refuse were burning on many of the plots, the dry weather favouring their combustion...As evening thickened some of the gardening men and women gave over for the night, but the greater number remained to get their planting done, Tess being among them...A few small nondescript stars were appearing elsewhere. In the distance a dog barked, and wheels occasionally rattled along the dry road. Still the prongs continued to click assiduously, for it was not late; and though the air was fresh and keen there was a whisper of spring in it that cheered the workers on. Nobody looked at his or her companions. The eyes of all were on the soil as its turned surface was revealed by the fires.

Tess of the Durbervilles (1891)

Thomas Hardy

For a county that was more than anything else agricultural, whose industries up to the nineteenth centuries were always light industries like lace-making, printing and publishing, shoemaking and the linen trade or connected to agriculture, the arrival of the railways from the 1840s was a significant development for the nature of work and had both direct and indirect effects on the history of allotments in Norfolk. The indirect effect was that there was an alternative to working in fields for the labourer and this meant that the farmer was for the first time in competition with other local employers. The direct effect was that the railway companies created allotments for their workers, perhaps importing a custom that had grown up with the industrialization of the midlands and north of England. Birmingham had **guinea gardens** on its outskirts from the 1750s until the town swelled to engulf them (NSALG, p3c) and there were other such at Coventry and Nottingham but factory hours were too long for urban allotments to become practicable until the 1880s and 1890s when an eight-hour shift was introduced (FHCRS Newsletter/2, p6).

In broad terms the early railways of the 1840s and 1850s ran from Norfolk's principal towns of Norwich, Kings Lynn and Great Yarmouth to the south to connect trade with London and the rest of East Anglia. The northern half of the county was not connected to the system until the 1880s (*Atlas* pp148–9). For its three stations (of which only one remains) Norwich certainly had allotments located to the side of the railways lines or at its depots. A map of 1873 of Thorpe which was then part of the city shows the railway station and workshops close to cottages with long gardens on the Great Yarmouth Turnpike Road and

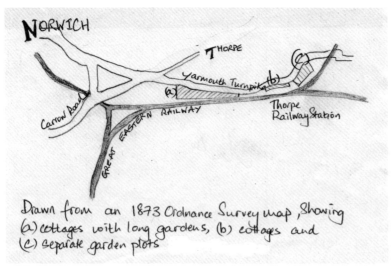

Figure 4.1

another set of cottages having separate plots. They are on land bordering the track of the Great Eastern Railway and must be on railway ground. The same is true of the other towns for which railway allotments have been confirmed: Aylsham, **East Dereham**, Melton Constable and Sheringham. **Harleston** is an exception: its pre-existing extensive allotment sites originate in 1844 and one was located on the outskirts of the town to the north, close to where the station was built in the 1880s so it may have been felt that there was no need for duplication.

Between 1875 and 1914 the Survey lists 38 towns and parishes that acquired allotments, some of them – Aylsham, **Dereham**, **Norwich** – had many more than a single site and in one case, Syderstone, the allotments were extended a few years after the original site was created. Some of the parishes, as we know, and especially in the south and east environs of Norwich, had allotments at a distance from the settlement – Arminghall, Blofield, **Docking**, **Little Melton**, Postwick, Great and Little Snoring, Stoke Holy Cross. For the same period in the whole of the county only eight sites appear that are not adjoining railway lines and these were linked to market towns. The sole

exception is **Castle Acre** which had its own peculiar problems, and would have again. This is not to say by any means that the railways brought allotments to Norfolk, except in the narrow sense already described, but they certainly made markets accessible, giving an added incentive to the demand for allotments.

Another feature of railway-led allotment foundation is the scale. Norfolk can only be described as having many large allotments whether that means the size of sites, or size of plots, or the area covered in totality, as in Fenland or along the north-east coastal railway, to cite just two areas. Such schemes emerged and evolved over decades and may have been due to legislative changes which permitted changes in terminology that brought large projects into the allotment category, as well as to economic developments in the locality which took advantage of Norfolk's expansive geography. The scale of the outcome, whatever the reason, was impressive.

Melton Constable was a railway village almost created from scratch, the base for the Midlands and Great Northern Joint Railway Company (fondly known as the Muddle and Go Nowhere Railway) built with alien midlands-yellow and grey brick: in 1881 its population was 118 and by 1911 it had grown to 1157. It is not surprising that the allotment site provided as part of the package which included terraces of houses, a grocer's shop, doctor and recreation ground provided by the company had two hundred plots (Wade-Martins/1, p95–6). Today that exists vestigially, but there is a parish site.

In 1873 occurred the first official 'census' of allotments which appeared as an appendix for the government crop returns for that year (Burchardt, p224–5). This showed

	Acres	Norfolk % of total	Plots	Norfolk % of total
Norfolk	1 628		6 400	
East Anglia*	12 255	13.3	46 735	13.7
England	58 966	2.3	242 542	2.7

Huntingdonshire, Suffolk, Essex, Cambridgeshire, Lincolnshire, Norfolk

These figures are remarkably consistent about the size of allotments, a neat quarter-acre. The Census may have used this statistic as a standard in order to define the garden allotments that they counted, distinguishing them from **field gardens** and **field allotments**. The Survey and other sources show that parishes described as 'allotments' sites which varied in size from half to one acre and even greater (see also Mozelle/1, p485 Figure1).

Unsurprisingly, the demand for allotments peaked when wages were lowest (Springall, p116) and so the years of good harvests, the 1860s to mid-1870s, do not see allotments being created. As we saw the Survey mirrors this with only two allotment sites appearing in the 1860s, one of which was **Costessey**, at enclosure, and the other was troublesome Swaffham, the site of one of only two major disturbances in Norfolk of that period. There in 1868 the Enclosure Commissioners came, intent on enclosing 2300 acres of commons on which local people had extensive rights, in some cases upon which their livelihoods depended. The Commisioners located labourers' allotments one-and-a-quarter miles from the town, on poor ground. Despite paying for legal representation, the Commissioners allowed no legal rights to the claimants, a decision that led Swaffham people to riot. An appeal to the Select Committee on Commons Enclosure led in 1869 to a meagre allocation of five acres for recreation and fifty acres for allotments. The lesson that combination brought results, however spare, was not lost on the Swaffham men.

In 1870 the Commissioners moved on to Fakenham. But claimants, evidently having watched the fate of their neighbours in Swaffham, staked their claims in advance and on a night in may 1870 made a bonfire around which men, women and children gathered. Property bought at public auction was threatened, stones were thrown. Some of those who encamped on the common overnight were charged, but not prosecuted. The disturbances persisted until july. The Association for the Defence of the Poor was formed and its instigator, a schoolteacher named Flaxman, was imprisoned for a short time in Norwich Castle Gaol. He was released on condition that he fomented no further trouble and with this he complied. But the Association which he had headed developed into the Eastern Counties' Union, the first of Norfolk's labourers' unions (Springall p79–81). Legislation reflected agitation in

the factories and towns more than in the countryside at that point and in 1871 an Act restoring the right of trades' unions to form was passed, putting beyond doubt questions of combination; and in 1875 peaceful picketing was permitted by Act of Parliament.

From the mid-1870s onwards weather had reverted to the dismal cold and wet that had characterized the first half of the century. 1879 was the wettest year on record, with tenant farmers abandoning agriculture through the 1880s.

VOLCANIC EVENTS/2

In 1883 an eruption of the Indonesian volcano Krakatau had a similar, though lesser, effect on european weather to that of Tambora in 1815: at six degrees south of the equator, the waste spewed into the atmosphere generated ash (247×10^{11}kg) and aerosols (55×10^{9}kg) around the globe and produced cooling in the northern hemisphere by a calculated $-0.5°C$ (Colling, p124, Table 4.3). As would be expected from a volcano that produced so much less material than that of Tambora, the effect on temperature and precipitation was not nearly so dramatic; but enough for its effect on the sunset skies to be recorded in paint by William Anscom in November 1883 and for Alfred Lord Tennyson in his poem Saint Telemachus to write:

Had the fierce ashes of some fiery peak
Been hurl'd so high they ranged about the globe?
For day by day, thro' many a blood-red eve
In that four-hundredth summer after Christ
The wrathful sunset glared against a cross ...

The Agricultural Depression, so-called, was at its worst in 1894. Although prices achieved for crops began to recover from then, with a further increase from 1900, the crisis in agriculture persisted until the 1940s. In terms of pay and working conditions the agricultural labourer in Norfolk started from a lower base than did those in other rural areas and by the 1900s the average wage had barely increased since the start of the nineteenth century, standing at an average of thirteen shillings per week.

The Survey records an upsurge in the number of parishes with allotments that were created between 1875 until the end of the century:

a total of 25 appear of which one was created by charitable donation (Shelfanger) and three through the generosity of private landlords (**Buxton**, Gillingham, **Docking**). The 1886 Agricultural Return recorded two hundred thousand allotments countrywide.

With the passage of unrest associated with poor weather through 1849–51, the railways gradually began to balance the equation of negotiating terms between the labourer and employer, by offering an alternative source of work. That was coupled with the general increase of work available in towns towards which the railways contributed, and a concomitant drop of population in rural areas in Norfolk as elsewhere, a trend that continued through the twentieth century as Britain became an urban nation (Miles, pp432–3). There was also a decline in migrant and casual harvest workers and from 1870 until the start of the World War 1 six million working men, including many agricultural workers, emigrated (Miles, p433) and so the major grievance of unemployment or underemployment did not threaten to the same extent in that period and farms had smaller, more regularly employed workforces.

> But much more powerful than the attraction of lucre, or dissipation and amusement, is the hope of a future which the towns hold out to the deserving. 'Tain't as if my son John lays by, as you may say; he's just as hard work to make two ends meet as Sam has here at home. But you see as Sam'll never be no better, and John'll never be no wuss!' That was Widow Rossin's way of putting it. John is in the police force in London, Sam is an agricultural labourer. The one has a future, the other has none. Therefore there is no difficulty in supplying the police force with the very best young men Arcady can breed. It is not the pay but the prospect, the promotion by merit, the recognition of faithful service, the appreciation of moral character, the pension for old age; these are the boons which the countryman knows nothing of. For the most skilful and trustworthy, equally as for the most drunken sot who is a byword to his neighbours, there is absolutely no career.
>
> Arcady, for better or worse (1887)
> Reverend August Jessop of Belaugh, near Dereham

Table 4.1: numbers of agricultural workers in Norfolk 1831–1911 (based on Howkins p8 combined with Mosby p190).

Year	Number
1831	37 466
1841	39 757
1851	47 693
1861	52 767
1871	45 198
1881	42 189
1891	37 839
1901	35 089
1911	33 091

A major engine of change in the relationship between farmer and labourer was the gradual development of workers' unions. The Chartists, with their six-point People's Charter of 1837, was an urban phenomenon, despite the creation of the Chartist Cooperative Land Society in 1845 which called for the resettlement of the urban working class on the land. The plan, which seems to have been devoid of detail, perished in 1848 with the Chartist movement. In the 1830s there was 'a scatter of Chartist branches in East Anglia and the south' (E P Thompson, p253) which perhaps alerted the agricultural worker to the benefits of combination although the transportation to Australia of the six Tolpuddle Martyrs in 1834, whose crime was to sign up to a union, must have deterred.

In Norfok the early days of trades unionism was chiefly connected to religious dissent. Nonconformism came to Norfolk in the seventeenth century. The **Quakers** were active there almost from their inception. The death of John Wesley in 1791 led to the splitting of Methodism from the Anglican church and to further divisions, including the Primitive Methodists in 1811. They preached in the open and had a clear, direct message that attracted many. The 1851 Religious Census shows Primitive Methodists to be in every nook and cranny of the county, and fifty per cent of the population of England and Wales to be nonconformist (*Atlas*, p40–41).

Nonconformist meetings provided a voice for working people and for those of intellectual heft and was an opportunity to develop skills of literacy and public speaking. There may not have been a chapel in every village but where there was it was used for meetings of militant agricultural workers who later formed the trades' unions. The circuit of chapels provided a network and a platform for the new message. At least thirty per cent of trades' union leaders were Methodists (Wade-Martins/2 p79). 'It was impossible to divorce labour from religion', according to **George Edwards**, whose strong voice insisted upon labourers' rights from the pulpit both as a Primitive Methodist and union man. However where workers were both dissenters and trades' unionists disputes did not lead to violence.

Village unions, seeking better conditions as well as an improvement in wages, began to be formed in Norfolk as in other parts of the United Kingdom. Eventually memberships combined and the East Dereham branch of Joseph Arch's National Agricultural Labour Union (NALU) was founded at Elsing Sand Pit on 22 april 1872. Its membership spread in west and central Norfolk and by 1874 there were branches throughout the county. In the same year farmers retaliated against increasing organization and strikes by locking-out 3116 members of the NALU. A contemporary newspaper reported that of that number 1176 went back to work, but 694 migrated, 415 emigrated, 415 remained unemployed and 402 left the Union (the remainder were untraceable).

From 1872 the Union had on its side the radical publication the *Eastern Weekly Press*, which had been founded in 1867 by a group of Liberal Norwich businessmen, including J J Colman, Thomas Jarrold and Henry Tillett. It aimed 'to guide the working classes politically and morally'. Its editor was James Spilling, a radical with particular interest in the rural poor. In 1872 it became 'the organ for the agricultural labourers' movement'. It reported disputes leading to withdrawal of labour for every year, some worse than others, between 1872 and 1889 inclusive. Allotments were not cited as the reason for the dispute in any except 1887, when there were four (Steadman, p282 and Howkins Table 3 pp72–3), from which **Castle Acre** and **Buxton** benefited. Norfolk labourers received help from Liberal politicians at a later date, the year 1900 and one of harvest strikes, when in the july Sir Richard Winfrey organized a group of fellow peers to purchase on behalf of the Norfolk Smallholdings Syndicate a farm of 132 acres near Swaffham.

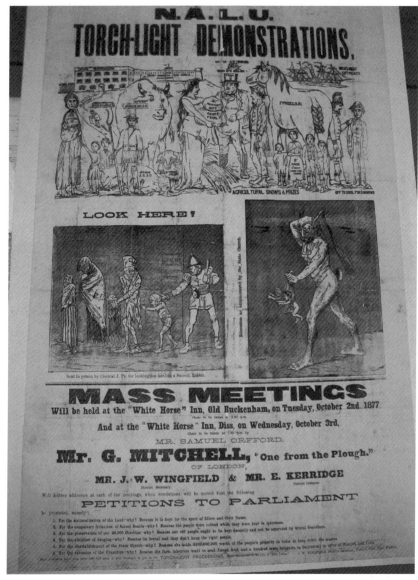

Figure 4.2: Thanks to Norfolk County Council Library and Information Service, at the Norfolk Heritage Centre, Norfolk and Norwich Millennium Library.

Winfrey was a nonconformist and newspaper owner, the proprietor of the *Spalding Guardian*, who committed his energies to the land question, as the rising demand from agricultural labourers had become known, as the key to eliminating rural poverty. From 1887, and the passing of the Allotments Act, Winfrey campaigned for the provision of allotments and smallholdings (Winfrey, p43)

Amongst those emerging from the rural poor – like Arch, none could have stronger credentials in this respect – and a background of nonconformism to create the Norfolk and Norwich Amalgated Labour Union in 1889 was **George Edwards**. Firstly as a Parish and then District Councillor, Edwards had made the provision of allotments a plank of his election campaigns and the allotments at Aylmerton, dating from the 1870s were introduced while he was Chair of the Parish Council:

'The objects of the Union were to be as follows: to improve the social and moral well-being of its members; to assist them to secure allotments and representation on local authorities and even in the Imperial Parliament; to assist members to migrate and emigrate (Edwards, p55).

Over the period of rising trades' unionism the legal status of unions changed, as has been noted, as did the body responsible for allotments; and as did the status of the allotment land itself.

Once the demise of enclosing rendered the 1845 General Enclosure Act obsolete, another legal instrument was needed to enable the demand for allotments to be met, and allotments were sufficiently part of the political itinerary for the **1882 Allotments Extension Act** to require charities of parishes to use charitably-donated land and poor's and fuel allotments to provide allotments where there was a demand for them (Crouch and Ward, p59). This divorced rural allotments from enclosures for the first time. If they failed to do so, appeal could be made to the Charity Commissioners. An example is found at Shelfanger, where in 1889 the **Shelfanger Charities** was formed from two local charities in order to provide allotments for local people but in general local authorities did not use the Act (Poole/2, p16). The Survey shows three other allotment sites having been created between 1882 and 1887

SIR GEORGE EDWARDS
The story of George Edwards is remarkable. born in Marsham, Norfolk in 1850 he started farm work at the age of six, scaring crows from a farmer's fields and from this unpromising start rose to become Member of Parliament for South Norfolk. He dedicated his long life to raising the standard of living of agricultural workers, mainly through the organization of the Agricultural Labourers' Union but he was also a local councillor, Alderman of Norfolk County Council and staunch Methodist.

George Edwards conducted campaigns on behalf of the persecuted and exploited farm workers of Norfolk and experienced victimization, the prejudice and hostility of those in authority and sometimes the indifference of those on whose behalf the battle was being fought. In 1896, for example, he lost his seat on Erpingham District Council and stated that 'this example of the ingratitude on the part of the working men in my own village after all I have done for them during my term of office was enough to crush the spirit of any man', this despite his success in bringing extra financial relief for the elderly and 'obtaining some few acres of allotments'. The provision of allotments for the rural poor was close to his heart and in his autobiography he recalls how when he was a councillor on Aylmerton-cum-Felbrigg Parish Council '...one of the first things we did on the Council was to obtain allotments for the labourers' for both Aylmerton and Felbrigg.

As a Member of Parliament he contributed to debates on all agricultural matters including the provision of smallholdings and allotments. George Edwards' story gives a fascinating glimpse into the conditions of agricultural Norfolk during the second half of the nineteenth and the beginning of the twentieth centuries, up to his death in 1933.

Bob Wilkinson

SHELFANGER CHARITIES

Roger Dade bequeathed 3 acres of land in 1596, for the benefit of the inhabitants of Shelfanger. The Land, known as the Old Town Land, is situated adjacent to the present allotments, opposite the Methodist Chapel on the Winfarthing Road.

Miss Sarah Franklin bequeathed £100 in her will dated 1703 to buy land for the benefit of the poor. She asked that the income be spent to provide bread for the poor of the parish, "every Lord's Day in the year, for ever". The two pieces of land were bought in 1937. The Freeboard Land, of 2 acres, (situated opposite 1 & 2 Hill Cottages, Heywood Road) was bought for £37. The New Town Land, near the Old Town Land (including the allotments) of 4 acres, was bought for £65.

In 1889 the Charity Commissioners established a scheme for the two charities, under the title of 'The Shelfanger Charities', and the giving of bread each Sunday ceased.

Five trustees now administer the Charities, the rent is collected in November from Villagers who have allotments, and Messrs Boult & Morley who farm the remainder. The trustees then decide how the income should be distributed.

Figure 4.3

when parish powers were extended, and all were on privately-owned land: in 1882 at **Scarning** and in 1883 at **Docking** and Hickling. The same appears to be true of **Norwich**. As well as railway allotments the beautiful first edition 1883 Ordnance Survey map on which every tree and feature was marked shows 26 allotments within the grounds of the Great Hospital, part of Cathedral land, whose eastern boundary is the River Wensum. Intriguingly in mediaeval times gardens were let by the Cathedral sacrist who had tenants for the Carnary gardens next to the charnel-house, for a garden near St Helen's Church called St Helen's garden and for a small lawned garden (Noble, p4); and these are in the exact position of gardens on George Cole's 1807 map (Frostick, pp63–5). They can still be identified on a later land-use map which post-dates the 1929 O/S Norwich map (identified as such because of streets and housing that have appeared since that date) but is not as late as maps of 1945. The 1883 O/S first edition shows another set of twenty or so allotments, also bordering the river to the north-east of Carrow Works and nearby another few, three or four, behind some cottages that lie between the Malthouse on Carrow Road and the Gothic Works (see maps in **Norwich** case-study).

Commentators have argued that nationally allotments continued to be provided by private landlords after 1882. As we have seen in Norfolk, as elsewhere, from 1875 the longest continual depression, lasting until the 1940s, had agriculture in its grip. Landowners as others were financially squeezed and many sold their estates during those years (**Costessey, Cley**). J J Colman, the mustard entrepreneur and public figure, gave a speech in 1892 in which he said that he did

'not wish to be harsh, or say anything hard of owners of land in Norfolk…[who]…have had their difficulties in past years…[but]…a large number of them have lamentably failed in their duty, in not voluntarily providing allotments, and cafes or reading rooms for people living in the country to resort to. I am quite sure there are individuals amongst them, and even combinations of individuals, who, if they had risen to their duty, could have provided some places in which the men could meet after a day's work, other than the public-houses which are scattered all about the country' (Colman, p356).

Perhaps Colman had rather less to fear and more to gain from providing opportunities for working men to meet and mardle at the end of the day.

Still the new legislation was not enough to persuade some of the great and the good to relinquish land to the poor for cultivation but momentum had been achieved. The *Gardeners' Chronicle* records that, since would-be tenants had been frustrated by parish Trustees' subterfuges of unrealistic rules and high rents, it was the **1887 Allotments for the Labouring Classes Act** that gave local authorities (whose chief responsibility then was to ensure that sanitary conditions prevailed in towns and villages) the power and the duty to compulsorily purchase land if six or more registered electors required allotments. Finally allotments on demand was guaranteed by law, but for one final piece of the jigsaw that needed to be put into place: it had to wait for the enfranchisement that made the 1894 Local Authorities Act a loaded piece of legislation for true reform and the establishment of rights to allotments to be ceded.

Following reform of rural local government in 1888, the **1890 Allotments Act** required County Councils to have a standing Committee on allotments; and through the 1892 Smallholdings Act to provide loans and acquire and offer smallholdings of up to fifty acres – legislation that was 'largely ineffectual' (Wade-Martins/2, p100). An example of self-help was that of the Friendly Society in Haverill which was convened to manage a plot of 25 allotments on land provided by the local authority. Its records run from 1890 to 1921 and refer chiefly to the setting out of the twenty-rod (quarter-acre) plots and to the lettings and income on the site. The allotments would have been a source of support in themselves as well as to other members through the income made from rents. Just as today some authorities are negotiating the responsibility of allotments away to local associations, the local authority in Haverill in Suffolk (for example, Great Yarmouth) delegated the task of running allotments to the Friendly Society (Percival, p239).

A residual paternalism in the 1880s and 1890s may have been partly responsible for the reluctance of local authorities to interfere in what was perceived as the landowners' right and responsibility. Articles in the *Gardeners' Chronicle* in the 1880s discussed whether the working classes were fit custodians of land and in 1886 an editorial recorded the formation of the Land Owners' Association for the Voluntary Extension of the Allotments System, whose aim it was to gather support for radical reform amongst landowners (Percival, p231), suggesting that Colman was not wide of the mark in his observations. One retort was, 'it is sometimes said that labourers do not care for plots of land. I can only say that I never knew a labourer who refused a suitable plot of suitable land in a convenient situation at a proper rent' and 'the natural love of gardening among all the best labourers and the ready means they possess of fertilizing the land by aid of pigs, road-scrapings and other gatherings, and the magic of the spade have long since occasioned the skilful cultivation of cottage gardens' (*Gardeners' Chronicle* III/63, p307). By the end of the nineteenth century the mood had changed with the *Gardeners' Chronicle* giving advice to County Council lecturers of evening classes in horticulture and books and journals of allotmenteering guidance being produced. Successful allotment schemes in urban situations vindicated the *Gardeners Chronicle* enthusiasm since by 1910 they were attracting a high level of praise: 'few better things have been done by those responsible for the government of our towns as the acquisition of land in their immediate neighbourhood for the purpose of

allotments'. The growing of flowers was also being mentioned at this time including sweet peas, Virginia stock and godetias.

By the time of allotments legislation there is evidence to show that some local authorities were taking their responsibilities seriously. Witnesses to the 1895 Report of the Royal Commission on Agriculture confirmed the existence of allotments in the Norfolk areas of King's Lynn, Swaffham, East Dereham, Aylsham and the Heydon Estate. To the question, 'Have the number of allotments increased of late, and to what extent?' Swaffham Board of Guardians replied, 'Yes, in some parishes' and the representatives of all but the Heydon Estate affirmed that the number had 'considerably increased'. Lord Leicester of Holkham gave evidence:

> 'In most parts of the County a considerable increase in the number of allotments was stated to have taken place in recent years, though in a few districts, it appears that there is a diminishing demand for them. Wherever the cottagers have good gardens there is not a keen demand for allotments. In the open village there are often no gardens with the cottages and in these cases allotments are naturally sought for... Generally on estates there are few allotments, because the cottagers have as much garden as the men require'.

He went on to state that in four open parishes he let land to the local authority for allotments; these parishes were Wells-next-the-Sea with 25 acres, Weasenham with 22 acres 1 rood 27 poles, Castle Acre with 29 acres 3 roods 6 poles, and Tittleshall with 15 acres (p46).

Lord Leicester's support for allotments can be inferred from the award made in 1875 by the Norfolk Agricultural Association (of which he was president) of Prize Essay to Alfred J Smith, who wrote:

> 'Much has been said about letting a portion of land to our cottagers...let every man have a good-sized garden and even allotment if it is not too large. But I find anything beyond what can be tilled by hand is of no benefit to him'.

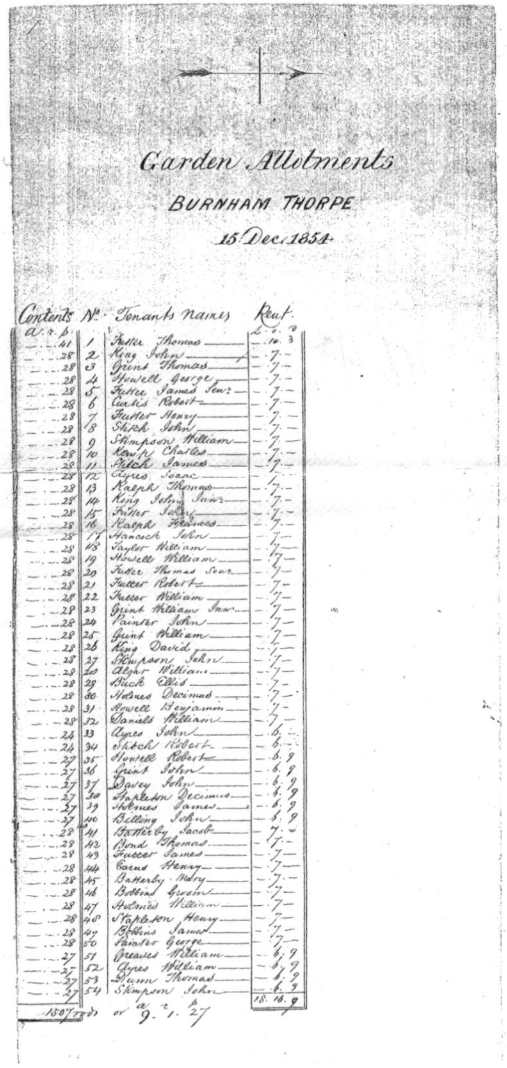

Garden Allotments
BURNHAM THORPE
15 Dec 1854

Contents a. r. p.	No.	Tenants names	Rent £. s. d.
- - 41	1	Futter Thomas	- 10 3
- - 28	2	King John	- 7 -
- - 28	3	Grint Thomas	- 7 -
- - 28	4	Howell George	- 7 -
- - 28	5	Futter James Senr.	- 7 -
- - 28	6	Curtis Robert	- 7 -
- - 28	7	Futter Henry	- 7 -
- - 28	8	Stitch John	- 7 -
- - 28	9	Stimpson William	- 7 -
- - 28	10	Kemp Charles	- 7 -
- - 28	11	Stitch James	- 7 -
- - 28	12	Ayres Isaac	- 7 -
- - 28	13	Ralph Thomas	- 7 -
- - 28	14	King John Junr.	- 7 -
- - 28	15	Futter John	- 7 -
- - 28	16	Ralph Frances	- 7 -
- - 28	17	Hancock John	- 7 -
- - 28	18	Taylor William	- 7 -
- - 28	19	Howell William	- 7 -
- - 28	20	Futter Thomas Senr.	- 7 -
- - 28	21	Futter Robert	- 7 -
- - 28	22	Futter William	- 7 -
- - 28	23	Grint William Junr.	- 7 -
- - 28	24	Painter John	- 7 -
- - 28	25	Grint William	- 7 -
- - 28	26	King David	- 7 -
- - 28	27	Stimpson John	- 7 -
- - 28	28	Algar William	- 7 -
- - 28	29	Buck Ellis	- 7 -
- - 28	30	Holmes Decimus	- 7 -
- - 28	31	Howell Benjamin	- 7 -
- - 28	32	Daniels William	- 7 -
- - 24	33	Ayres John	- 6 -
- - 24	34	Stitch Robert	- 6 -
- - 27	35	Howell Robert	- 6 9
- - 27	36	Grint John	- 6 9
- - 27	37	Davey John	- 6 9
- - 27	38	Stapleton Decimus	- 6 9
- - 27	39	Holmes James	- 6 9
- - 27	40	Billing John	- 6 9
- - 28	41	Batterby Jacob	- 7 -
- - 28	42	Bond Thomas	- 7 -
- - 28	43	Futter James	- 7 -
- - 28	44	Carns Henry	- 7 -
- - 28	45	Batterby Mary	- 7 -
- - 28	46	Bobbins Groom	- 7 -
- - 28	47	Holmes William	- 7 -
- - 28	48	Stapleton Henry	- 7 -
- - 28	49	Bobbins James	- 7 -
- - 28	50	Painter George	- 7 -
- - 27	51	Greaves William	- 6 9
- - 27	52	Ayres William	- 6 9
- - 27	53	Dunn Thomas	- 6 9
- - 27	54	Stimpson John	- 6 9
1507 rods		or a 9 r 1 p 27	18 16 9

Figure 4.4: The first page of Burnham Thorpe Allotments Rent Book. In 2005 there were still tenants named Futter, Ayres and Bobbins. (Thanks to Burnham Thorpe Parish Council.)

His direct involvement in allotments spanned 1888–1902 (Wade-Martins/1, p192) and beyond. South Creake obtained allotments from the Holkham Estate as early as the 'late nineteenth century' (Survey) and the relationship persists, and there are allotments on Holkham land in Burnham Thorpe, Burnham Overy Staithe, Burnham Market (dating back to the 1880s and still with some of the same families gardening there as did then, see Fig. 4.4), **Castle Acre** and Wighton (in 1914) (Survey).

In summary the 1895 Report said

> 'Farmers differ as to the desirability of allotments for their men. One witness observed that one-eighth of an acre of land near his home is advantageous to a man, so that he can grow all his own vegetables. When he gets beyond that, and has to have a plough and lose work for a day or two 'there is nothing in it'. This seemed to be the prevalent view. Some objection was taken to the fact that allotments are occupied mostly by non-agriculturalists. Thus on one lot of twelve acres laid out five years ago there are only three agricultural labourers, each of whom had a quarter-acre. A cowkeeper had three acres and a baker two acres' (p46).

Allotments had not been the route to social improvement which, perhaps, George Edwards and his colleagues had wished. To achieve financial independence as a small farmer the labourer needed to make sufficient profit from the produce of his allotment to invest in a smallholding and have capital for the equipment needed to work the greater acreage. Such profits could only be made when the labourer was not himself dependent for survival on the produce which, in those raw times, must have been rarely. Even supporters of the allotments system were mindful of its limitations (Ashby p6) and others were downright dismissive of the agricultural labourers' claim to independence, arguing that allotments' provision was best left to the landowners' discretion and that they should not be allowed parcels of land:

> 'While he is an agricultural labourer, let him remain an agricultural labourer. We have seen what are his deficiencies at the present day. He is ignorant of his duties and unwilling to be taught them (Kebbel, p61).

Others saw the necessity of all members of small communities to grow their own produce. The Reverend August Jessop, reflecting on his time as vicar of Bylaugh near Dereham, saw that for the agricultural worker 'surplus produce could be expected to pay half the rent, even in bad years' (Jessop, p244) Even without the pressures of unemployment or underemployment, living as they did in isolated circumstances and perhaps fulfilling different roles as well, of which examples can be seen in the community of **Oulton with Irmingland,** for agricultural worker and artisan alike the allotment provided life's staples.

use and value

OXFORDSHIRE, 1890s

On light evenings, after their tea-supper, the men worked for an hour or two in their gardens or on the allotments. They were first-class gardeners and it was their pride to have the earliest and best of the different kinds of vegetables. They were helped in this by good soil and plenty of manure from their pigsties; but good tilling also played its part. They considered keeping the soil constantly stirred about the roots of growing things the secret of success and used the Dutch hoe a good deal for this purpose. The process was called 'tickling'. "Tickle up old Mother Earth and make her bear!" they would shout to each other across the plots, or salute a busy neighbour in passing with: "Just tickling her up a bit, Jack!".

The energy they brought to their gardening after a hard day's work in the fields was marvellous. They grudged no effort and seemed never to tire. Often, on moonlight nights in spring, the solitary fork of someone who had not been able to tear himself away would be heard and the scent of his twitch fire smoke would float in at the windows. It was pleasant, too, in summer twilight, perhaps in hot weather when water was scarce, to hear the swish of water on parched earth in a garden – water which had been fetched from the brook a quarter of a mile distant. "It's no good stintin' th' land", they would say.

"If you wants anything out you've got to put summat in, if 'tis only elbow-grease".

The allotment plots were divided into two, and one half planted with potatoes and the other half with wheat or barley. The garden was reserved for green vegetables, currant and gooseberry bushes, and a few old-fashioned flowers. Proud as they were of their celery, peas and beans, cauliflowers and marrows, and fine as were the specimens they could show of these, their potatoes were their special care, for they had to grow enough to last the year round. They grew all the old-fashioned varieties – ashleaf kidney, early rose, American rose, magnum bonum, and the huge misshaped white elephant. Everybody knew the elephant was an unsatisfactory potato, that it was awkward to handle when paring and that it boiled down to a white pulp in cooking; but it produced tubers of such astonishing size that none of the men could resist the temptation to plant it. Every year specimens were taken to the inn to be weighed on the only pair of scales in the hamlet, then handed round for guesses to be made of the weight. As the men said, when a patch of elephants was dug up and spread out, "You'd got summat to put in your eye and look at".

Very little money was spent on seed; there was little to spend, and they depended mainly upon the seed saved from the previous year. Sometimes, to secure the advantage of fresh soil, they would exchange a bag of seed potatoes with friends living at a distance and sometimes a gardener at one of the big houses would give one of them a few tubers of a new variety. These would be carefully planted and tended, and, when the crop was dug up, specimens would be presented to neighbours.

Most of the men sang or whistled as they dug or hoed. There was a good deal of outdoor singing in those days. Workmen sang at their jobs; men with horses and carts sang on the road; the baker, the miller's man, and the fish-hawker sang as they went from door to door; even the doctor and parson on their rounds hummed a tune between their teeth. People were poorer and had not the comforts, amusements, or knowledge we have today; but they were happier. Which seems to suggest that happiness depends more upon the state of mind – and body, perhaps – than upon circumstances and events.

Lark Rise to Candleford, pp57–8
Flora Thompson

5 | town and country

'...each allotment holder had his little harvest...after we got the corn in we thrashed it as soon as we got a chance...Later on we used to stack our corn out there in front, by the road, just near the gate. Then a wagon came from the farm and took your small stack up there; and they threshed the corn out with the drum. The yield in from the quarter acre combined with the gleanings produced flour for the household. The middlings from grinding were fed to the pigs, whose manure had been dug into the quarter acre or passed on to the farmer if not needed'.

The farm and the village
George Ewart Evans

A review of enfranchisement which became a necessary condition for the creation of allotments on demand must start with 1832, a memorable year for legislation. With firstly the growing strength and division of urban living from rural parts and secondly the growth of the middle classes throughout the nineteenth century, the emphasis in national reform shifted. 1832 saw the First Reform Bill with which allotments was even then allied in the minds of some landowners, as in Lord Suffield's, by giving the vote to male 'ten pound householders' but it did little to address the grievances of the agricultural labourer for whom the new, Poor Law Amendment Act of 1834 had the greater significance. In 1835 the Municipal Reform Act gave local franchise to all ratepayers which encouraged the middle classes and nonconformists to enter the political fray. The Second Reform Act by which the working classes of the towns were allowed the vote did not appear until 1867. Finally the interests of the countryside (which had been addressed through legislation concerning enclosure and allotments) coalesced with those of the town (in places where allotments were demanded) in the 1884 Third Reform Act, extending the working class vote to the agricultural worker. Herbert Cozens-Hardy became a Liberal Member of Parliament for North Norfolk after 1895 through the voting power of the agricultural labourer. Having provided allotments at **Cley-next-the-Sea** as early as 1882, he was amongst those at Westminster who advocated allotments. Rural franchise and rights were further recognized by the 1888 Local Government Act by which County Councils were formed, ending the rule of the old Justices of the Peace. 'Light began to dawn with the county council elections for january 1889. Allotments were made the test question and upon 'allotments' or 'no allotments' every constituency was fought. The allotment party won by a small majority...'(Crouch and Ward, p62–3). The County Councils were composed of reformers:

'on the [Norfolk County] Council elected in 1892 there were ten or twelve Methodist local preachers...the Aylsham union leader became an alderman at the same time...(Springall, p118fn). The Councils achieved much during the first ten years of their existence. The Smallholdings and Allotments Committee gave many access to the land. Usually applicants were put in touch with landowners willing to let the land, for the Committee discovered quite soon that compulsory hiring was an expensive and irritating procedure, likely to harm the very men it desired to help' (Springall, p118).

And finally came the 1894 Local Government Act under which Parish Councils were created:

'The Rural District Councils...established at the end of 1894 had not the same chance of success. The RDCs became from the first the 'rural House of Lords', mainly composed of smaller farmers and clergy who were more obstinate and conservative in their outlook than their brethren on the County Council; occasionally a radical joined them but he had a hard fight to carry anything against such opposition...The Parish Council was the assembly which... in effect, 'disestablished the parson and the squire' in the village. At subsequent elections labouring members were reduced to a minority, though even then they seem to have watched effectively their interests in charities and allotments' (Springall, p119).

The 1894 Local Government Act created independent Parish Councils. It was they which had direct responsibility for providing land for allotments providing it was by agreement. A provision which raised the maximum size of an allotment from one to four acres only served to blur the distinction between an allotment and a smallholding, the distinction between cultivation for self and family or for purposes of trade and profit and this fuzziness was not clarified until the Allotment and Smallholding Act of 1908.

use and value
1910

Vegetables were grown for home and for sale: they were both 'fresh produce' and a 'cushion against unemployment'. 'This self-provision was the means by which many rural families survived in times of only casual labour or in old age' (p236).

Livestock kept on allotments included pigs, chickens, geese, goats and bees. Animals were moved around the allotment in order to progressively manure the plot. Pigs and chickens were especially valued for this (cf **Trowse**). Pig-killing was an annual ritual. Bee-keeping increased greatly in the early years of the twentieth century, so Norfolk became one of the main honey-producing areas of the country. Apiaries were located wherever space and the mutual benefit of the surroundings lent itself to such an arrangement, including the gardens of agricultural labourers, allotments and smallholdings, and orchards.

Flowers were permitted from 1900 onwards – sweet peas, mignonette. Virginia stock, godetias at that time – until the 1922 Allotment Act which prohibited them.

Pleasure was derived from allotments, as well as utility. 'The very nature of allotments – its separation from home, its solitude and the familiar presence of the cosy shed – offered for many a pleasure in itself...retreat from house, family and employment to a place where holders were their own bosses meant a great deal to many' (p237).

By 1910 the success of allotment schemes in urban situations was attracting a high level of praise. The *Gardeners' Chronicle* word on the subject was emphatically positive. 'Few better things have been done by those responsible for the government of our towns as than the acquisition of land in their immediate neighbourhood for the purpose of allotments' (p235).

Arts and Crafts influences in East Anglian gardens:
gardens and gardening in Norfolk and Suffolk
Elise Percival (unpublished doctoral thesis 1999, UEA)

The change came slowly in many cases: despite powers to provide garden allotments, as many record books attest, Trustees of the parish merge into councillors imperceptibly – same officials, same topics for discussion, same tone, same handwriting (**Toft Monks**). In other parishes civil council powers and railways were a heady mixture and many in Norfolk took advantage of speedy transport to become plot holders in order to grow and send produce to the towns and cities of Cambridge, Ipswich and London. This way of life persisted for many decades, as anecdotal evidence from Terrington-St-Clements and Aylsham relates. **Gresham** in North Norfolk and **Potter Heigham** on the Broads illustrate how significant was the change. **Castle Acre** is a parish where the Council took full advantage of its power to obtain many acres of allotments, even to the extent of renting land from a landowner in the neighbouring parish of South Acre. There are up to six sites there, some of them very large, which are still retained and used by the parish. Paston Parish Council negotiated with local landowners to obtain land for allotments. 'It is rather a difficult matter for the Council to satisfy all the applicants for land in the parish', wrote W N Andrews on 25 may 1895 from Paston Vicarage. Negotiations were conducted with two local landowners for a field of seven acres adjoining the Vicarage, of which half-an-acre would be sold to Andrews himself for cottages; and for allotments to be created in a long field adjacent to the Mundesley Road which would be rented through private agreement (Richard Watts letters). Norfolk became the market garden for London, sending vegetables, fruit and flowers – Norwich was famed for its carnations.

Still some water had to run under the bridge at that stage before an Act dealing specifically with allotments was in place. The 1905 Royal Commission had reported on its investigation into the *Decline in the Agricultural Population from 1881–1906* and gave reasons for the decline. The 1901 Census shows that only twelve per cent of the working population made up the force of agricultural labourers compared with about twenty-five per cent in 1851 and seventeen per cent in 1881. Between 1881 and 1901 land formerly used for arable cultivation, some two million acres of it, had been laid to grass. Of the remaining arable land machinery was used on 15.5 million acres. The result was sixty to eighty thousand unemployed agricultural workers.

Finally, working and housing conditions were so mean and the likelihood of becoming smallholders or tenant farmers in their own right so rare that many left agriculture for other prospects (May, p51–2). Opportunities for employment in other trades were increasing even in backwaters such as slow, rural Norfolk: ironically, the early part of the century saw a 'back to the land' movement of townees. Optimism glows from T Newsome's booklet *Gold-producing land – French Gardening* which advertised on its cover the prospect of '£700 per acre per annum'. French Gardening was an 'intensive market gardening' system reliant on deep manuring and cloches to extend the growing season. The same ploy emerged during World War 2. By the time of the 1908 Allotments Act there was sufficient enthusiasm amongst the public to support a number of publications: *One-and-all gardening – a popular annual for amateurs, allotment holders and working gardeners* appeared first in 1896. A magazine *The Gardener* appeared at the turn of the century. Together with the growth of towns there was more work and wealth in town and country in other than agrarian trades.

From the winter of 1902–3 onwards climatic conditions reverted to a state of misery for farmers and labourers alike. The latter experienced a return to low wages and unemployment. By 1909 Norfolk had the highest number of paupers, 38.5 per thousand in the population, of any agricultural county (Ashby, p5). 1905 saw the re-creation of trades' unions, a formal declaration taking place on 6 june 1906 in North Walsham. This time the links with the religious dissenting movement did not exist although many of the influential members came from that background. New connections had been established with politicians, or earlier collaborators had moved into politics. George Edwards was amongst others of the former movement who were present at the inauguration. The Liberal Richard Winfrey, now Member of Parliament, was there, as was another MP and former smallholder on Winfrey's Lincolnshire farm, George Nicholls together with the Socialist Herbert Day. Edwards' founding speech demanded not better wages and conditions for workers but their original requirement of allotments and smallholdings.

Between 1906 and 1910 Edwards worked tirelessly for the Eastern Counties Agricultural Labourers' and Smallholders' Union, as it was then called. His retirement followed in 1913, the same year that the Union was renamed the National Agricultural Labourers' Union. Over that period the Union shifted its argument from land-holding to the political, socialist case for wage rises and a national minimum wage. In 1911, a year of turmoil, the Union had linked itself to the railway workers and from 1913 the NALU held its annual demonstration at the village of Briston, next door to the railway town of Melton Constable. In the summer of 1913 the harvest was bountiful and labour scarce: Union members successfully went on strike for improved wages. The onset of World War 1 in 1914 meant that labour became still scarcer and by 1916 a national minimum wage for agricultural workers had been introduced and farmers grudgingly recognized the NALU. Membership of the Union increased rapidly.

Allotments having been firmly tied to locality by the 1894 Local Authorities Act, in **1907** came the **Allotment and Small Holdings Act** which strengthened it. The very title recognized that the need to alleviate poverty was no longer enough to satisfy the demands of rural people and that the possibility of satisfying their ambitions to move into the class of independent small farmer alone would stem the flow of emigration to other places and occupations and bring economic and political relief to the countryside. The Act 'became law and was strictly enforced…[it] was a great success as parish, urban district and borough councils were all equally responsible for providing allotments' (Poole/2, p16).

Just a year later, the **1908 Allotments and Smallholdings Act** made the Board of Agriculture '…the central authority for all matters related to allotments, except for finances which remained under the jurisdiction of the Local Government Board' (Poole/2, p17). The 1908 Act at last addressed the issue squarely and independently and transferred the 1887 conditions under which allotments should be created to satisfy local demand to the elected officers of the parish. Administration remained in the hands of the local councils, but with much of the detail of the Act spelling out and acknowledging the rights of the tenant while proscribing the liberties that might be taken by the unscrupulous or lackadaisical. The Act was the culmination of much agitation about land reform which dated back one hundred years or

more, which had been taken up by the agricultural unions in Norfolk and which had been linked finally to the enfranchisement of the labourer. This was finally a political stage on which men whose concern was the agricultural labourer could function.

In the county it is not evident from the Survey that the 1908 Act prompted a rash of local authority-run allotment sites. As we have noted, extant records of parishes having allotments that predate the 1895 Local Authorities Act show that the parish council took over the responsibilities of running an existing site (**Little Plumstead, Oulton**). There were parishes where the council introduced allotments, as at Potter Heigham in 1896, Denton in 1899 where the former fuel allotment was utilized and in 1906 at Toft Monks where the Town Estate Charity was registered for the purpose. Privately provided allotment sites continued to be formed, too. The Survey registers fourteen parishes acquiring new allotments between 1890–1899, of which three (including **Buxton**) were by private arrangement, and ten new rural sites being created between 1900–14 of which one (Stalham) was through a private arrangement with a landlord.

The 1908 Act had a number of important clauses. To begin with, allotments were to be provided if enough – six – people demanded them, who need not be agricultural labourers. This meant, in effect, that the link between pauperism and allotments had been broken once and for all and this is reflected in a number of texts. A picture of the benefits of allotments both to the labourer and artisan and of the acuity and enthusiasm with which plots were cultivated is found in the account of William Cullen, in his diary for the year 1909. That was the year he started shopwork in the Suffolk town of Bury St Edmunds and within days of acquiring his plot, which was within days of arriving in the town, it was planted:

'Entries record his early starts each day to garden before work, returning again in the evenings, of walking there for pleasure on a Sunday or in the winter and of taking time out of the shop to "go to a plant sale" or "…on such a fine day – slipped up to the allotment" '(Percival, p240).

Standards on allotments were encouraged by the Royal Horticultural Society by issuing guidance which would be used in competitions for judging allotments. Apart from the obvious points about quality of produce, the RHS emphasized 'originality of layout and planting', 'ingenuity in overcoming local problems', 'visual aspect of the plot' and 'condition of garden sheds' and other furniture (RHS Show Handbook 1909).

To have an allotment it was necessary to be employed. The bluntly-named *Report on the Administration of Out-Relief: the Destitute of Norwich and how they live* (on less than was required to keep body and soul together, was one answer given) made no mention of allotments. An allotment would have been an impossible dream for the destitute of Norwich in 1912, when the Report was produced. It had an introduction by B Seebohm Rowntree who co-authored a 1913 Report, *How the Labourer Lives* in which he casually remarked, 'In his spare time he works on the allotment, for which he pays at the rate of one penny per week'.

The record for Norwich gives ample evidence that once the local authority had the powers, they would seek opportunities to extend the allotment system and canvass demand in areas where formerly no allotments were found. Identifiable sites in Norwich emerge in 1903 through the Minutes of the Committee for Housing of the Working Class and Allotments (HWCA) (NRO N/TC 29/1) though naming of sites is erratic and some are difficult to tally with the current map of Norwich. Minutes make much of the 'insanitary' conditions of the houses for which the Committee was responsible, presumably following the Housing Act 1890, and it may be that combining housing and allotments under the auspices of one committee served the function of managing the disposal of night soil for those who lived in housing not connected to a sewerage system. Certainly gardens served the same purpose in council housing in **Reepham** as late as 1958 when it remained unconnected to mains water. In february and march 1908 the Corporation had received offers of land for sites near the Aylsham Road, Hellesdon, Hall Road, Lakenham and Earlham and were to place six notices in public places, inviting applications for allotments 'up to five acres in extent'. In may 1908 the Corporation advertised that allotments could be made available in Catton Grove following the offer of 35 acres from Mr S Gurney Buxton, a site on which at a later time rents were being taken.

At that time the HWCA Committee espoused the idealistic aims of Ebenezer Howard whose Garden City Scheme had come to fruition at Letchworth. In september 1905 the Chair of HWCA and the City Engineer attended the Annual Congress of the National Housing Reform Council at Letchworth, created in 1903, giving them an opportunity to see the model in practice. A resolution of september 1908 which squeaked through by eight votes to seven recorded that 'this Council views with constantly increasing regret the long lines of dull, same houses which disfigure nearly all the residential quarters of our city; and considers it most undesirable that nearly all new houses…should be let at the highest possible rental allowed. It therefore be an instruction to the HWCA Committee to obtain plans showing how to provide artistic dwellings on reasonable terms as is being done in Bourneville, Port Sunlight [the foundation of William Lever's "villages of vision" whose every house had an allotment (Brown, p154)] and Letchworth, in order that they may be carried out here' (NRO N/TC 29/1 for 7 september 1908). The City Engineer was once again despatched to Letchworth to obtain plans. Noticeably Norwich evolved a strong structural similarity to Howard's ideal, particularly in the post-World War 1 era with the placing of Waterloo Park and Eaton Park as recreational areas embedded in housing, adjoining 'The Avenues', the name a nod towards Howard's terminology, beyond which were extensive planned allotment sites.

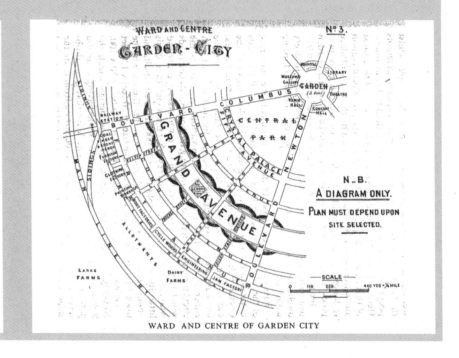

GARDEN CITY AND RURAL BELT

WARD AND CENTRE OF GARDEN CITY

Trowse was a later utopian expression. Norwich even acquired a small 'model town' at Thorpe but apparently without allotments – in may 1909 44 residents requested allotments. Mr Harvey of Thorpe Lodge offered twelve acres of land for purchase but at a price considered exorbitant by the Committee. In december 1910 the tenants had taken the initiative and found a field on a farm owned by Mr Martin Birkbeck and a prospective tenant for the farm who was willing to forego the use of the field. The residents were willing to pay fifty per cent more than the going rate, nine pence per rod, for their tenantry. By march 1911 a yet different deal was mooted which apparently failed; and despite a Corporation advertisement for four acres of land none was forthcoming.

Most of the Norwich City Corporation's Housing and Allotments Committee's business in these early days concerned negotiations about land tenure, rents and applications. The offer of land at Hellesdon was rejected because the charge on it was too high. Applications at Catton

Grove were few and for small amounts, and so the ambitious Mr S Gurney Buxton had to be content with a modest return on his investment. No further mention was made of Lakenham. In Earlham there was a robust response from the populace and an offer from Mr Bacon Frank of two fields amounting to forty acres was accepted. By february 1909 the Committee's deliberations had resulted in plans for 157 plots of twenty rods on the Earlham Road site and 153 plots of twenty rods on the Dereham Road site, roadways to be made down the centre of each site, £100 spent on fencing and staking out and a rental of sixpence per rod per year to be charged each tenant. By september 1909 all except five plots were let, and those were promised.

In contrast to rural areas water was laid on in the early days (Earlham 1910, Wall Road 1912, Angel Road 1913). Vandalism and theft seem to have been problems from the start and sites acquired barbed wire (Earlham 1912) and fences and gates with lock and key from 1914. Tenants complained about fences that were badly maintained and allowed in rabbits and bullocks to devastate their crops. Most of these depredations are familiar to allotment-holders today, although the predators may now be pheasants and foxes rather than bullocks. More unusual was the edict on Brickfields that there should be 'no bees, no pigs' and in 1913 that coppers were not permitted on site: plot-holders 'shall not boil bones or fat or any offensive matter'.

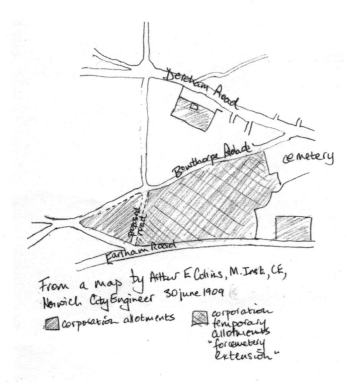

From a map by Arthur E Collins, M.Inst., CE, Norwich City Engineer 30 june 1909

▨ corporation allotments   ▨ corporation temporary allotments "for cemetery extension"

Table 5.1: Emergence of early Norwich allotments and fate, if possible to trace (based on Minutes of the Committee of the Housing of the Working Class and Allotments NRO N/TC 29/1 1903–16, from 1907 Housing and Allotments Committee – names used to the last date given)

Wild Road	1904–12	
Angel Road	1908–13	Became Elm Grove
Cemetery Allotments	1907–11	Tenants given notice 1911, when cemetery extended, but given preference in Earlham
Catton Grove	1908–present	
Earlham, consisting of		
Dereham Road	1908	Gurney-Brown offered two fields, forty acres in total
Earlham	1912	More plots required on closure Cemetery Allotments
Thorpe Hamlet	1909–12	Land acquired from Colonel Harvey (a site remains, no longer the responsibility of Norwich City Council)
Brickfield	1910–	Originally 3.75 acres, extended by 12.80 acres – 'certain work suitable for distress labour can be put in hand'
Martineau Lane	1912	Lakenham from 1925, now Lakenham Baths
Cottage Farm	1912–present	
Clare House Estate	1912–14	Described as 'part of Estate known as Walled-in-Close', referred to as Clare House 1923, possibly now Wall Road.

Earlham was a large site even in the early days where the Norwich Horticultural Society had a strong presence. In 1912 negotiations began with the Housing and Allotments Committee, as it had become from 1907, for further plots (perhaps to absorb those at Cemetery Road who had been displaced by the overflowing Cemetery) and it 'guaranteed to find tenants for thirty acres of allotments'. When the Committee appeared to be dragging its heels an open meeting was held at the Guildhall, at which 85 petitioners forced Councillors' hand so that a compulsory purchase order for a six-and-a-quarter acre field owned by J H Gurney was made. In 1915, when men went off to war, the Norwich Allotments Association agreed to take on its management for five years, if the Corporation would supply manure.

The clause which allowed the potential tenant up to five acres and that land must be compulsorily purchased if needs be was taken seriously, if only very rarely, by local authority and tenant alike. Despite the Corporation's invitation to would-be tenants to take up to five acres of land in some parts of the city, when the matter was put to the test the Corporation baulked. In Norwich the first of these was the quixotic Mr W Joice who requested two to five acres off the Newmarket Road, one of the more desirable locations. The application was rejected summarily by the City Council's Housing and Allotments Committee on 12 october 1908. Mr Joice 'persisted in asking', however, and the Committee agreed to approach local landowner, J H Gurney from whom allotment plots had been bought in the past. Somehow the matter was still pending in november 1911 when the Committee was rapped on the knuckles by the Board of Agriculture and Fisheries for not having met their statutory duty. Mr Gurney would be approached again. Eventually, on 26 april 1912, it was agreed that Mr Joice would have five acres of Gurney land at Eaton – once a report into his financial status had been obtained. Another seven months elapsed before the Committee insisted that two people must be found by Mr Joice to stand as surety for the lease of the land. Persistent Mr Joice. On 17 july 1912 the Committee approved the lease that had been drawn up. But on 22 october 1913 the Minutes show that Mr Joice refused to sign the lease! Beyond that date the record is silent.

6 World War 1 1914–18

The sole consolation of those antagonistic weeks was the young American airman, to whom I shall always be grateful for the sunny imperturbability which never seemed in the least shaken...Almost every day for a month or so he 'blew in' to the flat like a rush of wind from the wings of his own 'plane and extravagantly insisted upon taking me to the Savoy Grill... He also, with characteristic generosity, presented me with innumerable meat coupons, which by that time had become far more precious than all the winking diamonds in the empty luxury shops of deserted Bond Street.

Testament of Youth
Vera Brittain

World War 1 inevitably changed the conditions under which allotments operated, irrespective of the 1908 Allotments and Smallholdings Act, whereby, perhaps for the first time, allotments were seen by authorities as more than just the solution to rural poverty or a factor in negotiation between employee and worker, themes that in Norfolk were mostly identical. Ironically, wartime conditions forced Norwich City Corporation to revert to its former policy of using allotments as a means of providing out-relief.

In 1905 the British Government had written:

'We think that the effect of the naval and shipping evidence is conclusive as to the point that while there will be some interference with trade and some captures, not only is there no risk of a total cessation of our supplies but no reasonable problem of interference with them and that, even in a maritime war, there will be no material diminution in their volume...'
(*Report of the Royal Commission on Supply of Food and Raw Material in Time of War*, in May, p59).

The Norfolk countryside commentator, Rider Haggard, was scathing:

'...we seem to lay about £4 per head of the population on imported food, as against...about 7s per head of its population by Germany...To me, in face of the continued decrease in our agricultural output, these figures are simply terrifying...within a fortnight of the declaration of a war – which we must expect some day – corn would, I believe, stand at or near 100s a quarter. If we could think that the War Office was ready to meet such an emergency – to supply food, allay panic, etc., perhaps there would not be so much cause for alarm. But what intelligent person who has studied the action of that Department during our recent troubles…can conscientiously expect anything of the sort?' (in May, p60).

As Britain rolled closer to war, the Government tried to address the problems associated with the persistent agricultural depression – those of labour shortage and consequent loss of land to arable cropping – which had resulted for the prior ten years in 62% of wheat and flour being imported. In rural areas the Government sought to take commonland into production as garden allotments through local authority action but only one site, in Cornwall, was created in this way. Resistance was put up by the influential Commons Preservation Society and in 1910 ministers abandoned the plan (Birtles/3, p269).

Without providing the means to alleviate the inevitable food shortages suffered in Britain the public was asked to reduce their diet:

'We are asked to consume as little sugar as is possible…The Government have also appealed to the nation, time after time, to "eat less meat"…we also consume an inordinate amount of tea compared with other European nations…Last year we spent on Alcohol and Tobacco over £220 000 000. This expenditure is unjustifiable at a time when our country needs every penny' (George W Hall, p6).

Morale-sapping stuff. Support for the public came from the Royal Horticultural Society who produced a series of leaflets to help the amateur gardener. By 1915 *Vegetables and how to grow them* had run to a fifth edition. 1916 saw a run of heart-warming titles: *Vegetable bottling, storing and salting, Salads and Salad-making* and *Vegetable cookery* (already in its second edition by that date). But two titles had to wait for more propitious times when the Government finally put the mechanism in place to enable additional allotments to be created: for both *Cropping of an allotment or small kitchen garden* and *Cultivation of potatoes in gardens and allotments* it was 1917 before they were published for the first time.

Official anxiety to conceal the success of the Kaiser's threat 'to starve the british people until they who have refused peace will kneel and pray for it' lest the morale of the populace be threatened may have contributed to delays in making additional land available. Nonetheless in 1915 the Government revived their plan to have commons used as garden allotments. Up to five thousand acres were to be put to cultivation in remote and sparsely-populated districts. The President of the Board of Agriculture was a member of the Executive Committee of the Commons Preservation Society and was assured that reasonable claims would not be rejected (Birtles/3, 269–70).

In 1916 Germany intensified her submarine campaign, leading to the further loss of imports. A government investigation into the relative strengths of the german and british capacity for self-sufficiency contained the alarming news that the germans outstripped the british by 90% to 40% in its capability to provide food for its people, that german agriculture was far more efficient than british, being able to feed 70–75 people rather than 40–45 people per 100 acres of land, because Germany had more arable land than Britain (Dewey, p31). A poor harvest in summer 1916 resulting in plummeting imports from Canada and USA and german success in blockading ships entering Britain's ports contributed to a revolution in governmental thinking.

At one time in 1916 it was believed that there was only six weeks' supply of food left in Britain. This stimulated the new coalition government into reorganizing its agricultural policy. Powers to take over unoccupied land for cultivation with or without the owners' consent were awarded to local authorities by the Government through the Defence of the Realm Acquisition of Land Act in spring 1916. The Act created County Agricultural Executive Committees for the purpose. In Norfolk during World War 1 no common land was used for agriculture although some poor allotments were requisitioned; in Marsham twenty acres were taken and at Blo Norton eight-and-a-half acres of charity land were used. Resistance in parishes meant that no compulsory orders were executed (Birtles/3, p244–5).

TO INCREASE OUR FOOD SUPPLY, AND MAINTAIN OUR GARDENS INEXPENSIVELY DURING THE WAR.

The following popular practical Pamphlets have been prepared for the assistance of Amateurs and Cottage Gardeners, as well as for assisting those who have large gardens to upkeep during the present troubled times when labour is so scarce. They are simple, clear, and concise, and the whole series makes a very complete guide to outdoor gardening operations. The prices of each are as follows :—

Single Copy, 3d. ; 25, 6/- ; 50, 11/- ; 100, 20/-

ORDER FORM FOR R.H.S. DIARY AND PAMPHLETS.

		£	s.	d.
R.H.S. Gardeners' Diary for 1917 (in cloth) No..........@1/3				
" " " (in leather) 2/3				
PAMPHLETS :—				
(k) Fruit Bottling and Storing, and Vegetable Bottling, etc. .. .. No..........@ 3d.				
(e) Vegetables and How to Grow Them .. .. "				
(f) Autumn Vegetables from Seed sown in July .. .. "				
(q) The Cultivation and Manuring of the Kitchen Garden .. .. "				
(r) The Cultivation of Potatos in Gardens and Allotments .. .. "				
(v) Cropping the Allotment and Small Garden (with colored plan). .. .. "				
(a) A Selected List of Hardy Fruits, with Notes on Cultivation .. .. "				
(b) The Training of Fruit Trees .. .. "				
(c) The Pruning of Fruit Trees .. .. "				
(d) Keeping Fruit Trees Clean .. .. "				
(g) The Herbaceous Garden.. .. .. "				
(h) The Rose Garden .. .. "				
(i) Flowers for Small Gardens, Window Boxes, etc. .... "				
(j) Hardy and Half-Hardy Annuals in the Open Air .... "				
(m) Vegetable Cookery .. .. "				
(n) Salads and Salad Making .. .. "				
(o) War time Economy in Gardening .. .. "				
(p) Medicinal Plants and their Cultivation .. .. "				
(s) Fruit Cultivation under Glass .. .. "				
(t) The Pruning of Hardy Shrubs.. .. .. "				
(u) The Children's Garden .. .. "				
Rules and Regulations for Allotment Societies .... 2d.				
Rules for Judging Cottage and Allotment Gardens .... 2d.				
Companion Judges Sheet for ditto ... . 3d.				
Rules for Allotment and Vegetable Exhibitions .... 2d.				
Vegetable Bottling and Fruit Preserving without Sugar, by Mr. and Mrs. Banks (including valuable recipes for Jams and Jellies) 1/2				
A List of the most desirable varieties of Fruits 2/-				

To the SECRETARY, R.H.S., £
Vincent Square, London, S.W. 1.

The Royal Horticultural Society.

Incorporated by Royal Charter.

THE CROPPING OF AN ALLOTMENT

OR

SMALL KITCHEN GARDEN.

(WITH COLOURED PLAN).

1st EDITION, 1917.

Sold by WILLIAM WESLEY & SON,
28, Essex Street, London, W.C.

Copies of this Pamphlet for distribution may be obtained at the Society's Offices, Vincent Square, Westminster, S.W.

Price, post free, single copy, 3d.; or 25, 6/-; 50, 11/-; 100, 20/-

Smith & Ebbs, Ltd., Northumberland Alley, Fenchurch Street, E.C.

635.0

Roy

*Figure 6.1
(Courtesy of the
Linley Library, RHS)*

The 1916 Defence of the Realm Act created Allotment Committees and gave local authorities the powers to take over land for conversion to wartime allotments. Large and unwieldy County War Agricultural Committees were asked to form smaller Executive Committees of no more than seven members whose role was to promote an increase in the home production of food. Executive Committees were requested to pay particular attention to the use of female labour, the encouragement of allotment holding, pig keeping and the cultivation of waste ground. Government received the *Summaries of Evidence taken before the Agricultural Policy Sub-Committee, appointed in august 1916 to consider and report upon the methods of reflecting an increase in the home-grown food supplies, having regard to the need of such increase in the interest of national security* (Ministry of Reconstruction, HMSO 1918). Not only common land but parks and playing fields were sub-divided, dug and planted. A propaganda campaign by the government, 'Everyman a Gardener', involved King George V and the Archbishop of Canterbury and led to a huge increase in the home production of food. The King directed that potatoes, cabbages and other vegetables should replace geraniums in the royal parks. The Prime Minister, David Lloyd

Figure 6.2: Allotmenteers Frank Anderson, Blanche Anderson and daughter Joko in June 1917. (Thanks to Marian O'Hare)

George, let it be known that he was growing potatoes in his own garden. The Board of Agriculture made an appeal to the owners of private gardens to preserve their surplus stocks of vegetable seedlings for distribution to allotment holders and the RHS appointed a committee to assist in the distribution of these surplus plants. The railway companies strongly supported the war effort, helping 5 800 plotholders with seed and spraying machines by 1917(Poole/2 p28). 'The allotment movement is of national importance', declared the preface to Guide for holders of allotments leased from London and North Western Railway Company (published in October 1918) which let up to fourteen thousand plots at one shilling per year.

Figure 6.3: Allotments on a railway embankment, 1917.
(Courtesy of the Linley Library, RHS)

In addition allotment sites were protected by the Cultivation of Lands Act:

'The Food Production Department suggested that tenants patrolled their allotments on a voluntary basis or for a small fee from the Society funds...under the Defence of the Realm Act the Penalties for trespass and damage were severe' (Poole/2, p28).

A final measure which has become embodied as british eccentricity, rather as we still preserve the roman habit of driving on the left side of the road, was that of British Summer Time whereby the clocks were put forward by one hour between the spring and autumn equinoxes so that there was an extra hour's time for gardening or farming during the already long summer evenings. This innovation was deemed to be so successful that Double Summer Time came in at the start of World War 2.

World War 1 caused scarcely a ripple on the pond that was Parish Council business in **Little Plumstead**. In 1916 the Council was asked to consider anyone in the parish over the age of 41 as suitable for National Service but reported that it 'believed they were engaged on work of National importance' and there was no-one to spare. Anyone younger than 41 was answerable to the Military Authorities. At the same meeting the Council read out a letter from the Norfolk War Agricultural Committee (NWAC) about the full use of cottage gardens and allotments but deferred the business until a later meeting which never came. On 13 February 1917 the Parish Council in **Oulton** was called together to discuss a letter from the NWAC in which it was suggested that they should form a committee to ensure that all garden allotments were thoroughly cultivated. The Council thought about each of the gardens and allotments and decided that 'a few might want assistance' and it drew up a list of 'wives whose husbands were at the Front' and 'men who were too old to cultivate their land'. Still the parish would not need outside help and individual members of the Council agreed to see these people so that arrangements to help them could be made.

On 28 march 1917 at **Oulton** a further meeting to discuss wartime measures initiated by the NWAC agreed that all gardens should be cultivated, and the Council made plans for carting and distributing seed potatoes. With regard to the National Volunteering Service; 'the Meeting was of the opinion that the labourers should not volunteer as they were wanted on the land where they were and if they volunteered they might be sent somewhere else to do exactly the same work'. Again in 1918 a Food Production Department letter was 'ordered to be laid on the table'. All the allotments were in use, and the tenancies maintained. The Council also considered whether or not the parish needed to create a War Food Society. It decided that the NWAC should be told that 'it would not make any difference as everyone was doing as much as possible already'. In both parishes 'everything was being done that could reasonably be done'.

But of course the War took men away from the work and their plots. Norwich records show that plots were left untended and vacant and that tenancy turnover increased markedly. In february 1915 Norwich City Corporation minuted the existence of temporarily vacant plots 'due

Figure 6.4: Eloquent pages from the allotments rent book for Great Plumstead.

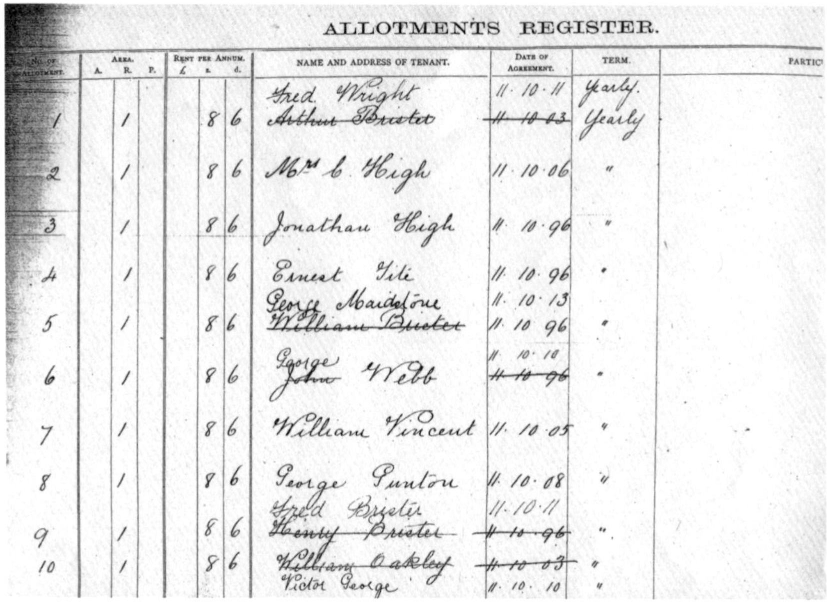

ALLOTMENTS REGISTER.

No. of Allotment	Area A.	R.	P.	Rent per Annum £	s.	d.	Name and Address of Tenant	Date of Agreement	Term	Partic
1		1			8	6	Fred Wright ~~Arthur Bristo~~	11·10·11 ~~11·10·03~~	Yearly Yearly	
2		1			8	6	Mrs C. High	11·10·06	"	
3		1			8	6	Jonathan High	11·10·96	"	
4		1			8	6	Ernest Tite	11·10·96	"	
5		1			8	6	George Maidstone ~~William Brister~~	11·10·13 11·10·96	"	
6		1			8	6	George ~~John~~ Webb	11·10·10 ~~11·10·96~~	"	
7		1			8	6	William Vincent	11·10·05	"	
8		1			8	6	George Punton	11·10·08	"	
9		1			8	6	Fred Brister ~~Henry Brister~~	11·10·11 ~~11·10·96~~	"	
10		1			8	6	~~William Oakley~~ Victor George	~~11·10·03~~ 11·10·10	"	

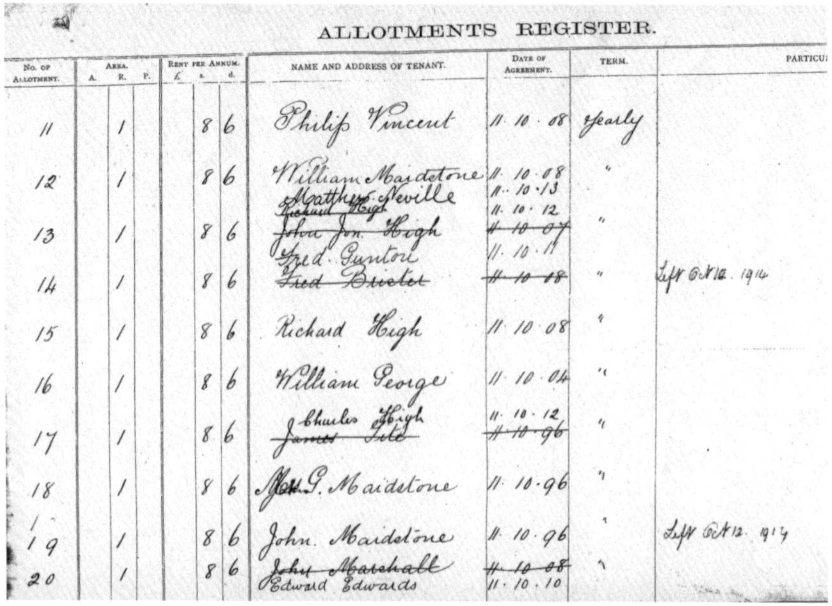

ALLOTMENTS REGISTER.

No. of Allotment	Area A.	R.	P.	Rent per Annum £	s.	d.	Name and Address of Tenant	Date of Agreement	Term	Particu
11		1			8	6	Philip Vincent	11·10·08	Yearly	
12		1			8	6	William Maidstone Matthew Neville Richard High	11·10·08 11·10·13 11·10·12	"	
13		1			8	6	~~John Jon. High~~ Fred Punton	~~11·10·07~~ 11·10·11	"	
14		1			8	6	~~Fred Brister~~	~~11·10·08~~	"	Left Oct 12. 1914
15		1			8	6	Richard High	11·10·08	"	
16		1			8	6	William George	11·10·04	"	
17		1			8	6	Charles High ~~James Tite~~	11·10·12 ~~11·10·96~~	"	
18		1			8	6	Mrs G. Maidstone	11·10·96	"	
19		1			8	6	John Maidstone	11·10·96	"	Left Oct 12. 1914
20		1			8	6	~~John Marshall~~ Edward Edwards	~~11·10·08~~ 11·10·10	"	

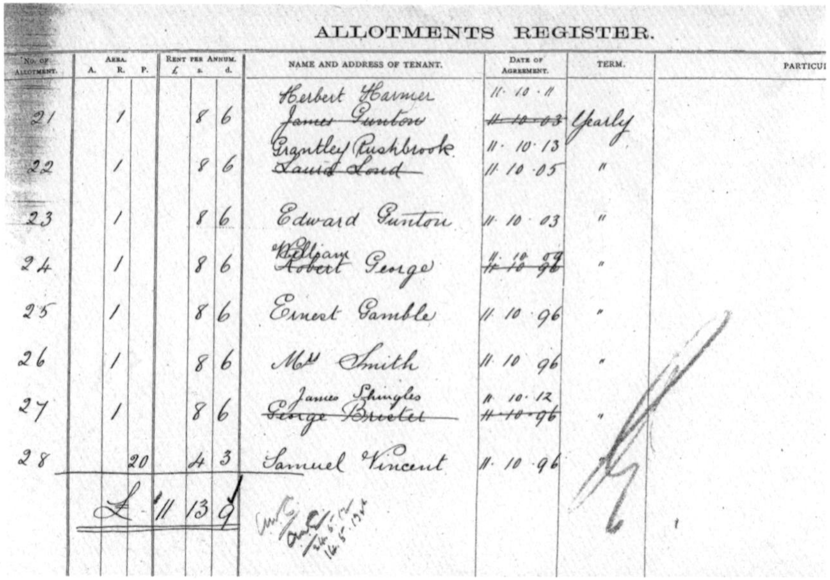

ALLOTMENTS REGISTER.

No. of Allotment	Area A.	R.	P.	Rent per Annum £	s.	d.	Name and Address of Tenant	Date of Agreement	Term	Particul
21		1			8	6	Herbert Harmer ~~James Punton~~	11·10·11 ~~11·10·03~~	Yearly	
22		1			8	6	Grantley Rushbrook ~~Lewis Lord~~	11·10·13 11·10·05	"	
23		1			8	6	Edward Punton	11·10·03	"	
24		1			8	6	William ~~Robert~~ George	~~11·10·97~~	"	
25		1			8	6	Ernest Gamble	11·10·96	"	
26		1			8	6	Mrs Smith	11·10·96	"	
27		1			8	6	James Shingles ~~George Brister~~	11·10·12 ~~11·10·96~~	"	
28			20		4	3	Samuel Vincent	11·10·96		
				£11	13	9				

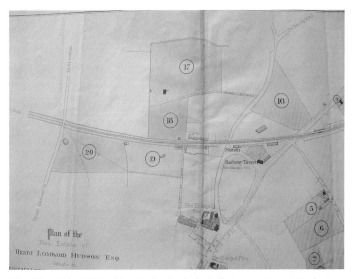

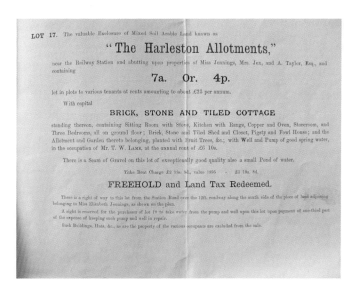

Plot 17 sold in 1895, of lands that included allotment sites at Harleston.

Pictured in 1980, Jack Bedingfield and Percy Chalker were tenants at the Station site.

A residual vegetable garden from Station Road allotments at Harleston.

Allotment sites at Aylsham are next to the railway line.

Gressenhall Workhouse, now a rural life museum, had a plot for vegetables and herbs in a walled garden.

to service by regular or distress labour' and of rents having fallen into arrears on the Earlham site. The Town Clerk was despatched to consult the Honorary Secretary of the Norwich Cooperative Allotments Association, to see if that body would undertake to cultivate temporarily empty plots while the tenants were away. The Distress Committee was alerted to the availability of plots. Sometimes they were let to adjoining plot-holders, sometimes to an outsider. In june 1915 the six-and-a-quarter acre Dereham Road site was offered to the Earlham Horticultural Association, but it was the Allotments Association which signed the five-year lease, manure to be supplied by the Corporation.

The Survey records no new allotments for the period of the War. Norwich City Corporation's records show that allotments were still those established around the periphery of the city, nineteen sites in all, a total of 279 acres 3 rods 13 poles and almost the same ones as are held today (NRO N/TC 30/1 for 8 may 1923. Of those that have not survived Recreation Road was vacated in 1923 and tenants transferred to South Heigham, and from the 1929 O/S map we learn that South Heigham and Plumstead Road still existed. Stanley Road was not mentioned beyond 1923). This satisfied 1821 plot-holders. 'The Town Clerk submitted [to the Council] an extract from the *Eastern Daily Press* of 31 may 1922 when it appeared that under a recent return of the Ministry of Agriculture in proportion to population Norwich is second on the list for the country in the matter of acreage of land provided for allotments, Leicester being the only place in which acreage per head of population is more than Norwich' (based on NRO N/TC 29/1 of 3 may 1922, in Haines letter and attachment of 10 january 2005 to Norfolk Recorders). Railway allotments increased from 27 860 to 93 473 and in England and Wales as a whole the number of allotments rose dramatically through WW1, from 674 000 in 1914 to one and a half million by 1918 (based on the *Thorpe Report* 1969, in *Memorandum by the Department of the Environment Transport and the Regions* (AL 23) 24 june 2004, p4). Allotments had become a fixed urban feature, an association which remains in the minds of most even today.

7 | between the wars

In 1926 Emma Noble of Swindon attended the Quaker Yearly Meeting, where the session on unemployment impressed her with the conviction that there was something <u>she</u> must do. She and her husband went to the Rhondda Valley where they lived for nearly twenty years. There with other Friends like Paul Matt and Peter Scott, they set up co-operative work schemes: boot and shoe factories, furniture making, pig and poultry farming, as well as organising social clubs. Children's drawings and embroidery… record the Allotment Committee, house repair schemes and basket making.

The Quaker Tapestry Souvenir Handbook

And then the men came back from the War, or not.

Far from returning to the dreamed-of 'land fit for heroes', many returning soldiers found that there was no employment for them. After 1918 a tragic combination of the aftermath of war – at **Cley-next-the-Sea** all the heirs to the Estate perished at the Front – and persistent agricultural depression meant that the numbers selling estates and farms rose, making many agricultural workers unemployed. There was a revolution in Norfolk, the greatest ever seen, in landownership. Many estate owners and farmers had to sell off their lands and others benefited. This resulted in the extension of owner-occupation of farms to many involved in agricultural work (**Hevingham, Oulton**), especially between the two World Wars and even more particularly between 1917 and 1922 when six million acres of formerly tenanted land (about one-fifth of the area under cultivation in the United Kingdom) was purchased by new landowners. Conditions were no more favourable for the new hopefuls than the experienced and many foreclosed on the mortgages that had been their passport to independence, about half of arrangements in Norfolk in the 1930s coming to grief (Barnes, pp29–30). The 1918 Sale Particulars of the **Costessey** Estate, not an especially grand one, show that included in the sale, apart from three lots of garden allotments in Bawburgh, were 33 cottages, many of them in pairs or triples or even four-at-a-time, with gardens, land, smithies or brick works attached; and small farms and smallholdings of several acres and a kitchen garden of over 22 acres. Between 1918 and 1930 more than at any other period in Britain's history thousands of acres of land went onto the market, initiating a massive transfer of ownership.

Norfolk had 10 089 acres of orchards and 1 413 acres of nurseries in 1938 as well as numerous smallholdings and allotments (Dudley Smith, p186).

Nationally demand for allotments exceeded supply with as many as seven thousand new applicants a week (Stokes, p24). To complicate matters further, some of the land for allotments which had been requisitioned during the War was reclaimed by its former owners so that many legal battles over possession ensued. Perversely the 1919 Cultivation of Land Act extended the tenancies of those who had held plots during World War 1 until after the growing season of 1920 whereas the 1919 Land Settlement (Facilities) Act belatedly recognized the desperation of ex-servicemen returning from the Front and gave them the right to hold allotments. The latter legislation had been assembled under the pressure, on the one hand, of the shame visited upon the government by the sight of thin, shivering former-trenchmen begging on the streets and standing in dole queues:

'*The Herald* spoiled our breakfast every morning. We read in it of unemployment all over the country due to the closing of munition factories; of ex-servicemen refused reinstatement in the jobs they had left when war broke out, of lockouts and abortive strikes' (Graves, p236).

Somehow by december 1918, barely a month after the Armistice, 26 local authorities provided five thousand new allotments (Poole/4, p28). Between 1918 and 1929 the Survey records nineteen country parishes in Norfolk that gained allotments, a veritable cluster for such a short period of time. Of those four had two sites and two had three sites each. The provenance of the allotment land was varied: it included estates (four, including Horning which acquired land from the Day Estate, and **Docking** and nearby Somerfield Estate which held large allotment sites from Hare lands), charity trusts (four), a churchyard trust (one) and private landlords at Sprowston whose tenants were the Food Protection League, at **North Elmham** which was given land in trust from a local landowner, and **Buxton** that benefited from the Quaker Sewells. A note to the Survey return for Shipdham (acquired 1918) adds that they were for 'World War 1 returning soldiers'. At Holt

fourteen acres were rented from a local private landlord on behalf of the Holt Discharged Soldiers' and Seamen's Federation Allotment Society which still runs the allotments today. Norwich created Elm Grove Lane allotments in march 1918 (Haines/1, p1).

In december 1920 Norwich experienced rioting – many returned soldiers were still reliant on charity. In october 1921 the agricultural workers' Union called a strike. Blacklegs with police protection rendered it pointless. The Repeal of a minimum wage in 1921 must have been a desperate attempt to gather more men into work, however mean its rewards, but a bad winter in 1921–2 nullified the effects of such a measure, as the payments to the unemployed for the Depwade Union show (Howkins Figure 4, p136). The recovery of work in Depwade for the 1922–3 season reflects a better winter but towards its end from january onwards employment was beginning to fail again. During march and april 1923 Norfolk was subject to a Great Strike of agricultural workers wanting an increase in wages. Flying pickets on bicycles were used to good effect and farmers were defeated, agreeing to workers' demands. Thrigby and Filby gained allotments in 1924. In 1924 the Agricultural Wages Act followed and the National Agricultural Labourers' Union was consolidated (Howkins, p159).

Against this dramatic background the Ministry of Agriculture and Fisheries (MAF) appointed a Committee of Enquiry into the need for allotments, which resulted in the **1922 Allotment Act**. The Act made it compulsory for Borough and Urban Councils of towns greater than ten thousand people to create an Allotment Committee; and to provide garden allotments which were defined as being not more than 40 poles (a quarter-acre); and for the production of vegetables or fruit for consumption, rather than sale; and which gave tenants greater security of tenure. A year later wartime measures allowing Councils to requisition land were curtailed and former occupiers reclaimed their lands (Stokes, p24). Published in 1922, the magnificent and comprehensive book *Allotment Gardening* by William Good, a Fellow of the Royal Horticultural Society, speaks of significant popular interest.

The 'not for sale' clause of the 1922 Act was presumably intended to protect the farming community but was unrealistic: an attempted ban

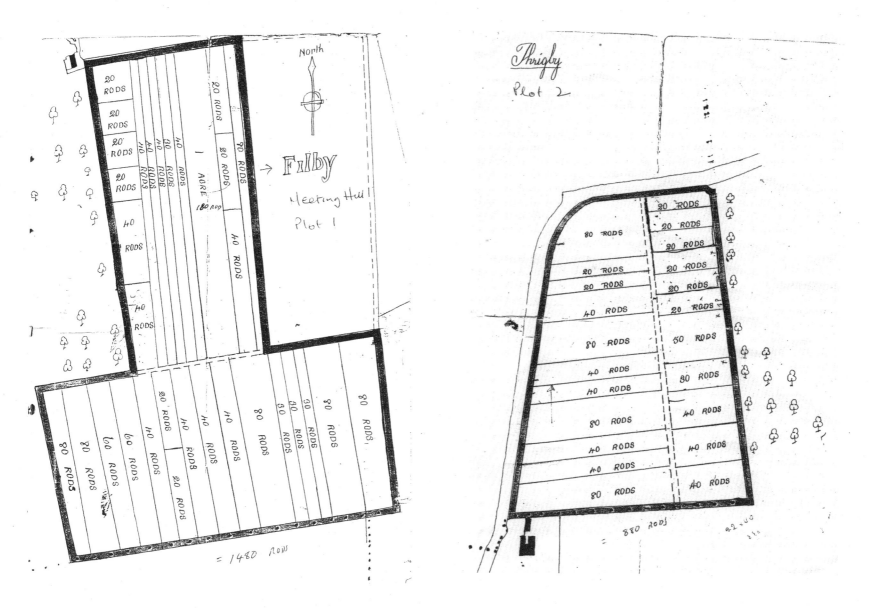

Figure 7.1: Allotment plans for Filby and Thrigby, acquired 1924.
(Thanks to Filby Parish Council)

on the sale of produce from allotments met the 'strongest possible objection' from the Norwich Co-operative Association. Evidently the 1922 Act threatened those in need who used their plots to earn income: in january 1923 the Norwich Cooperative Association 'would object most strongly about prevention' (NRO N/TC 30/1 of 1 january 1923). By may 1923 when applications for allotments in Norwich were 474 the Allotments Committee and Unemployment Committee turned to friendlier legislation to help out the unemployed by invoking the wartime Cultivation Of Lands Orders and Defence of the Realm (Acquisition of Land) Act 1916 to requisition allotment land on a number of sites, one of which was sub-let to the Food Protection League. At the start of 1924 applications were reduced to 67. The Corporation used allotments for an 'unemployment scheme' (ibid, 10 june 1924), certainly much-needed because even a policeman was found guilty of stealing two cabbages in 1924 from a site off the Dereham Road, for which he was found to have brought the City force into disrepute (anecdote from Mr Maurice MORSON). From 1925 the Allotments Superintendent is asked to report on rent arrears, a vexatious feature of Committee meetings that persists until World War 2 mopped up remaining unemployed men. The Allotments Committee was obliged to pursue people for money owed via notices to quit, writs and the whole legal paraphernalia until the bailiff was sent to claim such belongings as could produce a return. Many of those visits resulted in 'no effects upon which to levy. Many unemployed. Suggest this be written off' (ibid, 10 january 1928 and many, many other dates). The irreconcilability of a policy to pursue rent arrears and another to help the unemployed through allotments was never recorded, if discussed.

In the period following the 1922 Act Norwich created a number of new sites, all of which exist today: Hill Farm and Bluebell came in 1924, Hellesdon 1925 and Thorpe Estate 1930. The last two are now outside the city boundary. Bluebell accommodated the Earlham tenants as part of an ambitious development for the west side of the city. After WW1 the Corporation appointed the efficient Captain Sandys-Winch as Parks Superintendent, he to whom we owe the wealth of recorded detail on the progress of Norwich allotments from this period to the aftermath of WW2. Waterloo Park and Eaton Park are his legacy, and so are Bluebell North and South allotment sites. He planned five hundred twenty-rod plots 'on which a working man can produce sufficient to feed a family for a year' which are laid out on a grid design with roadways and paths giving access – for delivery of manure, care of the Allotments Committee, amongst other essentials – with water on tap and with huts ingeniously divided into four and standing on the crossing-point of four plots. The access lanes were lined with Norfolk varieties of pear, apple and plum trees, many of which still provide fruit for tenants (Haines, op cit). A similar scheme of fruit-trees, also Captain Sandys-Winch's initiative, exists at Hill Farm. These trees are landrace species and were catalogued a few years ago, and seeds were taken for the international seed bank which is maintained by the John Innes Centre at Colney.

With government support the **Quakers** helped to craft a private members bill which became the 1925 Allotments Act. It recognized that an allotment, which could be up to five acres, could be 'cultivated as a garden farm, or partly as a garden farm and partly as a farm' and it extended the provision of allotments beyond the 'labouring' classes. Further, local authorities were required to ascertain the demand for allotments in their areas and were to establish 'statutory allotments' which meant that the land dedicated to plots could not be sold or transferred to an alternative use without ministerial consent. But in **1926** a **Smallholdings and Allotment Act** reversed this position, explained in a Memorandum to the Act: there was

'no practical possibility under present financial conditions of satisfying the demand for further smallholdings owing to the fact that councils must only provide holdings on a self-supporting basis'.

So Councils were permitted to sell off smallholdings to those who wanted and could afford ownership, thus generating funds for the acquisition and provision of land for allotments and more tenanted smallholdings. According to Dr Alec Fisher of the University of East Anglia, a Labour Councillor from 1974 until the 1980s, 'Norfolk County Council owned thousands of acres of land, bought expressly to give a hand up to those working in agriculture who would not be able to afford to buy land, but could be offered tenancies which would

Figure 7.2: Thanks to Gressenhall Rural Life Museum, Norfolk.

eventually give them independence. The policy was supported by both Tories and Labour'. In total the Government's measures enabled 16 500 smallholdings, or 156 000 acres, to exist through County and Borough Councils but 6 600 ex-servicemen and unknown numbers of others remained unsupported. The popularity of this infringement upon landowners' traditional rights may be guessed by the following from Robert Graves, poet and novelist and biographer of the Great War, who became a parish councillor on his return from the trenches:

'Another caricature scene: myself in corduroys and a rough frieze coat sitting in the village schoolroom, debating...whether or not Farmer Tomkins could use a footpath across the allotments as a bridle path – having first overturned the decayed stile' (Graves p259-60).

The 1926 Act also created a new category, 'cottage holdings' with definitions of the amount of land attached to them and details of tenure specifically for agricultural workers.

Allowing that some benefited from the redistribution of land to become small independent farmers, for many in the countryside employment was their sole resource and allotments remained important. Norfolk, as the 1929 Ordnance Survey of Land Use reveals, had extended areas of allotments next to settlements throughout the county, amounting to many fields in many instances. The Survey for 1930–1939 records nine new parish acquisitions: one had two sites on land bought from Norwich Union of which one was administered by the Church of England. Three others, including **Cley**, were donated and managed by private landlords; under an agreement of 28 september 1931 the Gayton site is 'owned by Trustees of the Gayton Estate'. Published in 1938 the assessment called the *Land of Britain* (edited by L Dudley Smith) included a section on Norfolk allotments by John E G Mosby who wrote:

'The distribution of allotments is obviously connected with the distribution of close settlement. In Norwich there are over 450 acres of allotment gardens and there are allotments attached to almost every town in the county. But allotments are not restricted to towns for during the past decade it has become a fairly common thing for a field or smallholding near a village to be set aside for this purpose' (p186).

It emerges that in 1925 Norwich City Corporation was managing many acres of allotments in excess of those it owned (see Tables 7.2 and 7.3 below). Schemes for the unemployed were repeatedly introduced until the end of the decade when the Corporation received a letter from the Ministry of Agriculture asking that a demonstration allotment be created, supplemented by a course of lectures (NRO N/TC 30/1 of 11 february 1930). Norwich looked to Birmingham for guidance. Despite government initiatives unemployment in Britain rose to 22.5%. When the General Strike was called in 1926 allotments were of primary importance in meeting the crisis through the intervention of the **Quakers**. The Society of Friends worked locally by setting up, in many cases, local allotments' associations to provide allotments for people living in depressed areas and initially they provided free seed, tools, fertiliser and lime. In 1930 The Ministry of Agriculture formed a special Central Executive Committee which adopted the scheme and by 1936 urban sites where the need was greatest outnumbered rural by 4:1 (Poole/7, p26). Government aid ended in 1937 but by then the scheme was well-established and required less funding. By 1938 112 264 unemployed had been helped and were able to return funds to the scheme. All over the country local authorities had contributed land for allotments and, although the overall numbers of allotments had fallen at its lowest in 1937 to 589 015, the Society of Friends' statistics show how many hundreds of thousands of unemployed people they had helped.

FRIENDS LEND A HAND

IN ALLEVIATING UNEMPLOYMENT

*The Story of a Social Experiment
extending over 20 years, 1926-1946*

Compiled by

JOAN MARY FRY

With an Introduction by

A. C. RICHMOND

Controller and Vice-Chairman of
the Land Settlement Association

London
FRIENDS' BOOK CENTRE
Euston Road, N.W.1

1947

NUMBER OF SOCIETIES AND RECIPIENTS
IN ENGLAND AND WALES, 1935-6

Numbers in Brackets indicate Societies
Larger Numbers indicate Recipients

Total Number of Societies (2,671)
Total Number of Recipients 135,378

DIAGRAM MAP.   IN THE RECORD YEAR 1935-36.

*Figure 7.3: Acknowledgement to the Religious Society of Friends, Britain and thanks
to the Friends Library.*

With all this official determination, it might be supposed that the post-War resurgence in numbers of allotments would hold or increase; but in the ten years between 1920 and 1930 in the country as a whole the figure halved and continued to decline.

Table 7.1: Number of allotment plots in England and Wales 1873–1939

1873	244 268
1890	448 586
1914	674 000
*1914	130 526
1918	1 500 000
*1920	1 330 000
1928	1 024 000
1930	965 000
*1931	608 286
1934	936 000
*1937	589 015
1939	814 917

*figures taken from the official record of the Department of Environment. The remainder are found in a Memorandum by the Department of the Environment, Transport and the Regions (AL 23) *The Future for Allotments* on the Parliamentary website for 24.6.04, and are based on the Report of the Thorpe Committee of Inquiry into Allotments 1969. Replications are given to point up the discrepancies, which leave trends intact.

QUAKERS AND ALLOTMENTS IN NORFOLK/3
The Quakers most notable intervention between people and their sufferings used allotments and came in 1927 . In 1926 a miners' strike was followed by the General Strike called by the Trades Union Congress. The Friends' attention was drawn to the extreme poverty and deprivation of welsh miners. On 7 may 1926 the Meeting for Sufferings, the executive body of the Society of Friends, instantiated a Watching Committee, later replaced by the Friends' Industrial Crisis Committee (FICC), to report on the miners' plight: it met daily and was "in constant touch" with the two parties to the dispute. Visits were made to mining areas. Many miners had excluded themselves from the unemployment benefit through their thrift in buying their own back-to-back and hence were unable even to buy food. Shops closed for lack of trade. Local community centres were established and funds raised, for example to pay for boot-mending.

The strike ended in November 1926 without a satisfactory settlement for either side and in 1927 the FICC ended but "the thread of public work was never lost". The FICC had acted as a non-governmental organization, appealing through the BBC and press for donations and to march 1927 had distributed £5 000, the Christmas appeal raising £1 221. But with the economic trail culminating in the Great Crash and depression, unemployment and distress persisted in mining areas of Britain. By september 1928 there were demands for allotments, with the Friends once more acting as go-between with the government to obtain assurances that any sales from produce would not affect benefits. The Friends set aside £3 000 to start the scheme, providing free seed, seed potatoes, tools and lime, costing about ten shillings per plot. Some seed merchants helped out and pit owners gave wire for fencing. By 1929 local Friends organizations managed seven thousand applications for the allotments scheme in South Wales; it was the model for Yorkshire, Wigan, Durham, Northumberland and Staffordshire. When unemployment reached 1 066 000 the scheme was extended to the Lancashire cotton-workers.

Between 1929 and may 1930 the Friends established Training Clubs which provided a centre where the unemployed could meet, take a midday meal and receive talks and education. The Friends created a very successful scheme to find work for the unemployed through negotiating with the local authority that they carry out repairs on roads, playing fields, other publicly-owned sites. From these centres communal gardens developed.

The Friends formed a Central Allotments Committee in 1930: it published the *Penny Guide* to allotmenteering. As their scheme consolidated, free supplies were eliminated to encourage "self-help instead of charity". In October 1930, a total of £7 206 having been spent by the Society of Friends on the allotments scheme, the work passed to the Government. Under the Labour parliament of Ramsay MacDonald a committee was formed to continue the work of the Friends, which included three of its members. There were

Figure 7.4: Acknowledgement to the Religious Society of Friends, Britain and thanks to the Friends Library.

difficulties in finding land but "many vacant plots were brought into cultivation" and an estimated 20 000 new participants joined the scheme. The Minister for Agriculture introduced the Agricultural Land Utilization Bill which became law in july 1931.

The new National Coalition government of 1931, still headed by Ramsay MacDonald, did not vote through the funds for the allotments scheme; on 9 november 1931 the Committee ceased to function and its work was transferred to the Ministry of Agriculture. The Society of Friends took on the task of managing the, by then, 64 000 men involved. In 1932 they formed the Committee for Allotments Gardens for the Unemployed and raised money through allotment societies, through charities and with grants from the Government amounting to £42 833. In 1933–4, with 100 000 'subscribers' and 2 221 Societies £11 000 was required of Government monies.

This established movement became a fixture in national life. In July 1933 subscribers began to take part in shows, contributing to the Royal Show at Derby thereafter. In 1939 a model allotment plot was created at London Zoo. Grants were offered to replace scruffy huts with splendid Community Huts. An extension of the scheme, called the Group Holdings scheme, enabled larger plots to be taken, sufficient for market gardening but not for small-holding, which had its own legal category. Holders were encouraged to devote two-thirds of their land to vegetables and one-third to keeping poultry and grants helped to provide a model poultry-hut. Unemployment peaked in may 1935 at 2 044 753 but was still as high as 1 748 781 in march 1938.

This more ambitious scheme led in turn to the Land Settlement Association, a scheme for resettling the unemployed from Durham in the south of England, on five acres of land with which they would be self-sufficient. Together with the Group Holdings scheme, the Government and Carnegie Trust took over its running. This was a grand project, resulting in twenty estates contributing 9 817 acres, helping nearly eight hundred men as tenants or trainees. The cost of land, homes and stock buildings came to almost £1.5 millions. By 1946 there were more than six hundred holdings, generating produce to a total of £800 000. Verily from little acorns did magnificent oak trees grow.

Mary Joan Fry closes her account with these words:
> "When we consider the dual nature of man – 'a swinging wicket set between the Unseen and the Seen' – it is evident that for any person to be deprived of all possibility of work … is to imprison him within himself to a very dangerous extent … The isolation from other men, the home worries, the loss of physical aptitude as well as the utter uncertainty of the future are all calculated to tempt the strest character to give way to drift and discontent, if not worse.
>
> "To Friends, with their view of the sacramental nature of all life, it came as a peculiar call to bring some sense of fellowship and sympathy to those suffering such dire distress.
>
> "It is hoped that this account of one effort at using land culture as a cure for unemployment may encourage further efforts in making a wiser use of our countryside, recognizing that it must be with an understanding of, and a working with, nature rather than a ruthless conquest of her by mechanical means."

The National Allotments Society (NAS), as it was then called, was formed in 1930 'at a time when demand for allotments was falling after WW1 and more and more land was being used instead for housing, often in breach of the 1908 Act' (*Times*, p169). As the allotments had gone the associations went with them. One of these in 1924 was the Agricultural Organization Society, a coordinating body of over a thousand associations, to be replaced by the Allotments Organization Society which looked after a remnant 350 associations. Another leader in the field was the National Union of Allotment Holders whose fortunes had followed a similar pattern. Amalgamation of these two bodies into the National Allotments Society Ltd, the precursor to today's National Society of Allotment and Leisure Gardeners, was the logical if not inevitable solution. By 1939 there were 1800 and by 1941 the figure had increased to 2 300 societies affiliated to the national body (Crouch and Ward, p114–5). The Norwich Allotments Committee became affiliated in 1932, initiating an Allotments Garden Competition in 1935 (ibid 8 january 1935)

One of the National Allotments Society's projects for gaining greater acceptance, even enthusiasm, for allotments was publicized through its periodical. It ran an extensive piece on the *Model Allotment*, meaning a model site. The NAS was exercised by the dereliction of some sites: they were 'not merely ugly but revolting in their appearance'. NAS was not being finicky. It recognized the unpalatable reality that support for allotment schemes would never be forthcoming if order on site did not prevail. The hut was at the centre of objections. The solution was a 'well-constructed and attractive community hut, placed in the right position and the immediate surroundings well laid out' (p13). The Friends had supported the introduction of community huts by offering grants, 308 to august 1937 and the NAS had run a competition to 'encourage Societies to keep...[sites]...in good condition and make them attractive' (p13). For the future the NAS was to run a competition and amenity scheme 'to take account of the whole appearance of allotments in givèn areas' (p15).

Taking the concept to its extreme, a 1938 pamphlet by Lady Allen of Hurtwood, Fellow of the Institute of Landscape Architects, illustrated *How allotments could be made an asset to the community*. Lady Hurtwood produced an illustrated pamphlet whose object was 'to consider how allotment gardens can be made beautiful', nothing less.

This was a sympathetic attempt to reconcile public not-in-my-back-yard opinion to what was perceived to be and were, indeed, 'a great eyesore and blot on the countryside' (p6) in order that all those unemployed and the families on small wages should benefit materially and mentally. The fault lay in the 'haphazard system' whereby local authorities denied security of tenure on many sites. Lady Hurtwood advocated the linkage of productive and recreational spaces and parks so that they would become 'as decorative and as productive as were the best types of old cottage gardens' (p10), incorporating a community hut, childrens' gardens and playground and 'jungle gym'.

'Valiant efforts are being made by the National Allotments Society and the Society of Friends to stimulate the building of more seemly huts and to encourage their tidiness of individual plots', Lady Hurtwood concluded (p7).

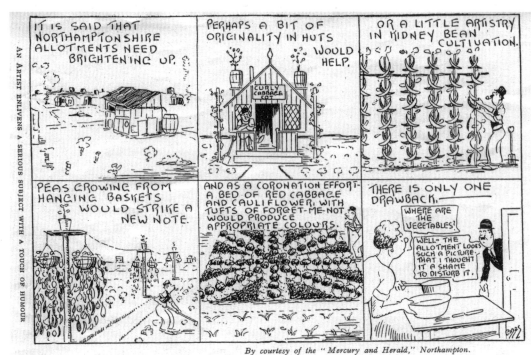

Figure 7.5: The National Allotments Society's take on the beautification of allotments.

Before the onset of war the acreage for allotments and the number of tenants it supported in towns like Norwich had risen substantially to meet the desperate need of the unemployed and partly-employed.

Table 7.2: Acreages and tenancies in Norwich 1923–1938 – allotments owned by the City Corporation (from NRO N/TC 30/1)

	acres	rods	poles	number of tenancies
1923	279	3	13	1 821
1924	295	1	33	1 756
1925				
1926				
1927	249	1	35	1 744
1928	248	6	0	1 722
1929	256	28	0	1 707
1930	260	2	20	1 718
*1931	253	3	37	1 724

* The decrease in acreage from 1930 but increase in tenancies reflects the policy of Norwich City Corporation to divide the larger allotments

Table 7.3: Acreages and tenancies in Norwich 1930–38 – allotments including those privately owned and hired/leased by the City Corporation (Source: NRO N/TC/30/1)

1925	473	3 181
1926	546	3 431
1927	534	3 228
1929	530	3 273
1929	502	3 286
+1930	491	3 209
1931	473	3 101
1932	458	3 207
1933	465	3 384
1934	452	3 370
1935	401	2 770
1936	382	2 972
1937	379	2 780
1938	366	2 681

Towards the latter half of the 1930s, the number of tenants began to reduce as well as vacancies to increase and the Allotments Committee sought to rationalize its holdings, a process that was interrupted by the 1939 Cultivation of Land Order commanding the Allotments Committee to create, once again, demonstration plots: Waterloo Park and Chapelfield Gardens were chosen for them.

Although *Amateur Gardening* appeared to be blissfully unaware of conflict even during wartime – it was strictly dedicated to gardening for pleasure and adornment – publications to help the plot-holder included journals like the weekly *Smallholder, poultry-keeper and gardener*. The issue for 16 september 1939 came out under the banner 'Your – and our – part in the War'. Accompanied by a fine photo, the Minister of Agriculture, Colonel Sir Reginald Dorman-Smith, addressed his 'Call to You':

> '...the assistance that smallholders, allotment holders and those with a reasonably-sized garden can render in the present emergency is to help – more perhaps than they realize – to feed themselves and others' (Issue No 1539, Vol 62, p2).

The next challenge and the one with which allotments will forever be connected was to be World War 2.

8 | World War 2 1939–45

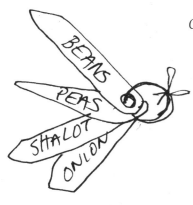

(c) MOH 23·6·04

On Monday we had Beans and Swedes,
On Tuesday Swedes and Beans,
On Wednesday we had Haricots
And some Swedes instead of greens.

On Thursday we had Beans again
With just a little soup
Made from some Swedes and Haricots
But we called it 'Cereal Soup'.

On Friday just by way of a change
We had Swedes fried in slices
And finished up with Butter Beans
Instead of nice cool ices.

On Saturday we've Swedes, mashed up,
And there's Beans again for Sunday
But we quite expect to have a change
From Beans to Swedes next Monday.

Allotments
(Anonymous)

When the wartime challenge to feed the country came in 1939 the allotment habit was already firmly embedded in the psyche of politician and public.

War planning had begun as early as 1936 when government recognized the continuing dependency of the United Kingdom on food imports: still eighty per cent of fruit consumed and, even more than at the start of World War 1, ninety per cent of cereals were imported (Griffiths, p89). Soon after World War 2 started food price inflation was at 84% and rationing was introduced to maintain a fair supply of staples to everyone, a practice that was not phased out until the early 1950s. In november 1936 the Food (Defence Plans) department of the Board of Trade was formed, partly in anticipation of a future role in the event of war, but also to collaborate with the Ministry of Agriculture and Fisheries in plans for improving home production, for which an increase in mechanization and labour needed to be secured. Deficits in agricultural practice were addressed in the Agriculture Acts of 1937 and 1939 which secured funds for improving the land and taking back into arable production unused and pasture land. The County War Agriculture Executive Commmittees – known as CAECs or WarAgs – were reconstituted (some of them with World War 1 veterans) in order to locally co-ordinate orders and regulations.

The Royal Horticultural Society was prescient. A Council memorandum dated 25 october 1938 considered what could be done to support Government efforts. 'The Ministry of Agriculture I have reason to believe would be very glad if this Society could undertake to look after the work in private gardens and allotments'. In anticipation the RHS would consider where vegetable shortages would occur and what seed needed to be saved; how fruits could be saved from losses to pests and in storing; and what advice through the medium of pamphlets could be disseminated through the BBC, Women's Institutes, horticultural societies and so on. 'The Society, with commendable foresight, saw the change that was coming and set itself from the early days of the war to co-operate with the Ministry of Agriculture in the campaign for an increased production of vegetables', so wrote the Minister, the Right Honorable R S Hudson M P in the foreword to the RHS's timely publication *The vegetable garden displayed*. By the ninth edition, the Minister of Food, the Right Honorable Lord Woolton put it starkly:

'This is a Food War. Every extra row of vegetables in allotments saves shipping. If we grow more Potatoes we need not import so much Wheat. Carrots and Swedes, which can be stored through the winter, help to replace imported fruit.

'We must grow our own Onions. We can no longer import ninety per cent of them, as we did before the War.

'The vegetable garden is also our National Medicine Chest – it yields a large proportion of the vitamins which protect us against infection.

'The battle on the Kitchen Front cannot be won without help from the Kitchen Garden.'

The Minister of Agriculture and Fisheries, Sir Reginald Hugh Doram-Smith, added encouraging words in a radio broadcast on 4 october 1939:

'Half a million more allotments properly worked will provide potatoes that will feed another million adults and one-and-a-half million children for eight months of the year, so let's get going and let "dig for victory" be the matter for everyone with a garden or allotment and every man capable of digging an allotment in their spare time."

Under the slogan 'cloches are true food weapons', Charles Wyse was quick to promote the value of the 'french gardening' technique that was imported to the UK from France pre-World War 1 with *Cloches versus Hitler*, published in October 1939 and with *Cloches month-by-month*. Others rushed to print, too, and Richard Sudell's *Practical gardening and food production* contained a section on allotment gardening while AGL Hellyer's book was solely devoted to *War-time gardening for home needs*.

Agriculture in Britain at the start of the War was described by Sir Daniel Hall FRS, formerly chief scientific adviser to the Minister for Agriculture and Fisheries (MAF) and Director of Norfolk's John Innes Horticultural Institute, in scathing terms. He warned:

'...a not inconsiderable proportion of the farming land of the country is not doing its duty. It is not merely that there is neglected and indeed derelict land that could be productive but that far greater areas are starved and half-farmed because they have lacked the capital expenditure on recondition which every flourishing industry regularly undertakes. This sad aspect of the

Allotments at Trowse were established by the Colman family as part of a model village. The original pig-shed, clinker built and with rooftiles, was provided to give tenants both food and manure for their plots.

Catton Grove in Norwich is one of its earliest sites.

Allotment sites in Norwich that date from the beginning of the twentieth century, Elm Grove Lane, Marston Lane and Brickfields.

Elm Grove Lane.

Marston Lane.

Brickfields.

(Thanks to Gressenhall Rural Life Museum, Norfolk).

countryside has been reported by many men but the work of the War Agricultural Committees has opened the eyes of farmers themselves to the extent of the waste that has been going on and to the way in which it can be repaired' (Hall, p267).

When the government came to consider land outside the towns its thoughts turned to commons. It remembered the rebuff of World War 1 and gave the reconstituted CAECs powers to requisition commons along with other unproductive lands. Irrespective of the emergency, the Open Space Society was as vigilant as ever:

'Under the Defence Regulations the process...[of sequestering commons for wartime purposes]...is being repeated on a greatly increased scale and large tracts of common land have been taken for...cultivation as allotments or otherwise...The Society pressed that this land should be restored immediately after the cessation of hostilities' (Birtles, p272).

In Norfolk thirteen commons and enclosure allotments used as commons were put under the plough, some 658 acres and 3.3% of the total for England and Wales (Birtles, p252). Although one case of garden allotments being offered to the CAEC for farming has come to light, at Tuckswood to the north of the City (returned to allotments at the end of the War), evidently no encroachment on rural garden allotments took place in Norfolk: in one case, Neatherd Moor in Dereham, when the land was offered to the CAEC by the Urban Council it was told that 'it might be put to better use as garden allotments' (Birtles, p261). However, a tenant-farmer was later found for its 49 acres and the land was part-cropped and later returned to common, just as the Open Space Society had asked. On the contrary, at Hickling in Broadland marshland was drained and cropped (Nelson, p47) and at Roydon, 'during the...War the eastern portion of the fen was divided into garden allotments' (Birtles/2, p88).

A **Cultivation of Land (Allotments) Act 1939** confirmed the Defence Orders of which two related to allotments: No. 61 said that theft from allotments was a statutory offence and No. 62A, intended primarily for towns and cities, gave local authorities powers to requisition unoccupied land and create allotments. In combination with a reduction of working hours from nine to five or five-thirty during weekdays and nine to twelve or twelve-thirty on saturdays, and with the introduction of double daylight saving an extra hour or two of daylight in the summer evenings could be achieved and even, arguably, a longer growing season so that output from gardens and allotments could be maximized and no-one had an excuse for not growing-their-own.

Believing that an example would motivate – they would prove to be 'of first-class educational, propaganda and psychological value' (Crouch and Ward, p75) – MAF created a demonstration plot and piggery in Hyde Park and urged local authorities to do the same. In Norwich the resourceful Captain Sandys-Winch complied with demonstration plots in Waterloo Park and Chapelfield Gardens, in the centre of the City. Since large numbers of urban allotments had been created to counteract unemployment levels following the economic slump of the 1930s, the Corporation for one was in a stronger position to launch a campaign than any plan could have anticipated (see Tables 7.2 and 7.3 above). One Norwich site, Harford Hall (now Marston Lane) went in the opposite direction: it was converted to farming land for the duration of the War and then returned to allotments (anecdote). Allotments were created in the royal parks in London and on the blitzed bombsites. Municipal parks, tennis clubs and golf courses were transformed into vegetable gardens, although in Norwich it was 1943 before the Municipal Golf Course relinquished land, just 30 poles of it! The nationalized industries made new space available – railways, the National Coal Board, British waterways and power utilities, the Church of England all transformed spaces from the meanest to the most hallowed into productive land. By 1950 there were seventy-five thousand railway allotments (Hyde, p49). In large centres of population local authorities established Horticultural Advisory Committees to help allotment-holders and they introduced higher education courses in vegetable-growing. The public needed help and education to develop new skills and the BBC produced *In Your Garden*. MAF commissioned striking and iconic posters of which one, urging people to *Dig for Victory*, introduced the slogan by which the movement is remembered. An initial attempt to help people through education was MAF's *Grow*

MANURE FROM GARDEN RUBBISH
HOW TO MAKE A COMPOST HEAP

BY means of a compost heap, demanding neither much time nor labour, and little or no expense, all the vegetable waste of the garden can be turned into valuable manure. Leaves, grass cuttings, sods, lawn mowings, pea or bean or potato haulms, outer leaves or tops of vegetables, hedge clippings, weeds and faded flowers ; in short, any plant refuse, green or otherwise, can be used for manurial purposes. Such a conversion of waste to good use, if widely adopted, can make a considerable contribution to the national effort for increased food production.

The process known as composting is based on the fact that if vegetable matter, soil, water and air are brought together and provided with a " starter," which may be animal manure or a chemical,

a fermentation or digestion takes place. Lime (especially slaked lime or chalk) is necessary to neutralize the acids which are formed. This action converts the materials to humus, a substance essential for maintaining the fertility of all soils.

Kitchen refuse, if it cannot be fed to pigs or other livestock, should be well mixed with the other material and added to the heap.

Autumn leaves, on account of their dryness, tend to decompose slowly, and should be mixed with sappy material or even dealt with in a separate heap. Decomposition of very fibrous matter, such as the stems of some herbaceous plants, cabbage stumps or potato haulms, will be hastened if it is chopped into short lengths and broken up.

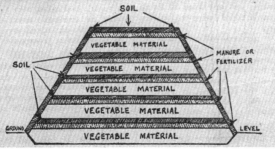

More Food bulletins, jointly produced with the Royal Horticultural Society. *Bulletin No 1 Food from the garden* gave a ten-rod cropping scheme which was criticized by experienced gardeners for being muddled and for simple errors. Millions of leaflets were issued and then re-issued with corrections, and this at a time when newspapers were reducing their sheets to save paper imports (Griffiths, p97).

In Norwich there were already 104 acres of private allotments serving 860 tenants by the 1939 Allotments Committee Return. By using the Cultivation of Lands Order 1939 the Committee increased the number of sites it managed by eight, providing just 22 acres extra for 268 tenants but the private tenancies had soared to 132 acres. Given that Norfolk was a launch-pad for the Battle of Britain and that Norwich was bombed, its allotments taking direct hits, that so much space should be successfully used for the war effort is a tribute to its people. Private sites totalled 39 by 1941, providing nearly 1100 people with fresh produce until at least 1944, after which the record is silent. In addition there were 38 acres hired for 190 people and 52 acres leased for 39, practices that ended soon after the finish of the War (NRO N/TC 30/1). At the peak the commitment of acreage to allotments was 473, sustaining 4 007 families, a tremendous achievement.

Table 8.1: Total allotment acreages in Norwich 1939–1946 (from NRO N/TC 30/1)

	acres	rods	poles	number of tenancies
1939	365	0	19	2 567
1940	415	2	28	3 085
1941	459	2	8	3 832
1942	473	0	0	4 007
1943	453	0	30	3 947
1944	"	"	"	3 892
1945	307	1	29	2 634
1946	298	0	8	2 498

Over the wartime period various devices were introduced in Norwich as elsewhere to educate and encourage its citizens to become self-sufficient. As well as creating demonstration plots, it collaborated with the East Anglian Horticultural Society to promote the production of vegetable crops in a way which would ensure a continuous supply of produce for the household. To stimulate intensive cultivation the Committee introduced smaller, five-rod plots from the beginning of 1942. In 1944 the Committee permitted plot-holders to erect Anderson Shelters on the plots, provided they were 'suitably painted or tarred'. A few remain.

Through the powerful medium of radio the government also launched two campaigns for involving the public in increased food production. The first was aimed at farmers and agricultural workers and was called *Ploughing Up*. The second campaign, *Grow More Food*, was initiated by the 4 october 1939 broadcast and exhorted people throughout the land to start producing vegetables instead of flowers and grass in their gardens and to take on an allotment where possible (Wilt, p188–9). The RHS anticipated Government advice with a *Companion Series to Growmore Bulletins* in 1940 with *Simple vegetable cooking*. There were at least 92 bulletins in all, including those for the specialist – No.16 *Shoot that pigeon*, No 44 *More drainage for heavy land*, No 91 *How to select a dairy bull*.

Faced with unexpected outcomes of their policies,

'...Typical of Ministry of Food ingenuity was the campaign when we had a glut of carrots at a time when other vegetables were scarce...[Lord Woolton's] master stroke was to spread the report that the night fighter and bomber aces of the RAF were eating carrots to enable them to see in the dark. The new airborne radar, and for that matter the powers of the older ground station radar detection, were at the time top secret. Success in bringing down enemy bombers at night was increasing...and the public was naturally asking how it was done. Some at least were quite convinced that it was all done by carrots' (Morrison).

It took longer to turn agriculture around than to create allotments. In 1943 a survey of manual workers showed that over fifty per cent kept either a garden or an allotment and by 1944 it was estimated that domestic hens were producing a quarter of the country's supply of fresh eggs. By the end of the war the Domestic Poultry Keepers' Council had over one-and-a-quarter million members owning twelve million birds. "You all went away so I talked to the hens instead', wrote Marion Longden to her daughter, then serving in Egypt. Pig-keeping was another craze – there were eventually 6 900 Pig Clubs with hundreds of thousands of members, feeding their beasts on kitchen waste and, as described at **Trowse**, allotment waste. The Government estimated in 1944 that food grown privately provided ten per cent of the nation's total production.

Women were a significant part of the war effort and with their children worked allotments alongside or without their menfolk as circumstance dictated. Not only were women increasingly assigned to jobs previously reserved for men, they were sent into critical trades where expansion was prevented by the new shortage of labour. The Land Army was one such occupation, of which Norfolk saw its share. The Women's Institute played a vital part in encouraging women to grow food, keep poultry and pigs and cook efficiently. They were the target of a MAF campaign conducted in the press to advise on creating 'appetizing' meals from limited resources and to make preserves. The *Dig for Victory* campaign for 1942 especially encouraged women to produce food and women's gardening associations started up in that year. In some towns more than fifty per cent of all allotments were held by women (Griffiths, p97). A member of the WI wrote:

'We dig for victory. We keep chickens and goats, we knit for troops, we keep our village merry and bright by handicrafts, music and drama and a hundred and one useful odds and ends' (in Wilt, p209).

Initially having sought to increase the number of allotments throughout the nation by half a million this figure was itself increased to one million when the success of the *Dig for Victory* campaign was evident: one estimate is that the number of allotments in Britain rose from 815 000 in 1939 to 1 400 000 in 1943 and that the acreage covered moved from 95 700 to 136 800 acres over that period. To accomplish this

DIG FOR VICTORY LEAFLET No. 15

POTATO GROWING IN ALLOTMENTS AND GARDENS

it took not only efficiency in government and enthusiasm in the country, as we have seen, but a radical change in eating expectations. Production of foods that were extravagant in inputs of land and feed – big animals and their products – was limited and staples were favoured, with farmers concentrating on wheat, barley, oats, rye, maize, beans, peas and potatoes. In Norfolk huge acreages were covered with blackcurrants to

WANTED FOR SEED — DO NOT TOUCH

TOMATO GROWING IS NOT DIFFICULT

How Amateurs Can Produce this Valuable Health-Giving Fruit

★ *In a greenhouse*
★ *In the open*

supply vitamin C. Amateurs used their gardens and allotments for green vegetables, onions, legumes, carrots, onions, pigs, poultry and potatoes. The potato was king – a poster campaign all to itself extolled its virtues. Having believed that an end to imports would mean an end to the tomato, people learned with some surprise how easy it was to grow tomatoes against a sunny wall, especially after town corporations started to sell dried sewage sludge as fertilizer (Griffiths, p93). Allotment tenants kept seed from one year to the next and shared. As well as having a big cottage garden, Alec Fisher's grandfather worked two of the five hundred allotments at Maldon, Essex:

'He had a special job and I was his assistant. He used the allotments to grow seedlings and everyone would come to him and say, "I'll have two dozen cabbages and thirty broad bean seedlings". They paid pence for them'.

Another wartime expedient to replace imported medicines was to grow herbs both on an agricultural and domestic scale for complaints which nowadays are treated only by drugs of synthetic manufacture. Herbs gave an uplift to a simple cuisine, too, and the wartime diet was surprisingly sophisticated.

What about some HERBS?

'No doubt owing to the American "invasion" of this country many gardeners became much interested in sweet corn' (Ministry of Agriculture *Allotment and Garden Guide* Vol 1 No 12, december 1945). Perhaps it was nostalgia for foods not normal for Norfolk but familiar to american servicemen that prompted this recollection:

'15th July, 1943: On the edges of American airfields and between the barracks of troops in England it is no unusual thing to see complicated and carefully tended vegetable gardens. No one seems to know where the idea originated but these gardens have been constantly increasing. It is fairly common now that a station furnishes a good part of its own vegetables and all of its own salad greens.

'The idea, which had as its basis, probably, the taking up of some of the free time of men when there were few entertainment facilities, has proved vastly successful. The gardens are run by the units and worked by the groups, but here and there a man may go out on his own and try and raise some strange

seed which is not ordinarily seen in this climate. In every unit there is usually some man who knows about such things who advises on the planting but even such men are often at a loss because vegetables are different here from the vegetables at home.

'The things that the men want to raise most, in order of choice, are green corn, tomatoes and peppers. None of these do very well in England unless there is a glass house to build up sufficient heat...

'The gardens usually start out ambitiously. Watermelons and cantaloupes are planted and they have practically no chance of maturing at this latitude, where even cucumbers are usually raised in glass houses, but gradually some order grows out of the confusion. Lettuce, peas, green beans, green onions, potatoes do very well here, as do cabbages and turnips and beets and carrots. The gardens are lush and well-tended. In the evenings which are very long now' – remember, the Government introduced double summer-time daylight saving, to extend the growing season as well as time available for cultivation – 'the men work in the beds. It does not get dark until eleven o'clock, there are only so many movies to be seen, English pubs are not exciting, but there does seem to be a constant excitement about the gardens and the produce that comes from them tastes much better than that purchased in the open market' (Steinbeck).

The Norfolk War Agriculture Committee Executive was up and running by October 1939 when it sent requests to town and parish councils to 'see that all allotments under their jurisdiction are cultivated in a proper husbandlike manner' and that all allotment tenants would be required to make the fullest use of their allotments (**Little Plumstead** Parish record).

In Norfolk the few allotment sites created during WW2 of which the Survey has been made aware were in the early days of the War and came by private treaty. In 1939 in **North Elmham** large pieces of land were gifted by Will, in Trunch in 1941 and in Overstrand in 1941 by private lease; and in **Thompson** in 1942 when Lord Walsingham gave land to one of his tenants. Despite an early wage agreement negotiated between government and the National Union of Agricultural Workers – 'food was never as short in the country as it could be in the towns but the wages of farm-workers showed little improvement'. Allotments remained important in the countryside: at the Lophams in south Norfolk where the Town Lands Charity provided quarter-acre allotments for 27 tenants on two sites,

> '…flowers and vegetables were matters of family pride. There was great rivalry for the earliest potatoes, the longest runner bean, the best grafted rose or apple of your own contriving and the biggest gooseberry' (Serpell, p252).

In april 1940 the **Little Plumstead** Parish Council was asked by the primary schoolteacher if allotments could be spared 'for the children to cultivate', under supervision, and a tenant agreed to let half of his plot to be used by them. 'Mr Jones very kindly offered to use his gyrotilla to break up the land, thus saving the children the hard labour of digging'. Similarly in **Reepham** children in the Primary School were handed out children-sized garden tools and on the extensive playing field, as well as land opposite the School, dug for victory.

By june 1940 the Sprowston War Agricultural Committee complained that some tenants in **Little Plumstead** had failed to cultivate their plots and the Parish Council responded summarily by immediately terminating the agreements of seven of the unenthusiastic tenants, with two others receiving notice. George Rushbrook, a tenant, and two Councillors, Mr Evan Jones (a market gardener) and Mr Henry Thomas Key (a farmer), collaborated to clear the 'trees and undergrowth' of one plot and the plots were distributed between them, remaining in multiple tenancy until after the War when there was a renewal of interest in allotments from returning servicemen.

In **Oulton**, some of whose land became an airfield dedicated to the Battle of Britain, the impact of war can hardly have escaped the parishioners. The parish record instances the wholehearted support that the village extended to any requests from government sources but a letter from the Ministry of

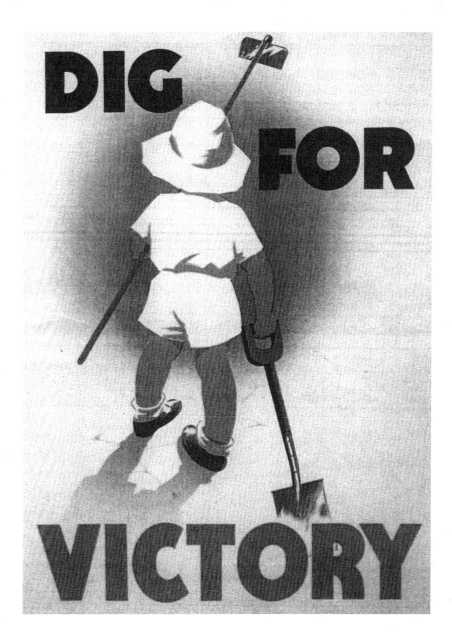

Agriculture asking if more land for allotments was needed returned a 'no'. The village's commitment to food production was exhausted in the course of a normal day and allotments and gardens were fully utilized.

At **Little Plumstead** matters were not so ordered. In September 1941 MAF agitated about the use of 'derelict gardens and waste land', but a piece of land owned by Mrs Pleasants was inspected and reported to be 'useless'. The Council also read out and answered the questions of a circular sent by the Norfolk Home Food Front.

It is believed that by the end of the War 1.75 million allotments existed in Britain (Department of Environment Policy Bulletin). Under the heading, 'Does vegetable growing pay?', Dr Joad opined that 'it all depends on what you mean by pay'(Ministry of Agriculture *Allotment and Garden Guide* Vol 1 No 12, december 1945). Using a sample of one hundred 10-rod plots over the country, 'crops to the value of anything from £20 to £30…had been grown' with produce weights each week varying between eleven pounds in spring to twenty pounds in winter, when the proportion of root crops increased.

Even in wartime, in dire emergency, allotments retained benefits beyond purely immediate demands. 'Of course, there is more to it than mere financial returns…The thrifty housewife…knows, too, how important a part vegetables pay in maintaining family health…No doubt the pre-war allotment holder felt the call of the land and the allotment was his pastime. The war-time cultivator would probably say that he wanted to make sure of vegetables for his family; in some cases he may have feared a food shortage or patriotically desired to help the national food situation. Whatever the motive that prompted the man to take on an allotment, he has benefited himself: he is generally better in health because of the exercise, better in spirit because cultivating his plot took his mind off the war or the burdens of office or workshop; he has benefited his family by providing fresh vegetables that kept them fit – and incidentally helped his wife in trying to make ends meet and avoid queues' (ibid).

Establishing gardens and allotments as an essential part of the national ethos had unpredicted effects. By 1944 when the Economist surveyed

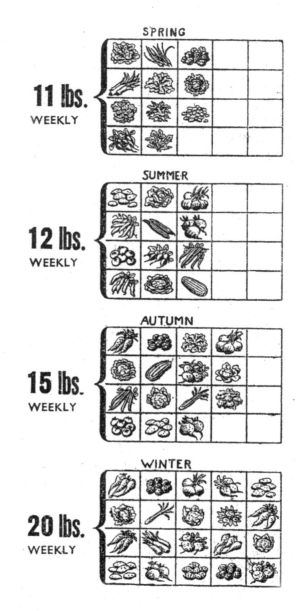

allotment-holders only twenty per cent claimed that they were there to help the war effort. Nearly eighteen per cent said that they wanted to save money, 55 per cent said that their main aim was to produce fresh food and sixteen per cent to acquire fresh air.

"Not yet must the flowers invade the fat green hinterland of the war-time allotment", a Northern newspaper recently declared' (Ministry of Agriculture Allotment and Garden Guide Vol 1 No 3, march 1945). The Ministry of Agriculture underlined the importance of maintaining allotment habits when the peace came: 'fresh allotment produce – garden stuff, too – is going to be of immense value during the first few years after the war, when there will be a great strain upon road, rail and all transport' (ibid). The Ministry was not prepared to be absolutely austere but allowed the country the sweet anticipation of peacetime: 'The Ministry does not rule out flowers altogether. As the Northern newspaper happily put it: "Now and again an allotment holder will disinterestedly set himself to cheer us all up by bedding out – in true peace-time parkland style – with lobelias, geraniums, pansies – just a happy fringe of them along the hem of his plot". The Ministry itself has said…that not more than one-tenth of peace-time flowers should be grown…"just a happy fringe"' (ibid).

9 | ridges and furrows: to the present day

We are a nation of flower-lovers, but also a nation of stamp-collectors, pigeon-fanciers, amateur carpenters, coupon-snippers, darts players, crossword-puzzle fans. All the culture that is most truly native centres round things which even when they are communal are not official – the pub, the football match, the back garden, the fireside and the 'nice cup of tea'. The liberty of the individual is still believed in... But this has nothing to do with economic liberty, the right to exploit others for profit. It is the liberty to have a home of your own, to do what you like in your spare time, to choose your own amusements instead of having them chosen for you from above.

England, your England (1953)

George Orwell

By the end of World War 2 the vegetable plot and allotment had become a way of life and, besides, the ration book stayed until 1954. Its termination was part of a general dismantling of structures relating to food production and hence land apportionment. Evidently by then a problem had been addressed that struck at the core of civil liberties, as well as a national addiction – the shortage of tobacco for smoking. A pamphlet *'Better Baccy – grow and smoke your own'*, one of a number on the same topic from 1948, was endorsed by the Reverend Hugh Cuthbertson, President of the National Amateur Tobacco Growers' Association and Vicar of Tilty in Essex who welcomed 'the opportunity of recommending to the public this study and competent little handbook which squarely faces the difficulties, as well as the delights, of attempting to grow your own smokes' (Foreword). It was produced on the occasion of a 'government concession...[to]home-growers to cooperate in airing and manufacture'.

In Norwich conflict arose between tenants on requisitioned and private land and the claims of landowners: Ministry of Agriculture Circular No. 2070 urged 'the continuance of wartime allotments', termination of agreement requiring Ministry approval first (NRO N/TC 30/1 of 12 march 1946). Where the Ministry consented to release land it asked the Council 'to leave allotment holders undisturbed for the longest possible time' (ibid 9 july 1946) and a year later it launched its 'Dig for Plenty' campaign. Private land ceased to be used as allotments in 1948 whereas land held under the Cultivation of Land Order was held until 1959, even as the acreage of allotments on City land diminished until in 1961 there was a total of 275 acres for 2350 tenants.

It was not until the mid-1960s that matters concerning allotments, open spaces and parks and commons became fully a local responsibility once more (Poole/3, p16) though powers to provide spaces for allotments remained with district and urban councils for some years:

'Some individuals noticed the muddle surrounding the provision and maintenance of allotments. In January 1948 Mr C W Whatley of Wroughton in Swindon noted that acres of rural allotments lay abandoned during a serious potato shortage. He attributed the problem to the shortage of parish council funds…Under existing legislation local authorities could utilize their far-reaching powers to obtain more allotments with funding from the Public Works Loan Commissioners…But George W Giles, Secretary of the National Allotment and Garden Society drew attention to the lack of allotment sites in regions where land was readily available…Although councils could still acquire land under the Defence Regulations, the Ministry of Agriculture preferred to adopt the slower but more permanent method to establish allotments' (Poole/6, p28).

WarAgs and the hierarchy maintaining them were disbanded in 1947, leaving the Allotments Advisory Committee which, in 1948, was asked to report and recommend changes that would take allotments into the future. Amongst those consulted was the National Allotments and Gardens Society who had redirected a grant of £1 500 from Government to support the thousands of allotment associations formed during the needy years of war. The Society appealed for the grant to be improved to £10 000 to take account of monetary inflation and for it to be extended. It was not. NAGS pressed for the acceptance of the terms in their Allotment Holders' Charter which saw security of tenure a motivator of tidy and productive ground: even in 1947 the contrast between the long-standing sites where water and sheds and order prevailed and the temporary spaces which were already abandoned and tumbled down (Poole/6, p28) was becoming widespread. NAGS pressed for four acres of land per thousand people to be reserved for allotments. The **1950 Allotments Act**, the most recent legislation under that name, promoted both recommendations by holding local authorities to one year's notice for tenants and by confirming local authorities' statutory obligation to provide allotments, but only in towns of at least ten thousand people and for garden allotments only (Andrews, p17). Provision of smallholdings was no longer compulsory. Government had already utilized a tool which would become the favourite of new governments to the present: the nineteenth century burying of allotments law in local authority powers or in planning regulations . Under the Town and Country Planning Act 1947 the Government had repealed the requirement for local authorities to preserve land for allotments (Andrews, p16) so anything more than a garden allotment was a vain hope.

Population changes for the two world wars of the twentieth century make an interesting comparison: throughout World War 1 there were considerable losses born by the male population of England and Wales – the female population continued to increase over those years, though not greatly. In WW2 population overall continued to increase, albeit with the rate of gain reduced dramatically in the early years 1939–42. What the population vectors for the Wars have in common is serious loss of life in the first two years of war and then either reduction of the rate of decline or recovery of the rate of gain in the remaining years. So in simple terms Britain came out of WW2 with a far stronger workforce and potential for economic recovery than at the end of WW1. Not surprising that the allure of food earned by toil and sweat at the expense of leisure- and pleasure-time faded. Women went back to their homes and allotments became the domain of the mature male once more, men to whom present generations of allotment users owe a debt for having preserved the tradition as well as the availability of land for allotments.

Britain had also discovered planning as the 1947 Act evinces and the word was found throughout the land, as if in a stick of rock:

'This time Britain emerged with a socially engineered Planning machine (with a capital P) which has ruled the development of houses and gardens for the last fifty years…A house with a garden was still the national ideal but planners learned to engineer their way around this; the childless and the elderly in flats could have allotments if they so wished, the majority of new house-dwellers who were in redevelopments and new towns would be in terraces and three-storey blocks with small plots for washing and children's play' (Brown, p164).

Of course air raids had significantly altered many towns and cities through the land, including Norwich and the City was swift to wheel out its plan for 1947.

With another nod in the direction of the ideal, Norwich City Corporation's section on allotments in the Plan for the city began with an acknowledgement of its past 'garden glory' and of the continuing demand for allotments, even in addition to large gardens for some people. It made a bid for the Lady Hurtwood communal facilities and spaces model: part of a site 'should be laid out as rest gardens surrounded by trees and shrubs with paths, flower borders and seats and allotments in the centre, suitably arranged and controlled' – a bit chilling, that – and for small sites 'an attractive hut or pavilion for communal use'. It added its approval for the continental style which made sites 'an added attraction to its neighbourhood'.

Post-war the obligations laid on local councils to provide allotment land were ignored, and ignored largely without protest. Reconstruction and recovery was the most important work of councils, enabling development, planning towns with public amenities and recreation grounds and pushing through roadways so that all of us could have our own homes and cars. The creation of the welfare state after WW2 finally eliminated the need for allotments as a barrier and bludgeon against the depredations of climate or war. There could only be one reason for working an allotment and that was for enjoyment. It was a pleasure unlikely to be discovered by the youth for whom rock n' roll was rock n' roll or by the young who were busy with homes, children and careers, keeping on and getting on. Within the space of just over a decade the era of the Swingin' Sixties, baby-boomer hippiedom and the 'you've never had it so good' culture resulted in the abandonment of rural and urban allotment sites to all but the faithful who were, sad to say, becoming the elderly – not quite the old – codgers revered today.

Figure 9.1: Photo of Carrow Road allotments, 1953 flood. (Courtesy of Eastern Daily Press picture library).

National trends in interest are revealed by two sets of figures:

Table 9.1: Returns of allotment plots post-World War 2
(from the Department of Environment)

1948	1 117 308 allotment plots on	107 282 acres
1961	826 487	85 220
1975	471 260	51 625
1997	296 923	25 416

From the NSALG comes the following:

Table 9.2: Returns of allotment plots and membership post-World War 2
(on the UK Parliament website of the Select Committee on Environment, Transport and Regional Affairs/Minutes of Evidence: Memorandum (AL 23) by the DETR The Future for Allotments (24.06.04) pp4–5)

Year	Number of plots	Acreage	Vacant plot	Waiting list	% statutory
1970	532 964	58 242	111 126	5 870	49
1977	497 793	49 873	20 576	121 037	–
1978	479 301	49 105	23 178	–	54
1996	296 923	25 393	43 594	12 950	74

According to the Memorandum, the NSALG 'found that high numbers of vacant plots and long waiting lists do not generally coincide'.

How much more useful and interesting are the NSALG statistics? The acreages and numbers of allotments show steady and consistent decline over the years (the apparent lurch downward to 1996 is an artefact of the time-gap – plotted on a graph the rate of decline is constant). The other columns tell a different story. In 1970 there were many vacant plots, reflecting the loss of interest, and from then onwards the number of plots/acreages came down steadily (percentage decrease by 1970=21%, 1977=4%, 1978=5% on previous year's figure). However, in 1996 when the number of allotments was still lower than in 1978 the vacancies as a percentage had risen to 15%, indicating that interest was much less even than in the 1970s. In parallel with these movements the waiting-lists embellish the story a little further. In 1970 when there were many allotments and many vacancies the waiting-list was low (a mere 1% of the number of plots). By 1977 and 1978 the percentage of vacancies was a rational figure compared to the number of plots but for 1977 the waiting-list had shot up to 24% of the total number of plots. By 1996 when the number of vacant plots was high there were just 4% waiting for an allotment. Whichever way you slice it, there was an upsurge of interest in allotments in the 1970s and a subsequent decline by the mid-1990s.

In the 1960s sites that were not lost may have become reduced in size or shifted. In Norwich the pattern persisted of locating sites further towards the periphery of the city to make way for the expansion of business from the centre and of housing development at the outskirts. Some nibbling away at sites also took place, chiefly for road-building.

The simple pattern of declining interest in allotments from the end of WW2 to the mid-1990s underlies the Survey results for Norfolk but there are crucial differences: there are new acquisitions throughout the period, more during some phases than others, which begs interpretation. First, the summary of returns.

An unusual case is that of **Thompson**, part of the Walsingham Estate about which Lord Walsingham wrote (Survey), saying that a field 'at the Danish end of Thompson' became the allotment site 'after the War'. Having resisted attempts by Breckland District Council to fulfil the Deputy Prime Minister's 2004 pledge (to build a substantial quota of new housing in the south-east of England, loosely defined), the field is still rented by the son of an original tenant from the Estate. After Thompson there are no new allotments in Norfolk until 1958 when Aylmerton created them. Four other parishes claim to have allotments that date back to that period but these attributions are loose and from recollection: they are Happisburgh ('pre-1959'), Outwell with three sites, Scarning with two sites and Wood Dalling, all of which were known to be there 'in the 1950s'. Given that allotments in towns and cities contracted post-WW2 it is curious to see burgeonings in the countryside, especially when in the 1950s the railways, and especially the trans-Norfolk M&GNR stopped operating, being unable to compete with new bus services and the private car. Railway closures of uneconomical lines were followed between 1964–70 by the Beeching cuts which left Norfolk with a vestigial service connecting it to the rest of East Anglia and England. As at **Terrington-St-Clement** the days when commercial allotments on a grand scale were viable were long over.

Aylmerton allotments presaged a series of nine new sites from 1961 to 1970 of which most were in villages in the countryside but some like Wymondham were attached to towns. Four sites only appear in the 1970s, including one in Thetford. This last-mentioned may be the clue for the contrary evidence for Norfolk that the early and not, as in the rest of the country, the mid-1970s saw an upsurge of interest. Since allotment sites now follow population, broadly speaking, it is likely that net migration into Norfolk throughout the post-war period, the only county for which this is true, is the driving force behind allotment creation. Incomers included an influx of retirees into rural Norfolk and those brought in by Town Development Schemes which encouraged planned settlement into King's Lynn and Thetford (*Atlas*, pp168–9).

So it is possible to claim that Norfolk anticipated the boost given to allotments by the Ministry of Land and Resources when it commissioned Professor Harry Thorpe of Birmingham University to chair a committee of inquiry into the state of allotments and to make recommendations for allotment policy. A lengthy questionnaire, the first of a number about allotments to the present day, went out to town and parish councils. When the Report came in 1969 it set out two propositions: allotments were a Good Thing for those living in cities; and allotments should mimic the continental model of the community and leisure garden, where allotment sites were a community resource. Thorpe had spent much of the investigation visiting sites in Germany, Holland and Denmark.

'What Thorpe actually suggested was the import of the idea of leisure gardens' – and he went as far as to propose that the term 'allotment' be abolished to be replaced by 'leisure garden' as if language could convert thinking – 'whereby the plots were let to garden-less city dwellers who could choose to have vegetables, flowers or lawn with a small summerhouse on each site, and a central meeting room with kitchen and toilets. Leisure gardens were developed in Birmingham (under the wing of a research unit at the university)' (Brown, p167).

Birmingham had been at the forefront of allotments research during WW2, having developed the demonstration allotment. An International Leisure Gardeners' Federation congress was held there in 1976.

It may have seemed a strong possibility in 1969 that urban dwellings would become synonymous with high-rise flats as in the United States

Departmental Committee of Inquiry into Allotments

REPORT

Presented to Parliament by the Minister of Housing and Local Government and the Secretary of State for Wales by Command of Her Majesty October 1969

LONDON
HER MAJESTY'S STATIONERY OFFICE
£2 2s 0d. [£2·10] net

Cmnd. 4166

Figure 9.2: The Thorpe Report remains the most comprehensive review of allotment provision nationally to date.

and Europe and Britain may by then have looked as if it might go the same way. Perhaps the British never quite understood what was required to make high-rise living an attractive proposition but it is true both that high-rise buildings in the amounts found elsewhere have not materialized and that those who do occupy them in the United Kingdom do not clamour for a window-box, much less gardens, either for food production or presentation. And perhaps Thorpe did not realize that alongside continental leisure gardens, tucked into any small corner or water-margin, true allotment gardens were to be found, as much a part of european culture as of british. Rather, those who wanted allotments were contented by, actually preferred, the old model. The Thorpe Report was never implemented:

'Although [the Report's recommendations] received a sympathetic hearing and a promise of suitable legislative action 'when time permitted'…no steps to…consolidate the seven existing legislative Acts of Parliament relating to allotments and to implement the recommendations of the Thorpe Report have yet been undertaken' (NSALG, p9c).

Government signalled its disinterest in reviving the allotment movement in the 1972 Local Government Act which permitted councils to disband their allotment committees.

Thorpe's 1969 *Report* provides some detail for Norfolk:
- vacant plots were at 5.3% (one-third the mean) and water on site 7.0%, low figures both;
- total area of allotment land (acres per thousand population living in rural areas) was 12.7 (against a national average of 2.1);
- average number of plots per acre of allotment land was 2.2 (national average 4.2);
- decline in total acreage of allotments 1952–1964 was 4.1%, the lowest of any county in England and Wales, bar two, by many multiples (Thorpe, Table XVIII, p394).

In relation to the second and third of these measures, Norfolk was clumped with Cambridge/Ely and Lincoln – flat, East Anglia.

But the post-War *zeitgeist* that shunned allotments was about to be replaced with one that found them desirable, for a very different set of reasons. In the 1970s the 'green city' movement, a revival of nineteenth century Ebenezer Howard's Garden City movement and William Morris's desire to transform the city with planting, began to emerge. The new ingredient was a deeper understanding of the science underlying natural processes and a recognition of the need, for the health of all, to balance concrete with planted spaces:

'Inner-city vegetation has advantages in addition to the cosmetic: it absorbs rainfall and prevents flooding; reduces noise levels; and acts as 'used air' filters. Green spaces can also add to the urban food supply…people started turning wasteland into urban farms and tree-planting became popular again as the environmental value of trees became more apparent. Allotments experienced a revival. New mini-parks tucked away behind rows of houses came to life and disused rail lines were turned into linear parks…for walks and for wildlife to 'commute' between the countryside and the inner city…(Girardet, pp132 and 136–138).

Publication in 1962 of Rachel Carson's *Silent Spring* forcefully directed concerns to the problems caused by modern pesticides and their effect on the food chain. Intensive farming, artificial fertilizers and pest control sprays began to be seen as a threat to the environment and a danger to people. In addition the oil crisis of 1973 reinforced concerns that the planet was consuming the world's resources at an unsustainable rate and a steady stream of alarming reports on the state of the planet appeared. A report called *Losing Ground* produced by the Friends of the Earth in 1974 warned that Britain, whose population was estimated at twice the level that could be supported by the food it could produce, was vulnerable to world food shortages and rising food prices due to the rapidly escalating fuel costs. In the face of these perceived threats to their food supply many town-dwellers looked for an opportunity to grow their own vegetables and fruit and to use organic methods in doing so.

Protest in London found its reflection in concern for the countryside. Norfolk is a county ideally suited for the appreciation of another aspect

Norwich allotment sites created between the two world wars, Bluebell North and South and Hill Farm, were planted with apple, pear and plum trees.

Bluebell, North.

Hill Farm.

Everything is adapted, nothing is wasted on allotments. Age old needs are met by new materials and techniques.

of late-twentieth century life that turned people towards allotments. The 1970s had seen the demise of the small farmer and the industrialization of agriculture which, since Norfolk was one of the most affected areas, translated into the wholesale destruction of hedges to create vast open fields across which roared mechanical behemoths, alternately ploughing, crop-spraying, harvesting in a never-ending cycle, sometimes twice-yearly. Traditionally the stubble was burned so reducing still further the quality of the soil. In dry summer months it blew like clouds of smoke off the fields, in the wet season muddy rivers ran down the lanes and out to sea, staining coastal waters.

'…between 1946 and 1970 around 4 500 miles of hedge were removed each year in England and Wales…Norfolk probably lost around half its hedges in this period…reaching approximately 2 400 miles per year by 1962, in part because hedge removal was subsidized after 1957 by the Ministry of Agriculture's Farm Improvement Scheme…3 500 miles were removed each year, the rate gradually falling thereafter to around 2 000 miles by 1970, the year in which subsidies for removal were withdrawn' (Williamson, pp64–5).

Eventually the public perception was of insipid and worthless food and a new movement towards organic production emerged, of which self-sufficiency through allotment holding was a natural corollary.

By 1974 the demand for allotments far outstripped supply. *The Times* reported that, compared with a figure of 5 000 in 1969, the number of people on waiting lists for allotments was 27 000. Unfortunately increased demand coincided with reductions in the number of allotments under cultivation which fell to some 45 000 as the demands for housing, new roads and other developments chewed away at allotments allocations. In 1975 the Friends of the Earth organized a Dig-in Day in many large cities to encourage local authorities to release derelict land for allotment use. The allotment had been rediscovered, especially by the middle classes and had become associated with 'safe' food and a healthy lifestyle.

The media, as we had come to call the combined forces of publishing, press, radio and television, played its part in reflecting and stimulating

the greening of cities, its most famous product being BBCs *The Good Life. One Man and his Plot* by Michael Leapman, the *Times* diarist, and the very serious *Food crops from your garden or allotment* by a Fellow of the Linnaean Society of London and member of the Soil Association, Brian Turner, both appeared in 1976. The latter is full of sound advice to the novice:

'Never, unless you are willing to take the plunge, take on what is known as a 'temporary allotment'. Temporary allotments are sited on land scheduled for development at an unknown date. Seeing a vacant plot of land nearby and knowing that the local authority is very willing to have the site tidied up by you and cultivated as an allotment does seem a tempting invitation to get cracking and produce tasty, home-grown goods. But after you have cleared the site, fertilized the soil and started to get good crops, along may come a Notice to Quit. My first temporary allotment was buried under twenty feet of household rubbish; my second coated with a two-foot layer of concrete' (pp11–12).

And he goes on to relate other horrors awaiting the unwary, hazards that would be familiar today from rotovation by the council, thereby chopping the roots of perennial weeds into pieces and distributing them evenly over the entire plot; to acts of predation and vandalism by local animals, including humans.

Following Thorpe, in 1973 Norwich City Council purchased land for development in the west of the City at Bowthorpe. As well as becoming sensitive to the environmental impact of motor vehicles Britain was experiencing the fuel crisis at the time and an explicit aim of the Bowthorpe Master Plan was to reduce reliance on car travel for those who would be settled there. Bowthorpe would consist of three villages, each complete with work, shopping, educational, social contact and leisure amenities. Described as 'informal open space', the Master Plan shows three small sites of allotments, in total five acres out of 591 acres envisaged for all of Bowthorpe. Somehow they vanished between Master Plan and execution.

A new Conservative government of 1979 proposed a new Local Government Bill which prompted protesters from Friends of the Earth and NSALG to demonstrate outside the Department of Environment headquarters in London, hoping to persuade the Government to remove clauses from their pending Bill which it was believed would jeopardize rights to allotments. They claimed, 'the Bill contains six clauses which would allow local authorities to fail even more abysmally in the provision of allotments' (*Times Picture Guide to Gardens 1900–2000*, pp168–9). Although the 1980 Local Government Act removed any involvement of central Government in allotments and released councils from bureaucratic obligations such as keeping a separate account and statistics for allotments, it offered some protections for tenants, crucially that an allotment <u>must</u> be let at a rent which a tenant could reasonably be expected to pay and <u>could</u> be let at a lower rent if circumstances pointed towards it. So pensioners and the unemployed were enabled by most local authorities to hold allotments at a fifty per cent rate, one of many concessions that have become commonplace in public life.

Lord Wallace of Coslany, President of the London Association of Recreational Gardeners and a former allotmenteer, attempted to redress the balance in the interests of allotment-holding with a private members' Recreational Gardening Bill in january 1984. 'The Bill's main aim is to raise the status of allotment gardening and establish it, in law, as a recreation on a par with other recreations that local authorities fund and foster'(Hyde, p56). Sensing Government opposition, it was withdrawn and re-introduced on 3 december and on this occasion reached and passed the Committee Stage and a third reading on 18 february, when it '... was passed and sent to the Commons – "to the dangerous waters of another place", as Lord Wallace put it...'(ibid). A sad footnote described the Bill as 'long-gone'. The 1970s bump of interest persisted into the 1980s, according to the NSALG, but levelled off as the decade wore on. Beyond 1985 the south-east of England witnessed a new wave of vacant plots and government paternalism reasserted itself with a number of schemes for matching them with those who needed training or work:

'Lawrence Hills of the Henry Doubleday Research Association [the leading advocate of organic gardening methods, now Garden Organic]...is concerned at the over-50s who have become

redundant and for whom cooperative ventures might be a good thing on some of those vacant plots...[he] started a directory of vacant plots in the 1985 and early 1986 HDRA newsletters. He can see the good sense of setting up organic projects and cooperatives on unused allotments, thus saving the sites from those rapacious property developers' (Hyde, pp57–8).

Sinking NSALG membership figures reflect lack of interest countrywide in the nineties. Interestingly, the biggest fluctuation is in members, not societies (*Magazine* Issue 1/2006, p21). Partly this is because the number of members per society had almost halved from the 1980s but it is likely also to be that initial enthusiasm on the part of the novice is quickly dispelled. This is the experience reported by the NSALG and from anecdotal evidence in Norfolk and around the country mentoring schemes are being introduced to countermand novice disillusionment. One such was advertised in the newsletter for Norwich's Citiwide Cooperative in december 2005. In recognition of this worrisome trend and because its own remit did not reach waiting-list and potential gardeners, the NSALG formed a charitable arm, the National Allotment Gardens Trust in 2003 to proselytize and support new talent. It introduced a National Allotment Week to gain publicity, and prizes which include an award for the Best Newcomer. It will contribute to a new allotments television series in 2007 (conversation with Chairperson NAGT 17.1.07).

1997 visited a change of government upon Britain and, like governments as far back as 1894 when local government was given its modern shape, a new Local Government Bill followed. Crouch's *Survey* was the precursor to the Select Committee on the *Future of allotments* 1998; followed by debate in Parliament under the Local Agenda 21, where it was agreed that the role of allotments should be examined in 'promoting sustainability' (Baroness Hayman, Parliamentary Under-Secretary, Department for the Environment, Transport and the Regions (DETR), quoted in *Hansard* 11 april 1998); followed by the Local Government Association's (LGA) variation *A new future for allotments- an advocacy document for sustainable living* in 2000 which linked it to the Local Agenda 21, a policy that took in all aspects of environmental concern; followed by the Department of Environment's Policy Planning

Guidance (PPG) 17 on open space utilization which included allotments in its remit for the first time since the 1979 submerging of allotments in arcane local authority practices: it was '…a best practice guide on management of allotments…produced by the Local Government Association, DETR, GLA [Greater London Association] and the Shell Better Britain Campaign in 2001' (North Norfolk *Open Space and Recreation Study*, Section 8.13).

Other connections within this nexus of concerned parties included the virtual QED Allotments Group of allotment associations (partners of the Federation of City Farms and Community Gardens, the Esmee Fairbairn Foundation and NSALG) which lobbied for the inclusion of allotments in the Local Agenda 21 plans. The LGA had also involved the Greater London Authority in their consultation, whose Green Party Group in the London Assembly organized an Allotments Conference in july 2003. Under the auspices of the Green Party a resultant steering group

Figure 9.3: (Thanks to the National Society for Allotment and Leisure Gardeners, www.nsalg.org.uk)

Figure 9.4: (Thanks to Allotments Regeneration Initiative www.farmgarden.org.uk/ari)

emerged, and a second conference in 2004. Finally the national umbrella group Allotments Regeneration Initiative was formed to promote good practice on allotments and, as they would see it, in national and local government. Having disseminated news and guidance through their newsletter and undertaken training events now with the support of its new charity partner the National Allotments Gardens Trust, it is still going strong, and stronger.

To update Crouch's 1996 *Survey*, a further national study of allotments, community gardens and city farms was commissioned from the University of Derby (again under Professors David Crouch and Peter Rivers) by the Department for Communities and Local Government in july 2005, chiefly noteworthy for its comprehensiveness – the form sent to councils ran to several pages of detailed questions. The results of this investigation (based on 241 questionnaires, representing 62% of local authorities, so presumably urban) were published on the internet in September 2006: the Survey will inform a 'green space database' generated through a 'map-based internet tool' (University of Derby, p2). Three out of ten respondents said that they had an allotments policy, which mostly included the promotion of allotments, management and 'a commitment to social inclusion' (p3). This last in 72% of the original 30% represented incentives to plot-holders which might mean retired people, new plotholders and the unemployed. Even if in a small way social policy via allotments persists.

PPG 17 advised district and borough Councils around Britain to commission consultation documents on their open spaces, including allotments. Comparing their results with those of the Norfolk Recorders' Survey, certainly not all councils received comprehensive details of their allotments but rather based results on samples. Although at the last moment of contact (october 2006) councils had not received final reports the information produced by councils that have been forthcoming – all except Yarmouth Borough Council and South Norfolk District Council – up-dates and supplements the Survey.

Table 9.3: Norfolk allotment sites
(based on results of District Councils' consultations on open space utilization (*unpublished))

*Breckland	*Broadland	North Norfolk
Ashill	Brampton	Bodham
Attleborough (2)	Cawston	Briston
Colkirk	Gt & Lt Plumstead	East Runton
Dereham (5)	Hellesdon	Fakenham, North
East Harling (2)	Horsford (2)	Gt Snoring
East Tuddenham	Horstead	Happisburgh
Gressenhall	Old Catton	Hempton
Kenninghall	Sprowston	Hindolveston
Litcham (2)	Thorpe-St-Andrew	Hindringham
Mattishall	Weston Longville	Knapton
Mileham		Little London (Corpusty)
Narborough		Melton Constable
New Buckenham		North Walsham
Roudham		Sheringham
Scarning		Sutton
Swaffham (3)		Trunch (2)
Thetford (3)		Upper Sheringham
Watton		Wells-next-the-Sea (2)
Whissonsett		

North Norfolk's document shows that where the average number of plots per household in England is fifteen, for North Norfolk it is 22.5, equivalent to 10.3 plots per thousand people (Table 5.1). In the case of papers sent from King's Lynn and West Norfolk sites next to the town were detailed: the Borough Council managed nine such sites and a further site at Ferry Road rented from Norfolk County Council and a further four sites are managed by associations.

'We believe that there is a need for urgent action to protect existing allotment sites' (Select Committee, Section 28, 29 january 2003). Noting the increasing popularity of allotments their role was debated in the House of Commons on 9 december 2004. Members of Parliament addressed the issue of funding at local level and drew attention to the reluctance of local authorities to spend on allotments: 'unwilling to channel what little they have available' was the description (*Hansard* Column 1370). Ambiguity on the part of local authorities big and little

towards allotments finds expression in the Committee for the 2012 Olympics to be held in London who propose to 'relocate' 80 plots, as if it were possible to just pick them up and put them down somewhere else, (*The Garden*, Volume 131, Part 11 for November 2006, p276), despite grandiose promises that this would be the 'greenest' Olympics on record.

In Norwich ambivalence expressed itself in the elimination of allotments from the Bowthorpe Master Plan in 1973; and in recent changes in policy, reducing the position of Allotments Officer to a part-time post which has resulted in grumbles from allotment-holders as they see the Council's responsiveness to their needs atrophy. However, in tune with more recent trends and a new popularity for allotment gardening, the map accompanying the current Local Plan (shortly to become by New Labour Government edict the Local Development Framework – comments to ldf@norwich.gov.uk) adopted 2004 shows the existing complement for Norwich plus the reallocation of two small sites as part of the masterplan for the new Threescore development at Bowthorpe. The section of the Plan on Sports and Recreation SR9 (paragraph 10.39, p182) acknowledges the importance of allotments for recreation, healthy food, exercise and as an environmental resource. It affirms the City Council's commitment to the provision of allotments and states that 'development leading to the loss of existing allotments will not be permitted ' – unless, that is, 'an assessment of the long-term need for the site has been carried out' and 'alternative provision of a similar standard is available within the area'. Oh, well ... Anyway, the position of Allotment Officer for the City has been restored to a full-time post from january 2007 and 'from april 2007 the Council will have three combined Parks and Open Spaces Officers who will incorporate the role of Allotment Officer. Each of the three officers will cover one of three areas of the City which, with an increased resource, will provide an enhanced service to allotment holders' (note from NCC Allotments Officer, march 2007).

As if statistical measurements coming thick and fast were not enough to demonstrate the case, over the past years interest in allotments has been manifest in the media, just as in the 1970s. A plethora of articles in journals, magazines and sunday supplements, especially in 2005 and

2006 have appeared. Allotments have been sourced for television programmes, factual and fictional. They have been represented in artworks at Tate Britain, *The Art of the Garden 2004*, in a book by David Crouch *The art of allotments – culture and cultivation* (2003) and locally in Norfolk in an exhibition of *Allotment Sheds* by Duncan J Reekie (at the Norwich Arts Centre 2005). Where allotments were never mentioned in other than gardening books and magazines for the specialist, they are the proper subject of social history, the history of agriculture, garden history and, well, allotment history. Not to mention allotment management and what could be called modern culture.

'...another wave of allotment interest surrounds us. There have been a number of television films on allotment life. There is a resurgence of allotment photography and other artwork. Poetry, too! As we write, a six-month-long exhibition of allotment life and history opens at the Pump House People's History museum in Manchester. *Amateur Gardening's 2000* campaign has attracted attention to the threats posed to allotments. *Big Issue* has had a feature on allotment campaigners, the new magazine the *Kitchen Garden* has an allotment section. The subject has even reached the Ikea magazine, *Room*, and the *Sunday Telegraph* now has an allotment column (Hyde, p(iii)).

Radio 4's *Gardeners' Question Time* (16 april 2006) looked at allotments in the regions. In the Midlands and Wales uptake was high, up to 100% on the 'well-run' sites, a trend confirmed in south-west England where the majority of newcomers were young couples with children. Throughout Greater London, the home counties and south-east England there was 'huge demand' in towns and villages alike. In Northern Ireland 60% of plotholders were women, confirming a trend that is certainly seen in Norfolk which claims 50% female tenancy on sites in North Norfolk and Norwich, typically 30–35 years old (from Colin Nickerson, Eastern Region representative of NSALG, spoke 9 june

use and value

An interesting contribution under the last of these subject headings is *Allotted time: twelve months, two blokes, one shed, no idea* by Robin Shelton – the title tells a big part of the story but the twist is that the author is a sufferer from bipolar disorder and SAD (seasonal affective disorder) for whom working an allotment is effective therapy. Shenton quotes from the report generated by the DCLG: 'We recommend that health authorities recognize and exploit the therapeutic potential of allotments for people with mental or physical health problems' (Shenton, p327). This was also the finding of Luci Carnall, an occupational therapist connected to the University of Brighton Faculty of Health whose study categorized the benefits of allotments under headings prompted by the need to combat the frenzy of modern life. For participants the allotment was not just somewhere to grow vegetables – 'the vegetable is a bonus' (Section 4.6, p20). Being in touch with nature, with growing things and the seasons was important, too:

'...having this allotment it means I can have direct contact with nature, there's birds up here that you don't see in the city and frogs and newts and butterflies and insects' (p16).

By contrast, it was 'an environment removed from everyday life' (Section 4.3, p16):

'This is somewhere you can go and lock the gate behind you and just have a bit of privacy and peace and quiet away from the madness of the town...and you know nobody's going to call for you here or ring you or ask you to do anything, you can just escape all the sort of pressures of everyday life' (p17).

The real value of the allotment was that it was 'a place to call my own' (Section 4.5, p18), somewhere to be creative:

'It's your space to do with pretty much as you wish' (p19).

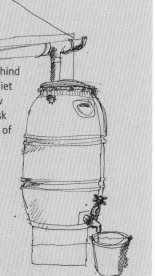

2005). Men who take on plots in Norfolk for the first time tend to be retired or coming up to retirement.

Regular printed contributions come from *Garden News* weekly and the *Ecologist* both of which have an allotments feature; and *The Garden*, the Royal Horticultural Society monthly, which has snippets of news. A significant lead in november 2006 related that more and more people are growing their own food on allotments in order to have 'healthy' food:

> '...Suttons Seeds said that when the company finalises figures this month they are likely to show a 60/40 vegetable/flower sales ratio for 2006. It is the first time since the Second World War that the company has witnessed such high demand for vegetables' (Volume 131 Part 11, p726).

Fothergill's and Thompson and Morgan have found the same, with the latter experiencing 55% of sales on the vegetable side.

Allotments exemplify a law of nature, or perhaps more specifically a facet of evolution: that forms that are essentially simple prove themselves. They are flexible, sturdy, adaptable, enduring. Through technology Britain has divorced itself from a dependence upon its native soil but not, it seems, from its relationship with the soil.

10 | Norfolk then and now

Old Joe was busy working his allotment one bright morning,
when the Vicar passed by.
'Mornin', Vicar', say Joe.
'Good morning, Joe. Fine day.'
'Yep'.
'The allotment's looking good, very good'.
'Ain't it', says Joe.
'That's a fine crop you've got there. A fine reward'.
'Yep'.
'That represents a lot of work'.
'That it do', says Joe.
Vicar smiles.
'And a bit of help from God, I suppose'.
'Oh, I dunno', says Joe. 'You should've seen it when he looked
after it on his own'.

Bernard Frankland

Where allotments were and are in Norfolk depends on the land, who owns the land and on their policy towards allotments.

If it were possible to generalize where demand for allotments would fall and where it would rise, based on history, at least two related conclusions might be offered:

- it depends on geography. In the fertile Fenland there remain many and large allotments. In the dry Breckland there are few.

- it depends on population levels, which is related to the first point, but also to other factors and trends. So, as usual, allotments are found in towns and especially where there has been and continues to be an influx of people. In Breckland householders have ample space for large gardens. In Norfolk it does not absolutely follow, however, that empty places have no allotments, or perhaps more accurately have never had allotments. The big open lands of the north-east during the heyday of the railways matched the Fenland for the number and size of allotment holdings; even now the Fenland has many large holdings that defy the rule elsewhere.

The existence of allotments used not to be obviously related to levels of population: looking at the case-study towns and villages population at the time that allotments were introduced varies from 5545 for Dereham and 1085 for Harleston (early railway towns), 1185 for Docking (where workhouse inmates were included) and 1123 for Castle Acre (an open parish) to a few hundreds – 217 for Salthouse, 284 for Little Melton, 360 for Oulton, 426 for Potter Heigham – rarely above 500. Reasons other than high population are needed to explain why allotments were introduced when they came to particular places. The current picture contrasts with this and now there is considerable consistency between population size and where allotments are found.

The first certain ascription is that of **Terrington-St-Clement** in 1816, a classic case exemplifying a number of historical factors common to early allotments throughout England: at a time of strife in rural communities they were the benevolent provision of the local estate-owner through the agency of the parish priest. Typically for Norfolk where land is flat or gently undulating, the individual allocation was a one-acre strip, a sizeable piece for a single holder but nothing less would have been adequate to sustain a man and his family. Labourers would have been unable to tend their plots daily and would have relied upon rainfall to water a crop: either potatoes or wheat would have met the demands both of sustenance and neglect, and commonly there would have been cooperation between labourers and their families, particularly at harvesttime.

Significant factors that applied later on included settlement pattern and so rural places having allotments were often market towns (**Reepham, Litcham, Harleston**) built around a central square. They are tight settlements where there is little or no space for householders to cultivate plots for their own use. A further advantage of the nucleated settlement is that allotments adjoining are close enough for routine access and within a man's capacity after a long hard day's work (the length of the working day in manufacturing industry delayed the popularity, or at least demand, for allotments in cities); this also would have been a factor that would have influenced what could be grown. As before, significant rainfall or a watercourse would have been essential: this may explain why early allotments like **Westfield** on boggy ground and others close to Rivers Waveney (Bressingham) and Nar (West Winch) and Wensum (Guist) were possible even though political or social motives drove their installation. Water must have continued to determine the viability of sites, as well as their crops, well into the twentieth century in most places.

Later the building of railways from the 1840s–1870s brought a revolution in demand and in the type of allotments demanded, making large sites as well as large plots amounting to smallholdings viable. In the 1870s an allotment plough needing only a single horse and able to turn in fairly small spaces was introduced enabling multiple or larger plots to be managed. The latter date saw the rise of trades associations in Norfolk. Demand for allotments was linked to early unions, giving the movement political overtones. Once allotments could be acquired through an elected local authority, at the end of the nineteenth century, allotment land whatever its provenance or ownership remained principally their responsibility.

Two world wars and severe economic depression in between meant that allotments became the resort of need and survival for the nation and not just individuals. Since then the rise of agribusiness and increased wealth has meant that allotments fell out of popularity, with planning policy a reflection of national mood. But the pendulum, albeit waveringly, has swung into a different orbit in recent decades and the same drivers, of agribusiness and wealth, translated now into loss of food quality and recreation time, are fostering increased demand for allotments.

The Survey shows in a sweep the varied picture of current allotment demand and provision in Norfolk. It appears that, by contrast with Thorpe's 1969 enquiry where, he remarked, North Walsham was the only town in the county that lacked allotments, lost by the 1990s are allotments to Cromer (where until recently there was ritual clamour at the Town Council's yearly open meeting) and Downham Market. Cromer, after many years of lobbying, acquired allotments again (a map from the eighteenth century shows allotment sites, as well as saffron fields) in 2005 on land adjoining the cemetery. They were oversubscribed from their opening. Downham Market is a puzzle. It is located at the edge of Fenland where the number and type of allotments is a feature: multiple sites attached to modest parishes of many tens of acreages both of garden and field allotments and holdings in between are found still, a feature which, if not unique to Norfolk is remarkable. Breckland and the open reclaimed land around Yarmouth cannot match Fenland for sheer scale of allotments, presumably a function of Fenland's flatness and rich loams that insist upon productivity, generating meaningful incomes for councils and landowners (which include estate, district council, County Council and diocese) and neither is there the temptation in an empty land to sell for development. The message from all these observations is that allotment-holding was popular and continued to be strong in rural Norfolk.

Norfolk lived up to its motto 'do different': the 1980s saw eleven sites created throughout the county, including a second one for Wymondham, indicating a renewal of demand and it was the 1990s which saw a downturn in new sites, with just five created in that decade. One of these was in a swanky new housing development on the eastern edge of Norwich, named Dussindale. Reflecting the then high demand for homes and land nationally, their gardens were handkerchief-sized, barely enough for a whirligig clothes line and some hard landscaping and so, in contrast to Bowthorpe in 1973 when the Plan indicated allotments but nothing materialized, allotments have been provided. Bowthorpe, attached to the western side of Norwich, is at last set to have some. A reduced number of sites of smaller size appear on the 2004 Plan and there is a waiting list for plots. The Allotments Officer for the City understands (january 2007) that there will be allotments in Bowthorpe. The Planning Department, to whom requests for information have been made, has not released details. There are waiting-lists for all allotment sites in Norwich. More land is apparently needed but Norwich comes into the government's catchment for new homes to be provided so there is a familiar clash of priorities, despite new homes tending nowadays to create a call for new allotments.

Since 2000 in Norfolk six including **Salthouse** (not captured by the Survey) new sites were made. In this series was Aldborough and Thurgarton which benefited from lottery money. Trustees of **Cley-next-the-Sea** have negotiated greatly improved conditions for their site. Additionally Hellesdon moved site from a tatty pightle on the A140 adjacent to the Norwich International Airport to make room for a MacDonalds to a much larger site a little further away from the city and next to the housing estate that it serves. With the money gained in compensation, the Parish Council was able to supply robust huts, running water, manure, access lanes and parking, a notice-board, and secure fences and gates for an increased number of tenants. The site was in full occupation from the moment it was opened. From stark and regimented

beginnings, in a year or two it was transformed into the comfortable variability familiar from allotment sites everywhere. Very recently Stalham has regained an allotment site (see 'before' and 'after' photos).

For Norwich the visual record (Norfolk Recorders photographs of Norwich 2004) shows that sites vary hugely in local involvement in them, an aspect reflected in the size and even existence of waiting lists. In a world that works seven whole days a week, particularly for those in public service or on lower wages (and the two are often synonymous) allotments require above all working flexibility or leisure. There are parts of the city where people have an abundance of leisure like the retired or whose time is more flexible, as with women, children, students, the self-employed – as an electrician said, 'it's a life-saver. I come here just for the odd hour, to escape the pressure'; and there are other parts of the city where Britain's new ethos of work-life balance seems not to have penetrated and where sites lie sadly neglected and untenanted. Allotments – the presumption is inevitable – are no longer the recourse of the needy. Norwich City Council policy had begun to catch up with this reality in a more thoughtful and energetic management policy which saw, as late as 2003, innovation in users and uses of allotments, such as the Art School which grew plants to harvest natural dyestuffs; segregation of plots committed to organic methods to ensure that they were free from contamination; letting on one site a twelve-acre chunk for adults with learning disability so that it was able to leave part of the allotment as a nature reserve, part for cropping and to have a permanent centre based on it. As visits to the city's eighteen sites made in 2004 and 2005 revealed, each has its own character. Some like Cottage Farm and Brickfield are workmanlike and no-nonsense, concentrating on the production of staples. A few verge on the untidy while evidently still being valued. Noteworthy are Bellacre and Woodlands, Harford Hill and Marston Lane and Mousehold which are extravagant in the abundance and variety of crops, methods and materials used on the sites. The Bluebell North and South sites are famed for their size, for the dedication of plotholders, for innovation and for variety of uses to which the plots are put. They are oases of colour in a sector of uniform housing development. Hill Farm is a delightful mix of the efficiently prosaic and the imaginative. Alongside landrace trees are grown a huge variety of crops, traditional, exotic, aromatic, colourful.

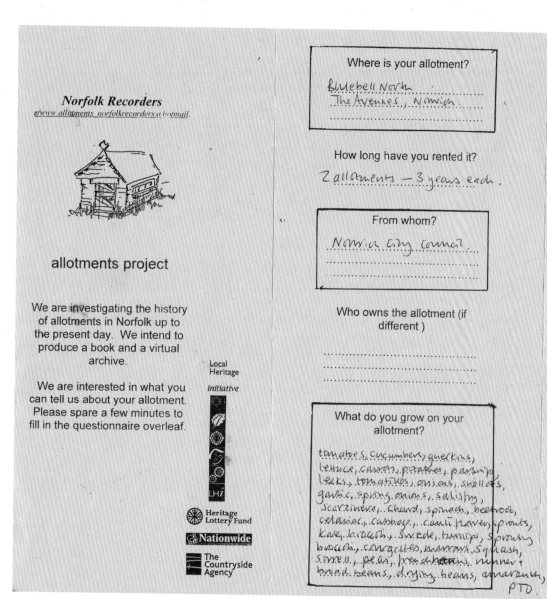

Norfolk Recorders
e/www.allotments_norfolkrecorders@hotmail.

allotments project

We are investigating the history of allotments in Norfolk up to the present day. We intend to produce a book and a virtual archive.

We are interested in what you can tell us about your allotment. Please spare a few minutes to fill in the questionnaire overleaf.

Local Heritage
initiative

LHi

Heritage Lottery Fund

Nationwide

The Countryside Agency

Where is your allotment?

Bluebell North
The Avenues, Norwich.

How long have you rented it?

2 allotments — 3 years each.

From whom?

Norwich City Council

Who owns the allotment (if different)

What do you grow on your allotment?

tomatoes, cucumbers, gherkins, lettuce, carrots, potatoes, parsnips, leeks, tomatillos, onions, shallots, garlic, spring onions, salsify, scorzinere, chard, spinach, beetroot, celariac, cabbage, cauliflower, sprouts, kale, brocoli, swede, turnips, sprouting brocoli, courgettes, marrows, squash, sorrell, peas, french beans, runner + broad beans, drying beans, amaranth, PTO

asparagus pea, tobacco, pumpkin, radishes, apples, pears, plums, strawberries, raspberries, blackberries, gooseberry/currant, rhubarb, oregano, marjoram, fennel, soapwort, thyme, rosemary, lavendar, chives, tarragon, caraway, cumin, coriander, St. Johns Wort, feverfew, camomile, mint, parsley, sage, basil, bergamot, clary sage, bay, yarrow, rocket, mizuna, woad, weld, madder, daffodils, tulips, sweet peas, nasturtiums, marigolds, hyacinths, lupin, comfrey, evening primrose, sunflowers, red sunflowers, chrysanthemums, phacelia, mustard, rye grass (green manures), orache, peppers, chillis, cat mint, jasmine.

Figure 10.1: When exhibiting at allotments and history fairs Norfolk Recorders surveyed the types of crops grown today. The range is extensive, but not exclusive or unrepresentative.

The rise and fall of interest in allotments in the City can be charted as follows:

Table 10: allotment acreages, tenancy, population and percentage population holding an allotment for Norwich 1921–2001
(Where data for the year listed is not available, figures for the nearest available date are given and the date shown in brackets. After 1972 Allotment Committees were not required and statistics for Norwich were not kept.)

	acreage	tenancies	population*	% population holding allotments
1921	279 3 13 (1923)	1 821 (1923)	120 661	1.50
1931	253 3 37	1 724	126 236	1.37
1941	459 2 8	3 832	–	–
1951	258 (1952)	2 189	121 236	1.80
1961	225	2 350	+120 096	1.97
1971			122 083	
1981			122 890	
1991	^100.22 (1996)	^1 426 (1996)	122 661	1.16
2001		++1 407 (2003)	121 553	1.16

* from the Office for National Statistics 17 february 2003
+ boundary changes
^ from David Crouch's *Report on the Survey on the Allotments of England*
++ Norwich City Council figures, from the Allotments Officer

The most recent, 2003 percentage of tenancies for the population of Norwich is the lowest of any available period.

The picture of losses gained through the Survey has been scrappy since no systematic enquiry was made into the issue, but such references as were offered by parish and town councils chime with the pattern of population movement and settlement alluded to already. That has been, roughly, an accumulation in and around the main towns, somewhat alleviated by incomers who have moved into some but by no means all rural areas – the favourites are to the south of Norwich around Wymondham especially, the north Norfolk coast (Burnham Market becoming Hampstead-by-the-Sea, although many if not most of these incomers are not residents) and the Broads. Where more detailed local

knowledge has been tapped sometimes it has been possible to confirm the widely-held suspicion that allotment land has been taken for building development (Roydon 1953, but replaced 1986 using glebe land (Birtles/2, p87), Reepham 1970s and 1980s, Toftwood 1980s, one of two sites at Narborough). In other words, where people have shifted away from a locality in Norfolk, allotment land has suffered one of a number of fates. It may have fallen into disuse and dereliction, when an alternative social use may have been found, especially that of bowling green (Thurlton) or recreation ground (**Little and Great Plumstead**, Weston Longville circa 2000, Brampton 2005). A number of Millennium Woods have been created, lottery money having been forthcoming (**Terrington-St-Clements, Costessey,** Coltishall). Alternatively garden allotments may have amalgamated to become field allotments, rented to local farmers or for grazing horses in the newly-isolated localities (**Terrington-St-Clements, Oulton, Westfield, Castle Acre**). From Gayton a Trustee of the Gayton Estate, owned by the Earl of Romney (who allocated land for allotments in 1931) and whose management moved to the Estate Office, on 11 october 2004 wrote,

'It is not the tidiest site in Gayton! But the Estate is happy to continue the allotments until such time as they are no longer needed. That appears to be accelerating. Parish Council allowed smallholder to 'farm' redundant allotments' (Survey).

Similarly Denton reported that two fields, seven acres in all, bequeathed by Reverend Thomas Rogerson, were taken as allotment plots from 1907 'until the 1950s when, as they became vacant, two farm workers in the village amalgamated the plots and began to grow corn on them. The last plots of allotments were vacated in 1996'. From 1980 two acres of land were allocated to a playing field, and in 1999 four acres were sold to become a Millennium Wood, known as 'Rogerson Wood'. One acre remained for provision of allotments but no applications had been forthcoming (Survey).

1999 also saw another allotment site affected by pressure on housing land in Norfolk, at North Walsham where, against much local protest supporting a permanent home, 'temporary garden plots' were created since it was envisaged that the land would be needed – the ultimate fate – for a cemetery in the future. The popularity of the area that underpins

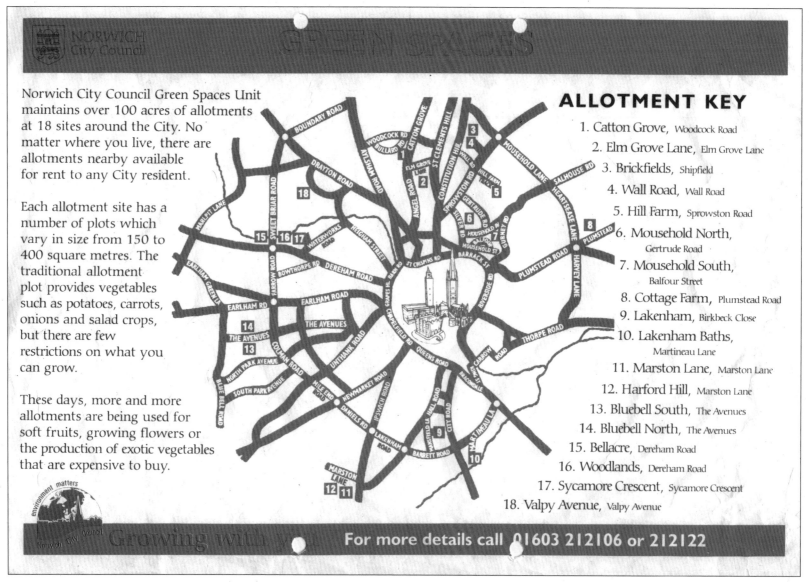

Figure 10.2: In 2005 Norwich City Council promoted its allotments through a publicity campaign.

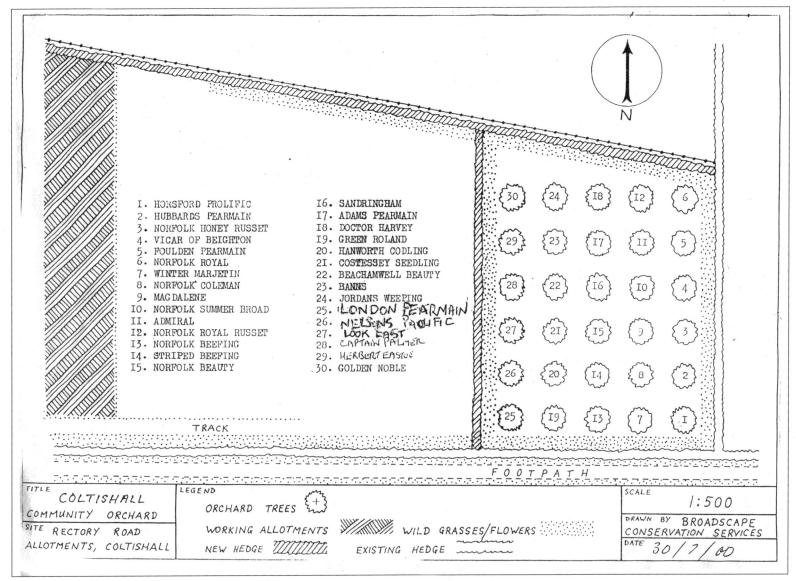

N

1. HORSFORD PROLIFIC
2. HUBBARDS PEARMAIN
3. NORFOLK HONEY RUSSET
4. VICAR OF BEIGHTON
5. FOULDEN PEARMAIN
6. NORFOLK ROYAL
7. WINTER MARJETIN
8. NORFOLK COLEMAN
9. MAGDALENE
10. NORFOLK SUMMER BROAD
11. ADMIRAL
12. NORFOLK ROYAL RUSSET
13. NORFOLK BEEFING
14. STRIPED BEEFING
15. NORFOLK BEAUTY

16. SANDRINGHAM
17. ADAMS PEARMAIN
18. DOCTOR HARVEY
19. GREEN ROLAND
20. HANWORTH CODLING
21. COSTESSEY SEEDLING
22. BEACHAMWELL BEAUTY
23. BANNS
24. JORDANS WEEPING
25. LONDON PEARMAIN
26. NELSONS PROLIFIC
27. LOOK EAST
28. CAPTAIN PALMER
29. HERBERT EASTOE
30. GOLDEN NOBLE

TRACK

FOOTPATH

TITLE	LEGEND		SCALE
COLTISHALL COMMUNITY ORCHARD	ORCHARD TREES		1:500
SITE RECTORY ROAD ALLOTMENTS, COLTISHALL	WORKING ALLOTMENTS — WILD GRASSES/FLOWERS NEW HEDGE — EXISTING HEDGE		DRAWN BY BROADSCAPE CONSERVATION SERVICES DATE 30/7/00

Figure 10.3: Coltishall Parish Council gave over part of its allotment site to an orchard of Norfolk varieties, and appointed a tree warden.

the existence of allotments will lead to its demise as former plotholders dig their own graves.

In Norfolk members of the **Dereham** group supported by the NSALG fought long and hard to preserve one of the town's allotment sites. Sadly a new dispute has broken out at Swaffham where a group has been formed to 'fight a threat to allotments in the centre...The local people think that the land was given to them in perpetuity but the Council think differently' (Norfolk Recorders email 12 february 2007). A notorious case that has rambled on in the press and elsewhere for the past two or more years is that of Sheringham. There the Weston Terrace Allotment Association has fought to preserve its land from Tesco's ambitions. In summer 2006 Tesco did not appeal against a decision to reject their application (NSALG Magazine Issue 2/2006, p24). This was consonant with North Norfolk District Council's commitment to allotments expressed in Policy 106 Local Plan 1998. So it came as a surprise to discover in september 2006 that North Norfolk District Council had found a 'secret agreement' between the Council and Tesco which gave the latter a 'free hand' (NSALG Magazine Issue 3/2006, p28). By november 2006 the Association, supported by the Mayor and a majority of the Council, were claiming that 'the site should revert to Town Council ownership' (NSALG Magazine Issue 4/2006, p22). In february 2007 Colin Nickerson, NSALG representative for the Eastern Region, reported:

'The depression has certainly lifted over Sheringham; ...[the] NSALG's Legal Consultant's interpretation of the 1972 Local Government Act which converted the Town Council to the allotment holders' cause proved to be the 'last straw'. North Norfolk District Council has decided to re-negotiate the 'secret' deal with Tesco for which an internal inquiry found 'no evidence of corruption'. The Weston Terrace site will be excluded from any settlement and will remain as allotments...even Tesco is not invincible'(NSALG Magazine, Issue 1 2007, p25).

Allotments, as ever, reflecting current concerns.

The NSALG has been working over the past two years to create a Federation of allotments associations. Norfolk has been notorious for not having associations and for their low incidence of affiliation to the National Society – another instance of 'do different', presumably. With notable enthusiasm being shown by a core group, the Federation was launched in 2005 and more and more associations are being formed, most recently at Hellesdon, Wiggenhall St Mary Magdalen, at Harleston at the Wortwell and Arburgh site, at Sheringham and in Norwich at the Cottage Farm site, with the aim of negotiating self-management with Norwich City Council (NSALG Magazine, Issue 1 2007, p25). **Litcham** has recently created an association in order to consolidate and revitalize the allotment holdings (phone 8.3.07).

The study carried out by North Norfolk District Council in response to the government's PPG 17 showed that allotments were worked by 1% of the population, one in one-hundred people. Numbers cannot express plotholders' dedication, enthusiasm, loyalty. It is both a solitary pursuit and a sociable one. Affairs on site are not always

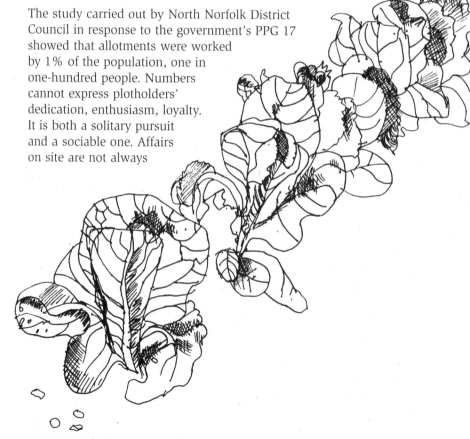

harmonious – people break the rules sometimes, sites are subject to damage from outside, management may not be as conscientious or alacritous as tenants would like – but relationships are mainly cordial. Support and guidance is offered to the novice by the experienced. Produce is shared, experiments in cropping and technique appraised. Allotments seem to marry the benefits and pleasures of solitary creativity and communality. The self-interested reasons for allotment gardening, the ones cited by planning authorities may be the ones that stimulate an interest, the commitment may come later. The value of allotments is out of all proportion to its statistical weight. What has attracted people to allotments, their reasons for working them has changed over the centuries; but what allotments have brought to people in quality of life has remained constant: a piece of land in which to invest time away from work and home, to use physical energy, to plan and create according to the limits of their own desires and inventiveness, time and space to share with other people and with nature. These are timeless virtues.

Crop varieties.

DISTRIBUTION OF ALLOTMENT SITES IN NORFOLK

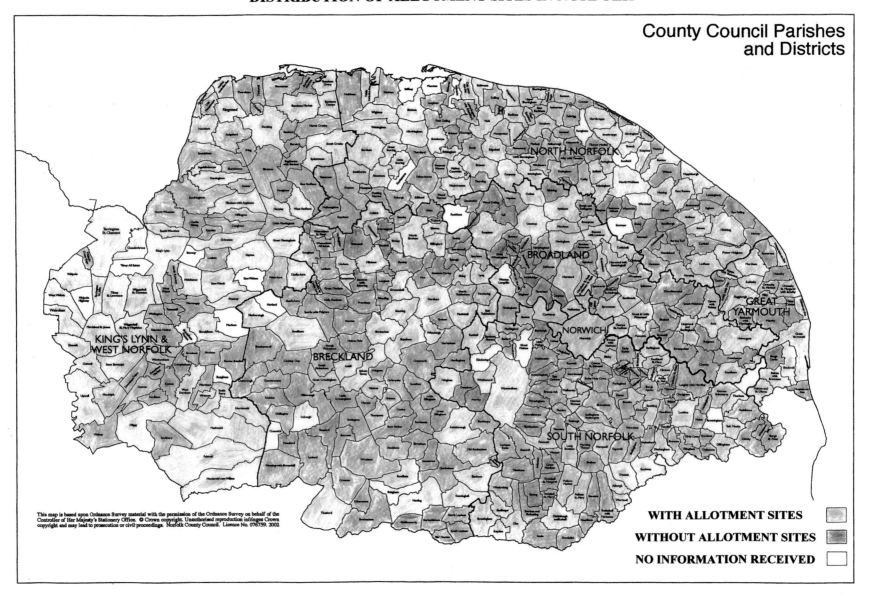

County Council Parishes
and Districts

WITH ALLOTMENT SITES

WITHOUT ALLOTMENT SITES

NO INFORMATION RECEIVED

This map is based upon Ordnance Survey material with the permission of the Ordnance Survey on behalf of the Controller of Her Majesty's Stationery Office. © Crown copyright. Unauthorised reproduction infringes Crown copyright and may lead to prosecution or civil proceedings. Norfolk County Council. Licence No. 076759. 2002

survey

of Parish Councils, Parish Meetings, Town Councils and Borough Councils for the County of Norfolk 2005–2007

Allotment Survey

When we considered researching the history of allotments in Norfolk our first thought was to contact the county council and the district councils for the location of all the current allotment sites in the county. We discovered that none of the local authorities, apart from Norwich City and King's Lynn, kept any record of allotment sites in their respective administrative areas. Further investigations revealed that the only people who could provide us with details of the current allotment sites were the parish and town clerks. We decided therefore to write to all 536 of them.

We initially sent a pilot questionnaire (see overleaf) to 22 different parishes and towns spread throughout the county. We were encouraged because we received 15 completed questionnaires nearly three quarters of our initial survey. King's Lynn Borough Council also sent us a detailed map illustrating the position of all the allotment sites in the borough.

As a result of the pilot study we wrote to all the other parishes and towns with a much simplified questionnaire. (Survey/1 see overleaf) We believed that a simple questionnaire would be more likely to be answered by the very busy town and parish clerks. Over a period of a few months we received replies from 359 clerks, a return of 67%. The stamped addressed envelope probably helped to boost the figure. We sent the same questionnaire a second time to those who had not replied and received a further 82. This raised our return to 82.3 %.

We became determined to increase this percentage. A further effort was made through press releases, magazine articles, exhibitions and finally a large number of telephone calls and our figure was boosted by a further 71 parishes. At present we have received information about 511 parishes and towns, a final return of 95.5 %. We are still hopeful that we will reach 100% by the time that the survey is closed.

To increase our knowledge we sent a further comprehensive survey form (Survey/2 see overleaf) to all those parishes which still had allotments. The return from this survey was 118 (56%).

The information we have collected for our Survey has been taken on face value. We have relied totally on the memories and records of the parish and town clerks and other members of the public for the history of their present and lost sites.

The statistical information we received was overwhelming. We were impressed by the enthusiasm of individual clerks. The information enabled us to target the individual parishes which had the most interesting histories, together with those which had archive material, for our case studies. Without the survey any such case studies would have been very hit and miss and many of them would not have been initiated at all.

We know that 213 (41.9%) of the parishes and towns we have received information from, have allotment sites and 299 (58.1%) do not. We suspect that the 24 parishes we have not heard from are far more likely not to have sites as they are predominately parishes with a small population and no parish council. Some only have a parish meeting every few years or so. Of the 299 who do not have sites, 130 said they had had them in the past, 50 said they did not know if they had ever had allotments and 119 reported that they had never had them. We know that the last figure is distorted as many of the clerks replied that "To their knowledge there had never been any allotments in their parish" indicating that they were drawing on the knowledge of the current council which would be the last 40 or 50 years only.

According to the population statistics supplied by Norfolk County Council, Norfolk has 285 (53.2%) parishes with a population of 500 persons or under. Our statistics show that in proportion to the larger parishes these smaller parishes are less likely to have allotment sites. We know that some of them have a scattered population living in houses with large gardens and that it was unlikely that there would have been a demand for an allotment site.

It is interesting to note that Parish Councils, in the form of the parish clerk, are responsible for the administration of nearly 50% of the allotment sites in Norfolk (177). This is a hugely valuable service to the allotment movement in the county. The other 50% are administered by local land owners, charities, churches and town, district and county councils. The district council sites tend to be of a temporary status and are on land which is already earmarked for future development. The parishes own about 29% of the sites that they administer, the rest are leased from local charities and land owners. Allotment Associations do not seem to be very active in Norfolk. Only 33 sites are run by associations and the majority of these are in Yarmouth (16), King's Lynn (6) Dereham (7).

We know of 356 sites with a total of just over 8500 plots making the size of the average site about 23 plots. The size of allotment plots in Norfolk can vary from 0.05 an acre to 5 acres. According to our survey the mean average size of the allotments in Norfolk is 0.192 of an acre. The Survey also indicated that there were very few vacant plots, although some of the larger plots are now let to local farmers. However we do not have enough information to estimate the number of vacant plots in Norfolk. Using the statistics from the Survey and making the following assumptions, that a rod is equivalent to one hundred and sixtieth of an acre and the average size of a plot is 0.192 of an acre it is possible to estimate that there are at least 1600 acres of allotment land in Norfolk.

Overall we were surprised and very pleased at the enthusiasm shown by the many people we contacted about our allotment Survey and would like to thank them all for their support and valuable assistance. Unfortunately we were not able to follow up as much of the interesting information as we were given. We know that without this Survey much of the information in this book would have been hidden away in the individual parish archives.

Christopher Hulse
Julie Hulse

<u>Norfolk Recorders – Allotment Questionnaire</u>

<u>PARISH</u>

Do you have allotments in your parish? Yes/No (If Yes please complete Section A)
Have you lost some or all of your allotments in the past? Yes /No (If yes please complete Section B)
You may find that both sections are applicable.

<u>Section A</u>

How many plots do you have?.........................
How many of the plots are vacant?.........................
How many on the waiting list?.........................
What is the size of the allotment site? (in hectares) ....
What is the location of the allotment site? (Map reference if possible).........................

When were the allotments first established?.........................
How was the land acquired and from whom?.........................
....
Do you have any written records or archive material for this?.........................

<u>Section B</u>

How many allotment plots have you lost in the past?.........................
What was their location? (Map reference if possible).........................

What was the approximate size of the allotment land lost? (in hectares).........................
When did you lose them and why and what was the land used for?.........................

How was this land originally acquired and from whom?.........................

Do you have any written records or archive material for this?.........................

<u>A and B please complete this section.</u>

Who administers/administered the allotments?   e.g. Parish Council, Charity or Other Organisation.........................
Who owns/owned the land?.........................
Do you know if your parish has or had a fuel allotment (It may well be run as a charity) Yes/No If Yes do you have a contact name?.........................
....

Thank you for completing this questionnaire.

May we contact you again if we have any further questions?.........................

Pilot Questionnaire

Norfolk Recorders – Allotment Questionnaire

PARISH

Are there any allotments in your parish?   Yes/No

If No. Have there been any allotments in the past?...............................

If Yes.

How many allotment sites are there?...............................

How many plots are there on each site?...............................

Who administers the allotment site(s)?...............................

....

Who owns the allotment site(s)?...............................

....

Who can we contact for further details?...............................

....

Please reply to   Norfolk Recorders
20 Broadwater Way
Horning
NR12 8LG
Norfolk

Telephone   01692 631436

e. mail   allotments_norfolkrecorders@hotmail.com

Survey Form 1

Norfolk Recorders Allotment Questionnaire

PARISH

History

When was the site first established?

How was the land acquired?

From who was the land acquired?

Do you have any written records or archive material that we can access?   Yes/No

Do you know of any other allotment sites in your parish which have been lost?   Yes/No

Current Information on your existing site

What is the name and/or address of the site?

What is the approximate size of the site?

How many plots does it have?

Is there a waiting list?   Yes/No

Are there any vacant plots and if so how many?

How many plot holders have more than one plot?

What is the annual rent for a plot

Survey Form 2 Page 1

P.T.O.

2

Does the site have any of these facilities?   Please circle those you have.

Piped water   Access road   Security gate   Fencing   Toilets   Community building

Trading hut   Skip for rubbish   Facilities for the disabled.

Do the plot holders have or belong to any relevant associations? Please would you provide ant details and/or the name and address of the secretary. (If known)

Is there anyone who has had a plot for a number of years to whom we can speak?

Do you have any photographs of your site that you would be prepared to let us copy?

Is there anything special or distinctive about your site that you feel should be recorded?

Thank you for completing this questionnaire.

Survey Form 2 Page 2

Guide for Survey Statistics

FIELDS

Parish	A list of parishes and towns in alphabetical order
Pop	Population of each parish or town (2001 Census)
Siz. Hec	Size of parish or town in hectares (2001 Census)
Recd	'Y' indicates that information has been received 'N' indicates that no information has been received
S.1	Survey form 1 (including pilot survey) has been completed and received '1' indicates first mailing '2' indicates second mailing '3' indicates by other means i.e. Telephone newspapers, exhibitions, serendipity etc.
S.2	Survey form 2 sent to all parishes and towns with allotments 'Y' indicates if form returned
Held	'Y' indicates allotments held at present 'N' indicates no allotments held at present
Lost	'Y' indicates allotments lost in the past 'DK' indicates that the parishes don't know if allotments were lost
Never	'Y' indicates that the parishes state they have never had allotments 'DK' indicates that the parishes don't know if they have had allotments in the past
Sites	Number indicates number of sites known 'DK' indicates that there was no information received
Plots	Number indicates number of plots known 'DK' indicates that there was no information received
Other use	States if the site is used for other purposes other than allotments
Site Size	Number indicates site size 'DK' indicates site size not known

FIELDS

Admin	Indicates who administers the site
	A.Ass (Allotment Association), A.Soc(Allotment Society), H.Soc(Horticultural Soc),
	CHA (Charity), CHU (Church), PC (Parish Clerk), TC (Town Clerk), City(Norwich)
	NCC (Norfolk County Council), LLO (Local land owner) DK (No information received)
Owner	Indicates who owns the site The abbreviations as in Admin fields
Est	Indicates date site established (if known)
Docs	Indicates if there is any further information other than the survey forms for this parish

#	Parish	District	Pop	Size Hec	Recd	S.1	S.2	Held	Lost	Never	Sites	Plots	O.Use	Site Size	Admin.	Owner	Est.	Docs
1	Acle	BRO	2732	946	Y	1	Y	Y	Y		1	22						
2	Alburgh	SN	349	642	Y	1		Y			1	3		0.5 Ac	A ASS	PC	1890 ?	
3	Alby with Thwaite	NN	223	581	Y	1		N		Y				DK	PC	PC	DK	
4	Aldborough/Thurgarton	NN	567	715	Y	1	Y	Y										
5	Aldeby	SN	437	1261	Y	1		N		Y	1	20		1 Ac	A ASS	LLO	2004	Y
6	Alpington/Yelverton	SN	646	439	Y	1		N		Y								
7	Anmer P.M.	WN	63	586	Y	3		N	DK	DK								
8	Antingham	NN	287	612	Y	3		Y			1	DK	Unused					
9	Ashby St Mary	SN	297	203	N									DK	DK	DK	DK	
10	Ashby with Oby P.M.	YAR	69	572	Y	2		N		Y								
11	Ashill	BRE	1426	1226	Y	2	Y	Y	Y		1	32		2 Ac	PC	PC	DK	Y
12	Ashmanhaugh	NN	197	482	Y	1		N		Y								
13	Ashwellthorpe	SN	756	974	Y	3		N	DK	DK								
14	Aslacton	SN	416	488	Y	2		N	DK	DK								
15	Attleborough T.C. 1	BRE	9702	2190	Y	1		Y			1	18		DK	TC	TC	DK	Y
16	Attleborough T.C. 2	BRE						Y			1	14		DK	TC	TC	DK	
17	Attlebridge	BRO	122	527	Y	1		N		Y								
18	Aylmerton	NN	435	686	Y	1	Y	Y			1	16		4 Ac	PC	LLO	1958	
19	Aylsham T.C. 1	BRO	5504	1752	Y	1		Y			1	12		DK	TC	TC	DK	
20	Aylsham T.C. 2	BRO						Y			1	20		DK	TC	LLO	DK	
21	Baconsthorpe	NN	232	553	Y	1	Y	Y			1	12		4 Ac	PC	LLO	DK	
22	Bacton	NN	1130	945	Y	1		Y	Y		1	19		DK	PC	PC	1895	
23	Bagthorpe P.M.	WN	53	905	Y	2		N	Y									
24	Banham	BRE	1443	1617	Y	1	Y	Y			1	11		1.09 Ac	PC	PC	1984	
25	Barford/Wramplingham	SN	618	785	Y	1		N		Y								
26	Barnham Broom	SN	552	724	Y	1		N		Y								
27	Barsham	NN	253	1940	Y	1	Y	Y	Y		1	6		0.37 Ac	PC	PC	1977	
28	Barton Bendish	WN	198	1592	Y	2		N		Y								
29	Barton Turf/Irstead	NN	480	1086	Y	3		N		Y								
30	Barwick P.M.	WN	21	527	Y	2		N	DK	DK								
31	Bawburgh	SN	466	582	Y	1		N		Y								
32	Bawdeswell	BRE	766	487	Y	1		N		Y								
33	Bawsey P.M.	WN	184	681	N													
34	Beachamwell	BRE	334	2215	Y	1		N		Y								
35	Bedingham	SN	216	552	Y	2		N		Y								
36	Beeston Regis 1	NN	1091	289	Y	1	Y	Y	Y		1	29		2.06 Ac	H.SOC	CHA	1946 ?	
37	Beeston Regis 2	NN			Y	3		Y			1	1		DK	TENANT	LLO	DK	
38	Beeston St. Andrew	BRO	39	256	Y	1		N		Y								
39	Beeston with Bittering	BRE	505	1080	Y	1		N		Y								
40	Beetley	BRE	1385	1102	Y	2		N		Y								
41	Beighton/Moulton St. Mary	BRO	412	763	Y	1		N		Y								
42	Belaugh P.M.	BRO	99	356	Y	1		N		Y								
43	Belton with Browston	YAR	4098	836	Y	1		Y			1	30						
44	Bergh Apton	SN	428	805	Y	2		N		Y				DK	PC	CHU	DK	
45	Besthorpe	BRE	561	887	Y	1		N	Y									
46	Billingford	BRE	223	736	Y	1		Y			1	DK		DK	LLO	LLO	DK	Y
47	Binham/Cockthorpe	NN	273	1152	Y	3		Y			1	3		DK	PC	LLO	DK	
48	Bintree	BRE	300	599	Y	1		Y			1	6		DK	CHA	CHA	DK	
49	Bircham	WN	586	2482	Y	1		N	Y									
50	Bixley	SN	144	542	Y	2		Y			1	4		DK	PC	CHA	DK	
51	Blakeney	NN	789	990	Y	1		N	Y									
52	Blickling	BRO	136	862	Y	2		N		Y								
53	Blo' Norton	BRE	270	462	Y	1		N		Y								

	Parish	District	Pop	Size Hec	Recd	S.1	S.2	Held	Lost	Never	Sites	Plots	O.Use	Site Size	Admin.	Owner	Est.	Docs
54	Blofield	BRO	3221	941	Y	2		N	DK	DK								
55	Bodham 1	NN	435	680	Y	2		Y			1	11		DK	PC	PC	DK	
56	Bodham 2	NN						Y			1	4		DK	PC	PC	DK	
57	Booton	BRO	100	437	Y	1		N	DK	DK								
58	Boughton P.M.	WN	213	548	N													
59	Bracon Ash/Hethel	SN	446	984	Y	1		N		Y								
60	Bradenham	BRE	722	1655	Y	2	Y	Y			1	17		3.12 Ac	PC	PC	1804	Y
61	Bradwell 1	YAR	10318	974	Y	1	Y	Y	Y		1	34		340 Rods	PC	PC	1970s	
62	Bradwell 2	YAR						Y			1	60		970 Rods	PC	PC	1979	
63	Bramerton	SN	350	296	Y	1	Y	Y			1	8		0.5 Ac	PC	PC	DK	
64	Brampton	BRO	162	478	Y	1	Y	Y			1	8	Pt. Ag.	0.75 Ac	CHU	CHU	1889	
65	Brancaster	WN	897	2143	Y	1		N	Y									
66	Brandiston	BRO	44	314	Y	2		N	DK	DK								
67	Bressingham/Fersfield	SN	751	1577	Y	2		Y	Y		1	DK		DK	PC	PC	DK	
68	Brettenham P.M.	BRE	475	2637	Y	1		N		Y								
69	Bridgham	BRE	328	1106	N													
70	Briningham 1	NN	122	496	Y	1	Y	Y			1	43		5 Ac	PC	PC	1920	
71	Briningham 2	NN						Y			1	4		DK	PC	PC	DK	
72	Brinton/Sharrington	NN	229	613	Y	1		N	Y									
73	Brisley	BRE	276	490	Y	1	Y	Y			1	30	Ag	27.91 Ac	PC	NCC	1920	
74	Briston	NN	2021	1196	Y	3		Y			1	DK		DK	DK	DK	1833	
75	Brockdish	SN	605	915	Y	3		N	Y								1830-3	
76	Brooke	SN	1242	872	Y	1		N		Y								
77	Broome	SN	475	591	Y	1		N	Y									
78	Brumstead	NN	84	322	Y	2		N		Y								
79	Brundall	BRO	3978	439	Y	2		N		Y								
80	Bunwell	SN	885	1011	Y	1		N	Y									
81	Burgh Castle	YAR	955	676	Y	1		N	Y									
82	Burgh St. Peter/Wheatacre	SN	386	1301	Y	2		N	DK	DK								
83	Burgh/Tuttington	BRO	255	670	Y	1		N		Y								
84	Burnham Market 1	WN	948	1843	Y	1		Y			1	18		DK	PC	LLO	DK	
85	Burnham Market 2	WN						Y			1	12		DK	PC	LLO	DK	
86	Burnham Norton	WN	76	1427	Y	1		N	Y									
87	Burnham Overy Staithe	WN	311	892	Y	1	Y	Y	Y		1	14		285 Rods	PC	LLO	1939/40	
88	Burnham Thorpe	WN	168	956	Y	1	Y	Y			1	36		9.73 Ac	LLO	LLO	1854	
89	Burston with Shrimpling	SN	538	917	Y	1		N		Y								
90	Buxton with Lamas	BRO	1685	874	Y	1		Y	Y		1	5		.29 Ac	DC	DC	DK	
91	Bylaugh P.M.	BRE	65	644	Y	3		N										
92	Caister on Sea	YAR	8756	412	Y	3		Y	Y		1	DK		DK	DK	DK	DK	
93	Caister St. Edmund	SN	270	655	Y	2		N	DK	DK								
94	Cantley	BRO	677	1290	Y	1		N	Y									
95	Carbrooke	BRE	1176	1266	Y	1		N	Y									
96	Carleton Rode	SN	727	1091	Y	1		N	Y									
97	Carleton St Peter	SN	29	319	Y	1		N		Y								
98	Castle Acre 1	WN	799	1318	Y	1	Y	Y			1	28		DK	PC	LLO	DK	Y
99	Castle Acre 2	WN						Y			1	DK		DK	LLO	LLO	DK	
100	Castle Rising	WN	225	865	Y	1		N		Y								
101	Caston	BRE	459	637	Y	1		N	Y									
102	Catfield	NN	848	1002	Y	3		N		Y								
103	Cawston	BRO	1390	1703	Y	1	Y	Y			1	13		0.5 Ac	PC	PC	1998	
104	Chedgrave	SN	985	354	Y	1		N		Y								
105	Choseley P.M.	WN	18	275	Y	1		N		Y								
106	Claxton	SN	244	407	Y	3		Y			1	4		DK	CHA	CHA	DK	

	Parish	District	Pop	Size Hec	Recd	S.1	S.2	Held	Lost	Never	Sites	Plots	O.Use	Site Size	Admin.	Owner	Est.	Docs
107	Clenchwarton	WN	2200	1277	Y	1		Y			1	18		DK	PC	PC	DK	
108	Cley	NN	376	863	Y	2	Y	Y	Y		1	38		5 Ac	PC	LLO	1880s	Y
109	Cockley Cley	BRE	138	1794	Y	1		N	Y									
110	Colby/Banningham	NN	524	834	Y	2		Y			1	5		DK	PC	PC	DK	
111	Colkirk	BRE	547	1060	Y	1	Y	Y			1	22		3 Ac	PC	PC	DK	Y
112	Colney	SN	124	383	Y	1		N		Y								
113	Coltishall	BRO	1405	727	Y	1		Y			1	80		DK	PC	PC	DK	Y
114	Congham	WN	227	1170	Y	1		N	Y									
115	Corpusty/Saxthorpe	NN	637	1273	Y	1	Y	Y			1	6		0.5 Hec	PC	PC	DK	Y
116	Costessey 1	SN	9822	1239	Y	1	Y	Y			1	34		10 Ac	PC	PC	1860	Y
117	Costessey 2	SN						Y			1	7				PC	PC	1860	
118	Cranwich P.M.	BRE	60	738	N													
119	Cranworth	BRE	440	2063	Y	1		N	Y									
120	Crimplesham	WN	221	663	Y	1		N	Y									
121	Cringleford	SN	2076	404	Y	1		N		Y								
122	Cromer T.C.	NN	7749	466	Y	1		N	Y									
123	Crostwick P.M.	BRO	97	282	Y	2		N	DK	DK								
124	Croxton	BRE	416	1896	Y	1		N	Y									
125	Denton	SN	352	1011	Y	1	Y	Y			1	4	No Lets	1 Ac	CHA	CHA	1907	
126	Denver	WN	847	1082	Y	1		N	Y									
127	Deopham/Hackford	SN	505	979	Y	1		N		Y								
128	Dereham T.C. 1	BRE	15659	2151	Y	1	Y	Y	Y		1	45		DK	TC	TC	Post 1945	Y
129	Dereham T.C. 2	BRE						Y			1	80		DK	TC	TC	Post 1900	
130	Dereham T.C. 3	BRE						Y			1	40		DK	TC	TC	Pre 1986	
131	Dereham T.C. 4	BRE						Y			1	DK		DK	TC	TC	DK	
132	Dereham T.C. 5	BRE						Y			1	DK		DK	TC	TC	DK	
133	Dereham T.C. 6	BRE						Y			1	DK		DK	TC	TC	DK	
134	Dereham T.C. 7	BRE						Y			1	DK		DK	TC	TC	DK	
135	Dersingham 1	WN	4502	1450	Y	2	Y	Y	Y		1	52		6 Ac	CHA	CHA	DK	Y
136	Dersingham 2	WN						Y			1	1		DK	LLO	LLO	DK	
137	Dickleburgh/Rushall 1	SN	1356	1431	Y	1	Y	Y			1	15		DK	PC	PC	DK	
138	Dickleburgh/Rushall 2	SN						Y			1	10		DK	PC	PC	DK	
139	Dickleburgh/Rushall 3	SN						Y			1	10		DK	CHA	CHA	DK	
140	Didlington P.M.	BRE	48	1107	Y	2		N		Y								
141	Dilham	NN	301	655	Y	1		N		Y								
142	Diss T.C.	SN	6742	532	Y	2		Y			1	54		DK	A.ASS	T.C.	DK	
143	Ditchingham	SN	1614	856	Y	1	Y	Y			1	14		3.4 Ac	PC	LLO	1930s ?	
144	Docking	WN	1150	2579	Y	1	Y	Y	Y		1	14	Pt. Ag.	3.5 Ac	PC	LLO	1919	
145	Downham Market	WN	6730	520	Y	1		N	Y									
147	Downham West	WN	285	0?	Y	1		N	Y									
148	Drayton	BRO	5150	556	Y	1		N	Y									
149	Dunton/Shereford/Toftrees	NN	115	1555	Y	1		N	Y									
150	Earsham	SN	907	1265	Y	1	Y	Y	Y		1	13		1.7 Ac	PC	LLO	1988	Y
151	East Beckham	NN	35	304	Y	3		Y			1	6		2.1 Ac	PC	DC	DK	
152	East Carleton/Ketteringham	SN	527	1146	Y	2		N	Y									
153	East Rudham	WN	525	1794	Y	1		N	Y								1849	
154	East Ruston	NN	497	1013	Y	1		Y			20	20		20 Ac	PC	NCC		
155	East Tuddenharn 1	BRE	436	847	Y	1	Y	Y			1	2		1.5 Ac	CHA	CHA	DK	Y
156	East Tuddenharn 2	BRE						Y			1	3		0.25 Ac	CHA	CHA	DK	
157	East Walton P.M.	WN	90	1081	N													
158	East Winch	WN	782	1995	Y	2	Y	Y			1	23		DK	CHA	CHA	Pre 1935	
159	Easton	SN	1141	625	Y	1	Y	Y			1	21		DK	PC	CHU	1980	
160	Edgefield	NN	393	1007	Y	1		Y			1	3		DK	PC	LLO	1833	

	Parish	District	Pop	Size Hec	Recd	S.1	S.2	Held	Lost	Never	Sites	Plots	O.Use	Site Size	Admin.	Owner	Est.	Docs
161	Ellingham	SN	532	565	Y	3		N		Y								
162	Elsing	BRE	229	634	Y	1		Y			DK	DK		DK	DK	DK	DK	
163	Emneth 1	WN	2466	1177	Y	1		Y			1	45		DK	PC	PC	DK	
164	Emneth 2	BRE						Y			1	23		DK	PC	PC	DK	
165	Emneth 3	BRE						Y			1	6		DK	PC	PC	DK	
166	Emneth 4	BRE						Y			1	19		DK	PC	PC	DK	
167	Emneth 5	BRE						Y			1	12		DK	PC	PC	DK	
168	Erpingham/Calthorpe	NN	541	1008	Y	1		N		Y								
169	Fakenham T.C.1	NN	7357	904	Y	3		Y			1	70		4.481 Ac	TC	TC	DK	
170	Fakenham T.C.2	NN						Y			1	15		1.456 Ac	TC	TC	DK	
171	Fakenham T.C.3	NN						Y			1	80		5 Ac	TC	TC	DK	
172	Felbrigg	NN	182	630	Y	1		N	Y									
173	Felmingham	NN	564	768	Y	1	Y	Y			1	11		8 Ac	PC	NCC	DK	
174	Felthorpe	BRO	710	870	Y	1		N	Y									
175	Feltwell 1	WN	2662	5216	Y	1	Y	Y			1	2	Pt. Ag.	20 Ac	PC	PC	DK	
176	Feltwell 2	WN						Y			1	3	Pt. Ag.	22 Ac	PC	PC	DK	
177	Field Dalling/Saxlingham	NN	273	1287	Y	1		N		Y								
178	Filby 1	YAR	740	580	Y	1	Y	Y			1	0	Ag.	12.42 Ac	PC	NCC	1924	Y
179	Filby 2	YAR						Y			1	0	Ag.	5.543 Ac	PC	NCC	1924	Y
180	Fincham	WN	474	1203	Y	2		N		Y								
181	Fleggburgh	YAR	909	1204	Y	3		Y	Y		1	DK		DK	DK	DK	DK	
182	Flitcham	WN	236	1708	Y	1		Y	Y		1	1		DK	TENANT	LLO	DK	Y
183	Flordon	SN	263	374	Y	2		N		Y								
184	Fordham P.M.	WN	71	894	Y	1		N	DK	DK								
185	Forncett	SN	1000	1076	Y	3		Y			1	10		.75 Ac	PC	DK	DK	
186	Foulden	BRE	444	1295	Y	1		N	Y									
187	Foulsham	BRO	860	1256	N													
188	Foxley	BRE	279	666	Y	3		N		Y								
189	Framingham Earl	SN	834	256	Y	1		N		Y								
190	Framingham Pigot	SN	167	257	Y	3		N	DK	DK								
191	Fransham	BRE	426	1214	Y	1		N	Y									
192	Freethorpe	BRO	906	951	Y	1		N	Y									
193	Frettenham	BRO	727	633	Y	1	Y	Y			1	12		DK	PC	LLO	1960s	
194	Fring P.M.	WN	94	693	Y	1		N		Y								
195	Fritton with St. Olaves	YAR	543	763	Y	1		Y			1	3		DK	DK	LLO	DK	
196	Fulmodeston/Barney	NN	431	1504	Y	1		N		Y								Y
197	Garboldisham	BRE	721	1117	Y	1		N	Y									
198	Garvestone	BRE	606	1452	Y	1		N		Y								
199	Gateley P.M.	BRE	65	614	Y	2		N		Y								
200	Gayton	WN	1396	2284	Y	2	Y	Y			1	22	Pt. Ag.	6 Ac	LLO	LLO	1931	Y
201	Geldeston	SN	398	345	Y	3		N		Y								
202	Gillingham	SN	650	829	Y	1	Y	Y			1	37		1.6 Hec	PC	PC	1895	
203	Gimingham 1	NN	462	604	Y	1		Y			1	14		DK	PC	PC	DK	
204	Gimingham 2	NN						Y			1	8		DK	PC	PC	DK	
205	Gissing	SN	254	811	Y	3		N	DK	DK								
206	Gooderstone	BRE	360	1129	Y	1		N	Y									
207	Great Cressingham	BRE	279	984	Y	3		Y			DK	DK		DK	DK	DK	DK	
208	Great Dunham	BRE	325	818	Y	1		N	Y									
209	Great Ellingham	BRE	1108	1114	Y	1		N		Y								
210	Great Massingham 1	WN	886	1717	Y	1	Y	Y			1	25		DK	PC	PC	DK	
211	Great Massingham 2	WN						Y			1	18	Unused	DK	PC	PC	DK	
212	Great Melton	SN	148	1024	N													
213	Great Moulton	SN	699	566	Y	2		N		Y								

	Parish	District	Pop	Size Hec	Recd	S.1	S.2	Held	Lost	Never	Sites	Plots	O.Use	Site Size	Admin.	Owner	Est.	Docs
214	Great Plumstead/Little Plumstead	BRO	2618	1104	Y	1	Y	Y			1	17		1 Ac	PC	PC	DK	Y
215	Great Snoring	NN	168	685	Y	1	Y	Y	Y		1	23	Pt. Am.	4 Ac	PC	PC	DK	
216	Great Witchingham	BRO	564	912	Y	1		N	Y						PC	LLO	1895	
217	Great Yarmouth 1	YAR	47288	2654	Y	2		Y			1	59		4 Ac			1830	
218	Great Yarmouth 2							Y			1	48		3 Ac	A.ASS	A.ASS	DK	
219	Great Yarmouth 3							Y			1	17		1 Ac				
220	Great Yarmouth 4							Y			1	50		3 Ac				
221	Great Yarmouth 5							Y			1	78		5 Ac				
222	Great Yarmouth 6							Y			1	53		3 Ac				
223	Great Yarmouth 7							Y			1	40		2 Ac				
224	Great Yarmouth 8							Y			1	12		0.75 Ac				
225	Great Yarmouth 9							Y			1	8		0.5 Ac				
226	Great Yarmouth 10							Y			1	8		0.5 Ac				
227	Great Yarmouth 11							Y			1	9		0.5 Ac				
228	Great Yarmouth 12							Y			3	162		10 Ac				
229	Great Yarmouth 13							Y			2	205		12 Ac				
230	Gresham	NN	443	869	Y	1		Y	Y		1	9		3.7 Hec	PC	LLO	DK	Y
231	Gressenhall	BRE	1008	1053	Y	1	Y	Y	Y		1	8		DK	PC	PC	1976	Y
232	Grimston 1	WN	1952	1808	Y	1	Y	Y			1	22		54 Ac	CHA	CHA	1779	Y
233	Grimston 2	WN						Y			1	12		3 Ac	CHU	CHU	1300?	
234	Grimston 3	WN						Y			1	DK		DK	CHA	CHA	DK	
235	Griston	BRE	1206	562	Y	1		N	Y									
236	Guestwick P.M.	BRO	135	745	Y	1		N		Y								
237	Guist	BRE	242	680	Y	3		N		Y								
238	Gunthorpe/Bale	NN	261	882	Y	1		Y	Y		1	DK		DK	LLO	LLO	DK	
239	Haddiscoe	SN	481	2042	Y	3		N	Y									
240	Hainford	BRO	951	694	Y	2		N		Y								
241	Hales/Heckingham	SN	622	847	Y	1		N		Y								
242	Halvergate	BRO	468	2465	Y	1		Y			DK	DK	Temp	DK	DC	DC	DK	Y
243	Hanworth/Gunton	NN	168	874	Y	1		N		Y								
244	Happisburgh/Walcott	NN	1372	1078	Y	1	Y	Y	Y		1	10		DK	PC	PC	Pre 1959	
245	Hardingham	BRE	274	978	Y	1		N		Y								
246	Harling 1	BRE	2201	2319	Y	1	Y	Y	Y		1	8		0.5 Ac	PC	PC	Post 1947	Y
247	Harling 2	BRE						Y			1	8		0.5 Ac	PC	PC	Post 1947	
248	Harling 3	BRE						Y			1	4		0.25 Ac	CHA	CHA	1893	
249	Harpley	WN	353	929	Y	1		Y			1	5		DK	LLO	LLO	DK	
250	Haveringland P.M.	BRO	187	891	Y	3		N		Y								
251	Heacham	WN	4611	1766	Y	1	Y	Y			1	25		6.33 Ac	PC	PC	1920s	
252	Hedenham	SN	173	730	Y	1		N	Y									
253	Helhoughton	NN	197	683	Y	1		N		Y								
254	Hellesdon	BRO	11177	524	Y	2		Y			1	60		DK	PC	PC	DK	Y
255	Hemblington	BRO	316	303	Y	1		N	DK	DK								
256	Hempnall 1	SN	1310	1482	Y	1					1	16		DK	CHA	CHA	DK	
257	Hempnall 2	SN						Y			1	2		DK	CHA	CHA	DK	
258	Hempstead	NN	179	719	Y	1		N		Y								
259	Hempton	NN	499	215	Y	1		Y			1	22		DK	DK	LLO	DK	
260	Hemsby	YAR	2973	714	Y	1		N		Y								
261	Hethersett	SN	5441	1092	Y	1		N		Y								
262	Hevingham	BRO	1150	1166	Y	1	Y	Y			1	34		17 Ac	PC	PC	1922	
263	Heydon P.M.	BRO	89	802	Y	1		N	Y								1830	
264	Heywood	SN	175	956	Y	3		N	DK	DK								
265	Hickling 1	NN	906	1711	Y	2		Y			1	5		DK	PC	LLO	DK	
266	Hickling 2	NN						Y			1	2		DK	PC	LLO	DK	

	Parish	District	Pop	Size Hec	Recd	S.1	S.2	Held	Lost	Never	Sites	Plots	O.Use	Site Size	Admin.	Owner	Est.	Docs
267	Hickling 3	NN						Y			1	4		DK	PC	LLO	DK	
268	Hickling 4	NN						Y			1	5		DK	PC	LLO	DK	
269	High Kelling	NN	515	146	Y	1		N		Y								
270	Hilborough	BRE	180	2408	Y	1		N	DK	DK								
271	Hilgay	WN	1174	3338	Y	1	Y	Y	Y		1	26		2 Ac	PC	DK	1920s	Y
272	Hillington	WN	287	1027	Y	3		N		Y								
273	Hindolveston	NN	505	1028	Y	1		Y			1	14		DK	PC	PC	Pre 1942	Y
274	Hindringham	NN	431	1372	Y	2	Y	Y	Y		1	14		3 Ac	CHA	CHA	Pre 1920s	
275	Hingham 1	SN	2078	1498	Y	1	Y	Y			1	30		DK	CHA	CHA	DK	
276	Hingham 2	SN						Y			1	3		DK	DC	DC	DK	
277	Hingham 3	SN						Y			1	DK		DK	CHA	CHA	DK	
278	Hockering	BRE	628	810	Y	1		N	Y									
279	Hockham	BRE	620	1336	Y	1		N	Y									
280	Hockwold 1	WN	1233	3105	Y	1	Y	Y			1	26	Ag	3.703 Ac	PC	PC	DK	
281	Hockwold 2	WN						Y			1	30	Ag	3.917 Ac	PC	PC	DK	
282	Hoe P.M.	BRE	219	925	Y	2		N		Y								
283	Holkham/Quarles	NN	236	2392	Y	1		N		Y								
284	Holme Hale	BRE	444	1069	Y	1	Y	N	Y									
285	Holme next Sea	WN	322	882	Y	1		Y			1	2		DK	PC	PC	DK	
286	Holt T.C. 1	NN	3550	1219	Y	1	Y	Y			1	120		8 Ac	A.SOC	A.SOC	1918	
287	Holt T.C. 2	NN						Y			1	4		DK	DC	DC	DK	
288	Holverston	SN	29	144	Y	1		N	DK	DK								
289	Honing/Crostwight	NN	319	880	Y	1	Y	Y	Y		1	2		.33 Ac	LLO	LLO	DK	
290	Honingham	BRO	342	1055	Y	2		N		Y								
291	Hopton on Sea	YAR	2706	563	Y	3		N		Y								
292	Horning 1	NN	1033	1104	Y	1		Y	Y		1	16		DK	PC	CHU	DK	
293	Horning 2	NN						Y			1	22		DK	PC	CHU	DK	
294	Horningtoft	BRE	135	573	Y	1		N		Y								
295	Horsey	NN	99	849	Y	1		N	Y									
296	Horsford 1	BRO	3965	1656	Y	1	Y	Y			1	38		DK	PC	PC	1991	
297	Horsford 2	BRO						Y			1	7		DK	PC	LLO	Early 20 C	
298	Horsham/Newton St. Faiths 1	BRO	1642	733	Y	1		Y			1	14		DK	PC	PC	DK	
299	Horsham/Newton St. Faiths 2	BRO						Y			1	36		DK	PC	PC	DK	
300	Horstead with Stanninghall 1	BRO	1007	1154	Y	1		Y			1	14		3 Ac	CHA	CHA	Pre 1900	
301	Horstead with Stanninghall 2	BRO						Y			1	6		1 Ac	CHA	CHA	Pre 1900	
302	Houghton	WN	69	764	Y	1		N		Y								
303	Hoveton	NN	1804	1020	Y	1		N		Y								
304	Howe	SN	54	320	Y	1		N		Y								
305	Hunstanton T.C. 1	WN	4961	607	Y	1	Y	Y	Y		1	38		4.822 Ac	TC	LLO	1935	Y
306	Hunstanton T.C. 2	WN						Y			1	DK		DK	A.SOC	LLO	1920	
307	ickburgh P.M.	BRE	245	1221	N													
308	Ingham	NN	376	613	Y	2		N	Y									
309	Ingoldsthorpe	WN	780	563	Y	1		Y			1	49		DK	PC	PC	DK	
310	Ingworth	NN	94	212	Y	1		N		Y								
311	Itteringham 1	NN	134	820	Y	2		Y			1	DK		DK	A.SOC	LLO	DK	
312	Itteringham 2	NN						Y			1	DK		DK	A.SOC	LLO	DK	
313	Itteringham 3	NN						Y			1	DK		DK	A.SOC	LLO	DK	
314	Itteringham 4	NN						Y			1	DK		DK	A.SOC	LLO	DK	
315	Kelling	NN	175	806	Y	1		N	Y									
316	Kempstone P.M.	BRE	18	331	N													
317	Kenninghall	BRE	878	1485	Y	3		Y			DK	DK		DK	LLO	LLO	DK	Y
318	Keswick/Intwood	SN	431	552	Y	2		N		Y								
319	Kettlestone	NN	177	755	N													

	Parish	District	Pop	Size Hec	Recd	S.1	S.2	Held	Lost	Never	Sites	Plots	O.Use	Site Size	Admin.	Owner	Est.	Docs
320	Kilverstone P.M.	BRE	60	746	Y	1		N		Y								
321	Kimberley/Carleton Forehoe	SN	121	933	N													
322	Kings Lynn T.C. 1	WN	34564	2841	Y	1		Y	Y		1	9		0.5 Ac	TC	TC	DK	Y
323	Kings Lynn T.C. 2	WN						Y			1	17		5.04 Ac	TC	TC	DK	
324	Kings Lynn T.C 3	WN						Y			1	7		0.64 Ac	TC	TC	DK	
325	Kings Lynn T.C 4	WN						Y			1	117		9.16 Ac	TC	TC	DK	
326	Kings Lynn T.C. 5	WN						Y	.		1	1		0.08 Ac	TC	TC	DK	
327	Kings Lynn T.C. 6	WN						Y			1	131		9.84 Ac	TC	TC	DK	
328	Kings Lynn T.C. 7	WN						Y			1	8		1.08 Ac	TC	TC	DK	
329	Kings Lynn T.C. 8	WN						Y			1	2		0.05 Ac	TC	TC	DK	
330	Kings Lynn T.C. 9	WN						Y			1	22		2.28 Ac	A.ASS	TC	DK	
331	Kings Lynn T.C. 10	WN						Y			1	19		1.42 Ac	A.ASS	TC	DK	
332	Kings Lynn T.C. 11	WN						Y			1	73		5.57 Ac	A.ASS	TC	DK	
333	Kings Lynn T.C. 12	WN						Y			1	35		3.55 Ac	A.ASS	TC	DK	
334	Kings Lynn T.C. 13	WN						Y			1	28		1.97 Ac	A.ASS	TC	DK	
335	Kings Lynn T.C. 14	WN						Y			1	67		5.08 Ac	A.ASS	TC	DK	
336	Kirby Bedon	SN	186	782	Y	1		N	DK	DK								
337	Kirby Cane	SN	375	613	Y	1		N	Y									
338	Kirstead	SN	247	419	Y	1		N		Y								
339	Knapton	NN	362	580	Y	1	Y	Y			1	23		3.34 Ac	PC	PC	1965	
340	Langham	NN	399	707	Y	1		N		Y								
341	Langley with Hardley	SN	489	1512	Y	1		N		Y								
342	Lessingham	NN	467	761	Y	1		N		Y								
343	Letheringsett/Glandford	NN	225	819	Y	1		N	Y									
344	Lexham P.M.	BRE	157	973	Y	2		N	Y									
345	Leziate	WN	581	1137	Y	1		N	DK	DK								
346	Lingwood/Burlingham 1	BRO	2504	939	Y	1	Y	Y			1	8		8.25 Ac	PC	CHA	1803	Y
347	Lingwood/Burlingham 2	BRO						Y			1	11		0.5 Hec	PC	NCC	1990s	
348	Litcham 1	BRE	592	789	Y	1	Y	Y	Y		1	0	Ag	6.0 Ac	CHA	CHA	DK	Y
349	Litcham 2	BRE						Y			1	10		DK	CHA	CHA	DK	
350	Litcham 3	BRE						Y			1	9		DK	CHA	CHA	DK	
351	Litcham 4	BRE						Y			1	4		DK	LLO	LLO	DK	
352	Little Barningham	NN	111	505	Y	3		Y			1	4		1.5 Ac	DC	DC	Pre 1950	
353	Little Cressingham	BRE	157	1190	Y	2		N	DK	DK								
354	Little Dunham	BRE	309	749	Y	1		N		Y								
355	Little Ellingham	BRE	271	624	Y	2		N		Y								
356	Little Massingham	WN	74	927	Y	1		N		Y								
357	Little Melton 1	SN	851	275	Y	1		Y			1	6		DK	CHA	CHA	DK	
358	Little Melton 2	SN						Y			1	4		DK	CHA	CHA	DK	
359	Little Melton 3	SN						Y			1	19		DK	CHA	CHA	DK	
360	Little Snoring	NN	603	731	Y	1		Y			1	1		DK	CHA	CHA	DK	
361	Little Witchingham	BRO	36	301	Y	3		N	DK	DK								
362	Loddon	SN	2578	1183	Y	1	Y	Y			1	18		2 Ac	PC	PC	DK	
363	Long Stratton	SN	3701	1049	Y	3		Y			1	18		3.8 Ac	CHA	CHA		
364	Longham	BRE	219	540	Y	1		N	Y									
365	Ludham 1	NN	1301	1218	Y	1	Y	Y			1	5		DK	PC	LLO	DK	Y
366	Ludham 2	NN						Y			1	5		DK	PC	LLO	2000	
367	Lynford P.M.	BRE	157	2472	Y	2		N		Y								
368	Lyng	BRE	806	799	Y	1		Y			1	12		DK	PC	CHA	DK	
369	Marham	WN	2951	1485	N													
370	Marlingford/Colton	SN	384	662	Y	1		N	Y									
371	Marsham	BRO	674	740	Y	1	Y	Y			1	11		1.5 Ac	PC	LLO	Pre 1930	
372	Marshland St James 1	WN	1137	2569	Y	1		Y			1	14		DK	PC	PC	DK	

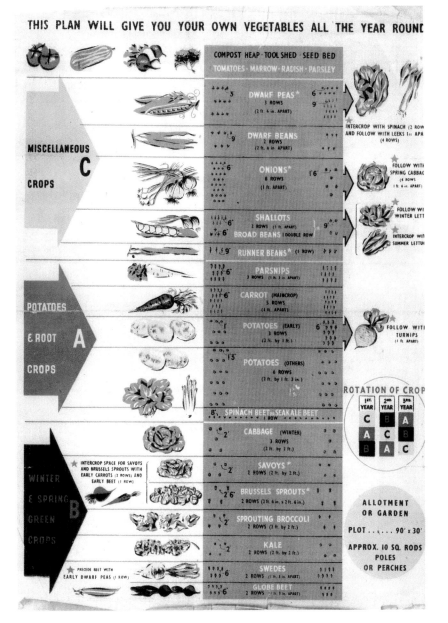

CROP	TIME OF SOWING	DISTANCE APART		PERIOD OF USE
		Rows	Plants	
BEANS (Broad)	Feb.-March	1 double row	6 in. by 9 in.	July
BEANS (Dwarf)	Late April-Early May	2½ ft.	9 in.	July-Aug.
BEANS (Dry Harvest)	Late April-Early May	2½ ft.	9 in.	Winter
BEANS (Runner)	Mid-May		9 in.	July-Oct.
BEET	(1) April	15 in.	6 in. (thin)	July-April
BROCCOLI (Sprouting)	(2) June Mid-Mar.			Feb.-May
	Plant Mid-June			
BRUSSELS SPROUTS	March	2½ ft.	2 ft.	Nov.-Mar.
	Plant May-June			
CABBAGE (Spring)	July-August	1½ ft.	1½ ft.	April-Jan.
	Plant Sept.-Early Oct.			
CABBAGE (Winter)	Mid-Mar.			
	Plant Mid.-Jun.			
CABBAGE (Cold Districts)	April	1½ ft.	1½ ft.	Autumn
CARROTS (Early)	April	1 ft.	6 in. (thin)	June-Sept.
CARROTS (Maincrop)	June-Early July	1 ft.	6 in. (thin)	Oct.-May
KALE	May	2 ft.	2 ft.	Mar.-May
	Plant May-June			
LEEKS	March		8 in.	Nov.-May
	Plant June-July			
LETTUCE (Summer)	March and every 14 days	Between other crops	9 in.	May-Oct.
LETTUCE (Winter Hardy)	Sept.	1 ft.	9 in.	Spring
MARROW	May		3-4 ft.	July-Feb.
ONIONS	March	1 ft.		Sept.-May
PARSNIPS	Feb.-March	15 in.	8 in. (thin)	Nov.-Mar.
PEAS (Early)	March and April	2½ ft.	3 in.	June-July
PEAS (Others)	March and April			
POTATOES (Early)	March	2 ft.	1 ft.	July-Aug.
POTATOES (Others)	April		2 in.	Sept.-May
RADISHES	March onwards	1 ft.		May-June
SAVOY	June-July			Dec.-Mar.
	Plant July-Aug.			
SHALLOTS	Feb.-March	1 ft.	9 in.	July-Oct.
SPINACH (Summer)	Mid-April	1 ft.	6 in. (thin)	Summer
SPINACH (Winter)	Sept.	1 ft.	6 in. (thin)	Spring
SPINACH BEET	April	18 in.		July-Oct. and Jan.-April
SEAKALE BEET	April	18 in.		
SWEDES	End June	15 in.	6 in. (thin)	Dec.-Mar.
TOMATOES	Plant end May		18 in.	Aug.-Oct.
TURNIP (Root)	July		6 in. (thin)	Oct.-Dec.
TURNIP (Tops)	End August	1 ft.	Sow thinly	April

Printed for H.M. Stationery Office by T. G. Porter (Printers) Ltd., Leeds. 51-1782

Grow for Winter
as well as Summer

DIG FOR VICTORY LEAFLET No. I.   New Series

Vegetables for you and your family every week of the year. Never a week without food from your garden or allotment. Not only fresh peas and lettuce in June— new potatoes in July, but all the health-giving vegetables in WINTER — when supplies are scarce - - - - SAVOYS, SPROUTS, KALE, SPROUTING BROCCOLI, ONIONS, LEEKS, CARROTS, PARSNIPS and BEET

Vegetables all the year round if you
DIG WELL
AND CROP WISELY

Follow this Plan

ISSUED BY THE MINISTRY OF AGRICULTURE

A World War 2 leaflet designed to help people 'Dig for Victory'.

Trowse (top left), and Norwich allotments: their surroundings give clues to their origins and show how much a part of the local community they are.

	Parish	District	Pop	Size Hec	Recd	S.1	S.2	Held	Lost	Never	Sites	Plots	O.Use	Site Size	Admin.	Owner	Est.	Docs
373	Marshland St James 2	WN						Y			1	12		DK	PC	PC	DK	
374	Marshland St James 3	WN						Y			1	9		DK	PC	NCC	DK	
375	Martham	YAR	3126	1184	Y	2		Y			1	83		DK	PC	NCC	DK	
376	Matlaske	NN	124	545	Y	1		N	Y									
377	Mattishall	BRE	2631	1189	Y	1		Y			1	11		DK	PC	PC	DK	Y
378	Mautby	YAR	395	1660	Y	3		N		Y								
379	Melton Constable	NN	518	696	Y	1	Y	Y	Y		1	79		6 Hec	PC	LLO	1896 ?	Y
380	Merton	BRE	113	594	Y	3		N	DK	DK								
381	Methwold	WN	1476	4912	Y	1	Y	Y			1	96		25 Ac	CHA	CHA	1660 ?	
382	Middleton	WN	1516	1301	Y	2		Y			1	8		DK	PC	CHU	DK	
383	Mileham	BRE	538	1166	Y	1	Y	Y			1	16		DK	CHA	CHA	Pre 1920	Y
384	Morley	SN	973	821	Y	1		N	Y									
385	Morningthorpe	SN	253	774	Y	2		N		Y								
386	Morston	NN	86	868	N													
387	Morton-on-the-Hill P.M.	BRO	85	409	Y	3		N		Y								
388	Mulbarton	SN	2827	534	Y	1	Y	Y	Y		1	12		1.5 Ac	CHA	CHA	1976	
389	Mundesley	NN	2695	284	Y	1		N	DK	DK								
390	Mundford	BRE	1591	832	Y	1		N		Y								
391	Mundham	SN	168	631	Y	1		N	Y									
392	Narborough 1	BRE	1095	1405	Y	1	Y	Y			1	4		1.25 Ac	PC	CHU	DK	Y
393	Narborough 2	BRE						Y			1	3		1.5 Ac	LLO	LLO	1960s	
394	Narford P.M.	BRE	41	970	N													
395	Neatishead	NN	537	771	Y	1		N	Y									
396	Necton	BRE	1865	1548	Y	3		N	DK	DK								
397	Needham	SN	310	469	Y	3		N	DK	DK								
398	New Buckenham	BRE	468	173	Y	2		Y			1	12		DK	PC	PC	DK	Y
399	Newton by Castle Acre P.M.	BRE	37	437	Y	3		N	DK	DK								
400	Newton Flotman	SN	1197	487	Y	1	Y	Y			1	21		.52 Hec	DK	PC	1981	
401	Nordelph	WN	375	1657	Y	1		N	Y									
402	North Creake	WN	414	1499	Y	1		N	Y									
403	North Elmham	BRE	1428	1920	Y	1	Y	Y	Y		1	27	Pt. Ag.	30 Ac	PC	PC	1831	Y
404	North Lopham	BRE	605	817	Y	3		N	Y									
405	North Pickenham	BRE	500	1015	Y	3		N	DK	DK								
406	North Runcton	WN	519	599	Y	1	Y	N		Y								
407	North Tuddenham	BRE	305	941	Y	1		N	Y									
408	North Walsham T.C.	NN	11998	1727	Y	1	Y	Y	Y		1	12		0.25 Ac	TC	TC	2000	
409	North Wootton	WN	2387	3233	Y	1		N		Y								
410	Northrepps 1	NN	839	1065	Y	1		Y			1	4		DK	PC	PC	DK	
411	Northrepps 2	NN						Y			1	4		DK	PC	LLO	DK	
412	Northwold 1	WN	1070	1952	Y	1	Y	Y			1	DK	Ag	DK	CHA	CHA	1777 ?	
413	Northwold 2	WN						Y			1	22		DK	CHA	CHA	1777 ?	
414	Norton Subcourse	SN	303	915	Y	2		N	Y									
415	Norwich 1	N	127600	3902	Y	2		Y			1	38		2.9 Ac	CITY	CITY	DK	
416	Norwich 2	N						Y			1	52		3.32 Ac	CITY	CITY	DK	
417	Norwich 3	N						Y			1	51		3.7 Ac	CITY	CITY	DK	
418	Norwich 4	N						Y			1	104		6.4 Ac	CITY	CITY	DK	
419	Norwich 5	N						Y			1	92		7.5 Ac	CITY	CITY	DK	
420	Norwich 6	N						Y			1	29		3.83 Ac	CITY	CITY	DK	
421	Norwich 7	N						Y			1	56		6.33 Ac	CITY	CITY	DK	
422	Norwich 8	N						Y			1	122		6.75 Ac	CITY	CITY	DK	
423	Norwich 9	N						Y			1	13		0.9 Ac	CITY	CITY	DK	
424	Norwich 10	N						Y			1	70		12.05 Ac	CITY	CITY	DK	
425	Norwich 11	N						Y			1	50		5.16 Ac	CITY	CITY	DK	

	Parish	District	Pop	Size Hec	Recd	S.1	S.2	Held	Lost	Never	Sites	Plots	O.Use	Site Size	Admin.	Owner	Est.	Docs
426	Norwich 12	N						Y			1	50		5.2 Ac	CITY	CITY	DK	
427	Norwich 13	N						Y			1	150		11.71 Ac	CITY	CITY	DK	
428	Norwich 14	N						Y			1	500		22.75 Ac	CITY	CITY	DK	
429	Norwich 15	N						Y			1	32		2.68 Ac	CITY	CITY	DK	
430	Norwich 16	N						Y			1	43		2.66 Ac	CITY	CITY	DK	
431	Norwich 17	N						Y			1	12		0.88 Ac	CITY	CITY	DK	
432	Norwich 18	N						Y			1	100		7.55 Ac	CITY	CITY	DK	
433	Old Buckenham	BRE	1294	2006	Y	1		N		Y								
434	Old Catton	BRO	5954	233	Y	1		Y			1	DK		DK	CHA	CHA	DK	
435	Old Hunstanton	WN	47	535	Y	1		N		Y								
436	Ormesby St. Margaret/Scratby	YAR	4021	732	Y	1		Y			1	53		DK	PC	LLO	DK	
437	Ormesby St. Michael	YAR	297	421	Y	1		Y			DK	DK		DK	CHU	CHU	DK	
438	Oulton	BRO	196	1058	Y	1	Y	Y	Y		1	0	Ag	DK	PC	PC	1987	Y
439	Outwell 1	WN	1880	1221	Y	1	Y	Y			1	19		18.5 Ac	PC	PC	1930s	
440	Outwell 2	WN						Y			1	10		11 Ac	PC	PC	1940s	
441	Outwell 3	WN						Y			1	24		15.5 Ac	PC	PC	1950s	
442	Outwell 4	WN						Y			1	38		38 Ac	PC	LLO	1940s	
443	Overstrand	NN	952	186	Y	1	Y	Y			1	26		3.28 Ac	PC	LLO	Pre 1941	Y
444	Ovington	BRE	239	644	Y	3		N	Y									1830	
445	Oxborough	BRE	240	1324	Y	1		N	DK	DK								
446	Paston	NN	265	566	Y	1		N		Y									Y
447	Pentney	WN	387	1039	Y	1		Y			1	14		DK	PC	CHU	DK	
448	Plumstead	NN	120	517	Y	1		N	Y									1830	
449	Poringland	SN	3261	632	Y	1		N		Y								
450	Postwick with Witton	BRO	323	829	Y	2		N	Y									1830	
451	Potterheigham 1	NN	961	1038	Y	1	Y	Y	Y		1	8		12.4 Ac	PC	PC	1909	
452	Potter Heigham 2	NN						Y			1	24		8.5 Ac	PC	NCC	1923	
453	Pudding Norton/Testerton	NN	267	595	Y	1		N		Y								
454	Pulham Market	SN	999	1208	Y	1	Y	Y	Y		1	8	Pt. Am.	1 Ac	LLO	LLO	1966	
455	Pulham St. Mary	SN	866	1226	Y	1	Y	Y			1	22		DK	PC	LLO	DK	
456	Quidenham	BRE	576	2251	Y	3		N	Y									1830-3	
457	Rackheath	BRO	1551	752	Y	1		Y			1	DK		DK	DC	DC	DK	
458	Raveningham	SN	157	805	N													
459	Raynham	NN	257	1675	Y	1		N	Y									
460	Redenhall with Harleston	SN	4058	1373	Y	1		N	Y									
461	Reedham	BRO	925	1245	Y	1		Y			1	4			DC	DC		
462	Reepham T.C.	BRO	2455	1909	Y	2	Y	Y	Y		1	6		DK	TC	TC	1990	
463	Repps with Bastwick	YAR	401	510	Y	1	Y	Y			1	25		8.53 Ac	PC	LLO	1960s ?	
464	Riddlesworth P.M.	BRE	147	826	Y	3		N	DK	DK								
465	Ringland	BRO	217	505	Y	1		N	Y									
466	Ringstead	WN	355	1113	Y	1	Y	Y	Y		1	3		DK	LLO	LLO	Pre 1887	
467	Rockland St. Mary/Hellington	SN	893	764	Y	1		Y			1	15		DK	CHA	CHA	DK	
468	Rocklands	BRE	702	1097	Y	1		N	DK	DK								
469	Rollesby 1	YAR	995	591	Y	1	2	Y			1	20		2 Ac	PC	LLO	1946	
470	Rollesby 2	YAR						Y			1	4		DK	DC	DC	DK	
471	Roudham/Larling	BRE	278	1520	Y	3		Y			1	DK		DK	DK	DK	DK	Y
472	Rougham	BRE	152	1085	Y	2		N	Y										Y
473	Roughton	NN	866	723	N													
474	Roydon	SN	2358	522	Y	1	Y	Y			1	12		0.93 Ac	PC & DK	PC & DK	1986	
475	Roydon	WN	368	462	Y	1		N	Y									1830-3	
476	Runcton Holme	WN	676	1389	Y	2		N		Y								
477	Runhall	SN	365	1198	Y	1		Y			1	11		DK	CHA	CHA	DK	
478	Runton 1	NN	1633	544	Y	1		Y			1	16		DK	PC	PC	DK	

	Parish	District	Pop	Size Hec	Recd	S.1	S.2	Held	Lost	Never	Sites	Plots	O.Use	Site Size	Admin.	Owner	Est.	Docs
479	Runton 2	NN						Y			1	34		DK	PC	PC	DK	
480	Runton 3	NN						Y			1	8		DK	PC	PC	DK	
481	Runton 4	NN						Y			1	24		DK	PC	PC	DK	
482	Ryburgh	NN	668	1004	Y	1		N	Y									
483	Ryston P.M.	WN	93	936	Y	1		N	DK	DK								
484	Saham Toney	BRE	1565	1651	Y	1	Y	Y	Y		1	6	No Lets	1.5 Ac	PC	PC	1930s ?	
485	Salhouse	BRO	1462	896	Y	3		N	DK	DK								
486	Salle P.M.	BRO	50	821	Y	2		N	Y									
487	Salthouse	NN	196	622	Y	1	Y	Y			1	10	Pt Ag	21 Ac	PC	NCC	1940s	
488	Sandringham	WN	402	4191	Y	3		N		Y								
489	Saxlingham Nethergate	SN	676	855	Y	2		N	Y									
490	Scarning	BRE	2932	1413	Y	1		Y			1	20		DK	CHA	CHA	20th C	Y
491	Scole	SN	1339	1490	Y	3		N	Y									
492	Scottow	NN	1774	859	N													
493	Scoulton	BRE	241	902	Y	1		N	Y									
494	Sculthorpe 1	NN	744	852	Y	1		Y			1	12		DK	CHA	CHA	DK	
495	Sculthorpe 2	NN						Y			1	5		DK	CHA	CHA	DK	
496	Sea Palling	NN	488	1105	Y	1		N	DK	DK								
497	Sedgeford	WN	540	1706	Y	1		N	Y									
498	Seething 1	SN	341	678	Y	1		Y			1	1		DK	CHA	CHA	DK	
499	Seething 2	SN						Y			1	5		DK	CHA	CHA	DK	
500	Shelfanger	SN	362	699	Y	1	Y	Y			1	11	Pt. Ag.	9 Ac	CHA	CHA	1879	Y
501	Shelton with Hardwick	SN	283	890	Y	1		N		Y								
502	Sheringham T.C.	NN	7143	400	Y	1	Y	Y	Y		1	61		4 Ac	TC	TC	1954 ?	
503	Shernborne P.M.	WN	59	563	Y	1		N		Y								
504	Shipdham 1	BRE	2145	1869	Y	2	Y	Y			1	12	Pt. Ag.	32 Ac	PC	PC	1918	Y
505	Shipdham 2	BRE						Y			1	14		DK	PC	PC	DK	
506	Shotesham	SN	539	1450	Y	1		N	Y									
507	Shouldham 1	WN	608	1604	Y	1		Y			1	1		DK	PC	PC	DK	
508	Shouldham 2	WN						Y			1	1		DK	PC	PC	DK	
509	Shouldham 3	WN						Y			1	1		DK	PC	PC	Dk	
510	Shouldham Thorpe P.M.	WN	157	587	N													
511	Shropham	BRE	351	1112	Y	1		N		Y								
512	Sidestrand	NN	83	173	Y	1		N		Y								
513	Sisland	SN	44	190	Y	1		N	DK	DK								
514	Skeyton	NN	200	528	Y	2		N		Y								
515	Sloley	NN	255	304	Y	3		N	Y									
516	Smallburgh	NN	518	502	Y	1		N		Y								
517	Snetterton	BRE	202	894	Y	1		N		Y								
518	Snettisham	WN	2374	2803	Y	1		N	DK	DK								
519	Somerton	YAR	257	825	Y	3		N		Y								
520	South Acre P.M.	BRE	32	1015	Y	2		N		Y								
521	South Creake 1	WN	536	2018	Y	1	Y	Y			1	25		7.708 Ac	PC	PC	1890s?	
522	South Creake 2	WN						Y			1	30	Pt. Ag	10.14 Ac	PC	PC	1890s?	
523	South Lopham	BRE	371	791	Y	1		N	Y									
524	South Pickenham	BRE	101	758	Y	1		N	Y									
525	South Walsham	BRO	738	1143	Y	1		N	Y									
526	South Wootton	WN	3717	854	Y	1	Y	Y			1	109		4 Ac	PC	PC	1850	
527	Southery	WN	1161	1812	Y	1		N		Y								
528	Southrepps	NN	758	845	Y	1		Y			1	9		DK	PC	PC	DK	
529	Sparham	BRE	291	722	Y	1		N	Y									
530	Spixworth	BRO	3769	480	Y	1		N	Y									
531	Sporle with Palgrave	BRE	1038	1721	Y	1		N	Y									

	Parish	District	Pop	Size Hec	Recd	S.1	S.2	Held	Lost	Never	Sites	Plots	O.Use	Site Size	Admin.	Owner	Est.	Docs
532	Sprowston	BRO	14027	946	Y	1	Y	Y			1	91		5 Ac	PC	PC	1979	
533	Stalham T.C.	NN	2951	730	Y	1	Y	Y	Y		1	16	1 in use	3 Ac	TC	LLO	DK	
534	Stanfield	BRE	144	380	Y	2		N		Y								
535	Stanford P.M.	BRE	0	1362	Y	3		N		Y								
536	Stanhoe	WN	196	606	Y	1		N	Y									
537	Starston	SN	321	902	Y	3		N	Y									
538	Stibbard	NN	365	668	Y	1	Y	Y			1	5		0.5 Ac	CHA	CHA	Pre 1961	
539	Stiffkey	NN	223	1455	N													
540	Stockton	SN	59	365	Y	1		N	DK	DK								
541	Stody/Hunworth	NN	181	799	Y	1		N	Y									
542	Stoke Ferry	WN	896	915	Y	1		Y			1	DK		DK	DK	LLO	DK	
543	Stoke Holy Cross	SN	1568	927	Y	1		N	Y									
544	Stokesby	YAR	293	861	Y	3		N	Y									
545	Stow Bardolph 1	WN	1014	2468	Y	1		Y			1	7		DK	PC	CHA	DK	
546	Stow Bardolph 2	WN						Y			1	4		DK	PC	CHA	DK	
547	Stow Bardolph 3	WN						Y			1	2		DK	PC	CHA	DK	
548	Stow Bardolph 4	WN						Y			1	3		DK	PC	CHA	DK	
549	Stow Bedon	BRE	287	1368	Y	1		N		Y								
550	Stradsette P.M.	WN	42	545	Y	2		N	Y									
551	Stratton Strawless	BRO	495	714	Y	1		N	Y									
552	Strumpshaw	BRO	602	1169	Y	2		N		Y								
553	Sturston P.M.	BRE	0	781	Y	3		N		Y								
554	Suffield	NN	138	594	Y	2	Y	Y			1	3		DK	LLO	LLO	DK	
555	Surlingham	SN	637	732	Y	3		Y			DK	DK		DK	DK	DK	DK	
556	Sustead/Bessingham/Metton	NN	218	684	Y	1		N	Y									
557	Sutton	NN	1226	634	Y	2		Y			1	DK		DK	DK	DK	1831	
558	Swaffham T.C. 1	BRE	6935	2957	Y	2		Y			1	20		DK	TC	TC	DK	Y
559	Swaffham T.C. 2	BRE						Y			1	105		DK	TC	TC	DK	
560	Swaffham T.C. 3	BRE						Y			1	27		DK	TC	TC	DK	
561	Swaffham T.C. 4	BRE						Y			1	42		DK	TC	TC	DK	
562	Swaffham T.C. 5	BRE						Y			1	50		DK	TC	TC	DK	
563	Swafield/Bradfield	NN	273	643	N													
564	Swainsthorpe	SN	374	338	Y	1	Y	Y			1	3		DK	CHA	CHA	Pre 1943	
565	Swannington/Alderford	BRO	330	770	Y	2		N	Y									
566	Swanton Abbott	NN	436	476	Y	3		N	Y									
567	Swanton Morley	BRE	2415	1114	Y	1		N	Y									
568	Swanton Novers	NN	263	545	Y	1		N	Y									
569	Swardeston	SN	540	395	Y	1		N	Y									
570	Syderstone	WN	532	994	Y	1		Y			DK	DK		DK	CHA	CHA	DK	
571	Tacolneston	SN	699	645	Y	1		N	Y									
572	Tasburgh	SN	1070	371	Y	1		N	DK	DK								
573	Tattersett	NN	902	1138	Y	2		N		Y								
574	Taverham	BRO	10233	870	Y	1		N	Y									
575	Terrington St. Clement 1	WN	3902	4538	Y	1		Y	Y		1	84	Pt. Ag.	22.29 Ac	PC	PC	1816	Y
576	Terrington St. Clement 2	WN						Y			1	45		12.034 Ac	PC	PC	DK	
577	Terrington St. John 1	WN	882	826	Y	1		Y			1	28	Ag	DK	PC	PC	DK	
578	Terrington St. John 2	WN						Y			1	28	Ag	DK	PC	PC	DK	
579	Tharston / Hapton	SN	599	926	Y	1		N	DK	DK								
580	Thelmelthorpe P.M.	BRO	65	269	Y	2		N		Y								
581	Thetford T.C. 1	BRE	21588	2955	Y	2	Y	Y			1	21		DK	TC	TC	Pre 1974	Y
582	Thetford T.C. 2	BRE						Y			1	44		DK	TC	TC	Pre 1974	
583	Thetford T.C. 3	BRE						Y			1	34		DK	TC	TC	Pre 1974	
584	Thetford T.C. 4	BRE						Y			1	11		DK	TC	TC	Pre 1974	

	Parish	District	Pop	Size Hec	Recd	S.1	S.2	Held	Lost	Never	Sites	Plots	O.Use	Site Size	Admin.	Owner	Est.	Docs
585	Thetford T.C. 5	BRE						Y			1	85		DK	TC	TC	Pre 1974	
586	Thetford T.C. 6	BRE						Y			1	8		DK	TC	TC	Pre 1974	
587	Thompson	BRE	341	920	Y	1	Y	Y			1	1		DK	LLO	LLO	DK	
588	Thornage	NN	218	512	Y	1		N	Y									
589	Thornham	WN	478	1347	Y	1		N	Y									
590	Thorpe Market	NN	284	589	Y	1		N		Y								
591	Thorpe St Andrew 1	BRO	13762	9?	Y	1		Y			1	37		DK	PC	NCC	DK	
592	Thorpe St. Andrew 2	BRO						Y			1	67		DK	PC	PC	DK	
593	Thurlton	SN	720	522	Y	1	Y	Y			1	15	Pt. Am.	2.662 Ac	PC	PC	Pre 1989	
594	Thurne	YAR	116	269	Y	1		N	Y									
595	Thurning P.M.	NN	43	647	Y	2		N		Y								
596	Thursford	NN	224	602	Y	3		N	DK	DK								
597	Thurton	SN	567	318	Y	2		N	Y									
598	Thwaite	SN	111	276	Y	1		N		Y								
599	Tibenham	SN	453	1334	Y	3		N	DK	DK								
600	Tilney All Saints	WN	563	1156	N													
601	Tilney St Lawrence	WN	1536	2048	Y	1		Y			1	1		DK	PC	PC	DK	
602	Titchwell P.M.	WN	91	646	Y	1		N	DK	DK								
603	Tittleshall	BRE	407	1382	Y	3		N		Y								
604	Tivetshall St Margaret	SN	266	690	Y	1		N	Y									
605	Tivetshall St Mary	SN	302	465	Y	1		N	DK	DK								
606	Toft Monks	SN	324	687	Y	1	Y	Y			1	10	Ag. Let.	DK	CHA	PC	1906	Y
607	Topcroft	SN	268	776	Y	3		N	Y									
608	Tottenhill	WN	231	590	Y	1		N	Y									
609	Tottington P.M.	BRE	0	1312	Y	3		N		Y								
610	Trimingham	NN	370	233	Y	3		N	Y									
611	Trowse with Newton 1	SN	479	450	Y	2	Y	Y	Y		1	54		DK	PC	LLO	1921	
612	Trowse with Newton 2	SN						Y			1	20		DK	PC	LLO	1921	
613	Trunch 1	NN	805	549	Y	2	Y	Y			1	14		0.5 Ac	PC	CHU	1941	Y
614	Trunch 2	NN						Y			1	8		0.25 Ac	PC	CHU	1941	
615	Tunstead	NN	674	1132	Y	1		N		Y								
616	Twyford P.M.	BRE	26	213	Y	3		N	DK	DK								
617	Upper Sheringham	NN	214	619	Y	2		Y			DK	DK		DK	CHA	CHA	DK	
618	Upton with Fishley 1	BRO	660	893	Y	1	Y	Y	Y		1	20	Ag.	11.76 Ac	PC	PC	DK	
619	Upton with Fishley 2	BRO						Y			1	1		.125 Ac	PC	LLO	1930s	
620	Upwell 1	WN	2456	2765	Y	1		Y			1	25		DK	PC	PC	DK	
621	Upwell 2	WN						Y			1	16		DK	PC	PC	DK	
622	Upwell 3	WN						Y			1	15		DK	PC	CHU	DK	
623	Upwell 4	WN						Y			1	18		DK	PC	CHA	DK	
624	Wacton	SN	319	454	Y	3		N		Y								
625	Walpole 1	WN	1707	1927	Y	1	Y	Y			1	7		DK	PC	DC	DK	
626	Walpole 2	WN						Y			1	16		16 Ac	PC	PC	Pre 1920	
627	Walpole 3	WN						Y			1	22		23 Ac	PC	PC	Pre 1920	
628	Walpole Cross Keys	WN	469	403	Y	1		N	Y									
629	Walpole Highway	WN	685	1048	N													
630	Walsingham/Egmere	NN	864	1898	Y	1		Y			DK	DK		DK	LLO	LLO	DK	
631	Walsoken	WN	1484	1257	Y	1	Y	Y			1	27	1 Tenant	DK	PC	NCC	1934	
632	Warham	NN	193	1865	Y	1		N	Y									
633	Watlington	WN	2031	693	Y	1		N	Y									
634	Watton T.C.	BRE	6819	720	Y	1	Y	Y			1	18		0.242 Hec	TC	TC	1990	Y
635	Weasenham All Saints	BRE	178	816	Y	1		N	Y									
636	Weasenham St. Peter	BRE	166	579	Y	3		N	Y									
637	Weeting with Broomhill	BRE	1751	2516	Y	1		N	DK	DK								

	Parish	District	Pop	Size Hec	Recd	S.1	S.2	Held	Lost	Never	Sites	Plots	O.Use	Site Size	Admin.	Owner	Est.	Docs
638	Wellingham	BRE	55	439	Y	1		N		Y								
639	Wells T.C. 1	NN	2451	1631	Y	1	Y	Y			1	90		DK	TC	TC	1875	Y
640	Wells T.C. 2	NN						Y			1	112		DK	TC	TC	1875	
641	Welney	WN	528	2073	Y	1		N	Y									
642	Wendling	BRE	323	525	Y	2		N		Y								
643	Wereham	WN	626	859	Y	1		N	Y									
644	West Acre	WN	187	1449	Y	3		N	DK	DK								
645	West Beckham	NN	222	311	Y	3		Y			1	10		4.3 Ac	PC	DC	DK	
646	West Caister	YAR	195	685	Y	3		N										
647	West Dereham	WN	440	1351	Y	1	Y	Y			1	26	Pt. Ag.	20 Ac	PC	PC	Pre 1922	
648	West Rudham	WN	213	1181	Y	1	Y	Y	Y		1	5		0.35 Ac	PC	LLO	1983	
649	West Walton 1	WN	1659	1577	Y	1		Y			1	64		DK	PC	PC	DK	
650	West Walton 2	WN						Y			1	40		DK	PC	PC	DK	
651	West Winch	WN	2596	802	Y	1		N	Y									
652	Weston Longville	BRO	303	1124	Y	1	Y	Y			1	6		0.48 Ac	PC	PC	1982	
653	Westwick P.M.	NN	72	488	Y	1		N		Y								
654	Weybourne	NN	518	691	Y	1		Y			1	18		DK	PC	PC	DK	
655	Whinburgh / Westfield	BRE	307	756	Y	1	Y	Y	Y		1	12	Pt. Ag.	2 Ac	CHA	CHA	Pre 1966	Y
656	Whissonsett	BRE	483	557	Y	1	Y	Y			1	33	5 Let	5 Ac	PC	PC	Pre 1930s	Y
657	Wicklewood 1	SN	886	875	Y	1	Y	Y			1	DK	Ag Let	10 Ac	PC	PC	Pre 1962	
658	Wicklewood 2	SN						Y			1	33	Pt Ag	8.5 Ac	PC	PC	Pre 1962	
659	Wickmere / Mannington	NN	125	707	Y	1		N		Y								
660	Wiggenhall St. Germans	WN	1155	1898	Y	3		Y	Y		1	10		0.5 Ac	LLO	LLO	1971	
661	Wiggenhall St. Mary	WN	687	1776	Y	2	Y	Y			1	60		30 Ac	PC	PC	1900	
662	Wighton 1	NN	203	1193	Y	1	Y	Y			1	2	Pt Ag	6 Ac	LLO	LLO	1913	
663	Wighton 2	NN						Y			1	1		DK	CHA	CHA	DK	
664	Wimbotsham 1	WN	558	604	Y	1	Y	Y			1	9		6.105 Ac	A.Ass	LLO	1900	
665	Wimbotsham 2	WN						Y			1	2		11.125 Ac	A.Ass	LLO	DK	
666	Wimbotsham 3	WN						Y			1	0	Ag Let	3.25 Ac	A.Ass	LLO	DK	
667	Winfarthing	SN	403	1080	Y	1		N		Y								
668	Winterton on Sea	YAR	1359	570	Y	1	Y	Y			1	69		DK	PC	PC	DK	
669	Witton / Ridlington	NN	298	977	Y	3		N	DK	DK								
670	Wiveton	NN	158	425	N													
671	Wood Dalling	BRO	181	989	Y	3		N		Y								
672	Wood Norton	NN	221	699	Y	1		N		Y								
673	Woodbastwick	BRO	362	1904	Y	1		N		Y								
674	Woodton	SN	472	885	Y	2		N	Y									
675	Wormegay	WN	339	1218	Y	1		N	Y									
676	Worstead 1	NN	862	1065	Y	1		Y			1	5		DK	CHU	CHU	DK	
677	Worstead 2	NN						Y			1	3		DK	DC	DC	DK	
678	Wortwell	SN	574	460	Y	2	Y	Y			1	12		1.18 Ac	PC	PC	DK	
679	Wreningham	SN	493	624	Y	1		N		Y								
680	Wretham	BRE	366	3225	Y	2		N		Y								
681	Wretton	WN	392	470	Y	3		Y			1	DK	Ag Let	5 Ac	DK	DK	DK	
682	Wroxham	BRO	1532	621	Y	1		N	Y									
683	Wymondham T.C. 1	SN	12539	4431	Y	1	Y	Y			1	15		145 Rods	TC	TC	1964	
684	Wymondham T.C 2	SN						Y			1	8		80 Rods	TC	LLO	1980	
685	Yaxham	BRE	677	664	Y	1		N	DK	DK								

case studies

Buxton
Castle Acre
Cley-next-the-Sea
Costessey Estate
Dereham and District Allotment and Leisure Garden Association
incorporating   Cemetery Road   Scarning
                   Dumpfield   Toftwood
                   Cherry Lane 1 and 2   Westfield
                   Southend   North Elmham

Docking
Great Snoring
Gresham
Harleston
Litcham
Little Melton
Little Plumstead
Methwold
Norwich
Oulton with Irmingland
Potter Heigham
Reepham
Salthouse
Terrington-St-Clement
Thompson
Toft Monks
Topcroft
Trowse
West Winch

Buxton

In the nineteenth century Dudswick House was owned by Quakers, the Wrights. At enclosure in 1809 it was John Wright, Esq (died 1830) and in 1845 White's *Trade Directory* records that his son, also named John, was a benefactor who created school rooms for the village in 1833. White's makes no mention of allotments but family papers from the 1880s include a rent record for the year 1881 which show that there were nineteen tenants, of whom eight paid the full rent of 10s-6d per year, nine paid a half-rent of 5s-3d and the remaining three paid 7s each. Two of the tenants were widows, following normal practice for the period, and suggesting that the site had been in existence for many years prior to the 1880s. A twentieth century map shows the site, part of the estate bounded by Lion Road to the north of the village, as being of 1.80 acres.

After World War 2 interest in allotment-holding declined until in the 1980s only two plot-holders remained. The current owner converted the site into woodland.

Thanks to Mr Charles Briscoe

Castle Acre [pictures]

In 1843, when the town was an open parish and prey to a large shifting population, the Reverend J H Bloom of Castle Acre wrote:

'It has been the fashion to single out the parish of Castle Acre as the most conspicuous in point of demoralisation and general depravity within the circuit of many miles and until within the last few years there has been, we fear, but too strong ground for the conclusion; but then it is only justice to indicate the main source of evil and the still-existing obstacle to its effectual eradication. It is simply this: a custom has for many years prevailed in the place and been encouraged by the occupiers in adjacent parishes, to farm out the work necessary to be done on their respective lands to one or two individuals who shall provide hands to accomplish it in the best manner and on the most reasonable terms. These parties are termed *gang* masters, and a very significant term it is, for surely no gang of wretched slaves beneath the sweltering sun of the tropics could materially fall beneath the generality of persons thus assembled together in intellectual debasement and moral depravity. The gang-masters, anxious to reap as much advantage to themselves as possible from their bargain with their employers, seek about in all directions for idle hands to execute their work on the cheapest terms they can procure them at. What is the result? – Vagrants – the very scum and refuse of the county jails – homeless, houseless wanderers with perhaps the brand of infamy upon them…Short as their term of service might prove, it has been sufficient to inoculate the place, in the congenial hot-bed of the ale-house, with the virus of depravity, vice and cunning…' (Bloom, p308).

It is not surprising to find that there are no references to charities other than small disbursements of money to the poor until as late as 1883. Zachary Clark in 1811 lists the seventeenth century bequest of Mr Coney from rents of land, shrunk to ten shillings per year, according to Brougham in 1843; and Brougham also records Allee's Charity of £7-16s per year to be divided among the poor of Castle Acre, East and North Lexham, Great Dunham, Beeston, **Litcham** and Newton. In 1845

White's *Trade Directory* refers to two commons for pasturage, amounting to 32 acres in the 1880s. Castle Acre is also notable for its spread of nonconformist chapels, representing Wesleyans (for a few years only) and Primitive Methodists as well as having a Baptist Meeting Room. The Odd Fellows' Hall was used later, in the 1920s, as the meeting place of the Agricultural Workers' Union.

By the time of the first record of allotments Castle Acre was no longer swelled by transients seeking work and tenants were drawn from a stable population. In 1880 'most but not all agricultural land in the parish belonged to the Holkham Estate, the first year allotment rents appear in the Audit Books'. Rent for the first allotments was £3-10s for the year. In 1889 'W D Everington, the Holkham tenant at the Lodge Farm had £15-11s-2d deducted from his rent, for Labourers' Allotments, an area of 14 acres 3 roods 2 poles. He was paid 17s-6d for fencing the allotments...' (Garry, letter of 10 october 2006). By 1890 the total of rents collected for allotments in the parish was £41-12s-1d.

In 1894 the Local Authorities Act created parish councils and Castle Acre, already with a substantial acreage of garden or strip allotments to its credit, became even more active in seeking lands for that purpose. 'The early Minute Books of the Parish Council, that is from january 1895 onwards, are almost entirely devoted to matters to do with allotments'. Even at this early stage the land given to allotments was extensive: 'at one point there were c.77 acres of land used as allotments, let in quarter-acre plots. The administration was so great that the Parish Council appointed an Allotment Overseer in may 1895, a Mr E Hunsley' (Garry, ibid).

'During the 1890s the Parish Council actively sought land for allotments outside the parish. They approached Mr H Gayford of Raynham, the agent for the Fountaine family of Narford Hall, requesting the rent of a three-acre field called White Post Break at eighteen shillings per year and more land in South Acre, probably Castle Acre Break. These lands in the parish of South Acre were and continue to be let by the Narford Estate. They appear on the 1905 O/S map as land south-east of the town towards Hungry Hill. (Garry, ibid).

'In 1897 the Parish Council again wrote to Mr H Gayford, wishing to rent land in the centre of the village of Castle Acre but owned by the Narford Estate known as School Gardens and the rent was agreed at £15 per year. In 1905 the Holkham Estate purchased School Gardens from Narford. The rents collected by the Parish Council in 1897 amounted to £55' (Garry, ibid).

There are no hints in the civil parish authority's records why Castle Acre was so fertile a parish for the creation of garden allotments. Based on figures provided by trade directories for the period, the parish population was at the high end of the density spectrum for a rural settlement but not exceptional. Evidently there was symbiosis between the local landowners and parish residents: the Holkham Estate, as we have seen from the evidence given to Poor Law Commissioners and the Survey, favoured allotments. There must have been a great local demand in the 1890s given that site maps of Kitchen Close, Guannocks (dating to as early as 1897 (NRO ACC 2005/95)) and Taylor's Pightle are marked with 96 plots, 40 plots and 19 plots each and Minutes talk of quarter-acre and half-acre usually, mention one-acre plots rarely. Demand continued into the 1900s, even though tenancies were severed through non-payment of rents or when tenants moved away from Castle Acre, there being a steady supply of applicants.

1906 Ordnance Survey maps for the area give five sites

(a) 53.67 acres to the south-east of the town, towards Hungry Hill (Narford Estate Land, in the parish of South Acre);

(b) 22.283 acres south-west of Pale's Green, bounding Dyke Hills (School Gardens);

(c) 27.199 acres to the east of the Peddar's Way, north of the town (Kitchen Close);

(d) 10.570 acres to the north-east of the town, off Orchard Lane (Guannocks);

(e) 4.824 acres on the east side of the town, east of Sandy Lane (Taylor's Pightle).

This gives a magnificent total of at least 118.546 acres of allotments.

In 2005 the Parish Clerk notified the Norfolk Recorders of five allotment sites.

'...we have two types of allotments in the village:

(i)   'garden allotments – small areas used for growing vegetables and there are two sites for these. One of these sites is administered by the Parish Council and has 28 plots [known as School Gardens]. The second lot of garden allotments, approximately one acre overlooked by the church, is administered directly by Holkham Estate. The Court Rolls 'revealed that Holkham owned a small percentage of the land in the north-east corner of the allotments nearest the churchyard boundary by 1840 but the main part belonged to the Morley family till at least 1914. There is no record of when the Morleys or their descendants sold the land [to the Holkham Estate]' (Garry, email 18 december 2006);

(ii)   'agricultural allotments. There are three fields of these, once upon a time divided into strips and worked in small numbers by numerous residents often co-operating to grow a field crop. These fields are known as Taylor's Pightle with nineteen plots, Guannocks Field with forty plots and Kitchen Close with 96 plots. Today these fields are worked by only four people.

'All of the allotments, both garden and agricultural are owned by Holkham Estate with the Parish Council administering School Gardens and the three agricultural fields' (letter from Rosita Sheen, Clerk to the Castle Acre Parish Council, dated 2 march 2004).

Thanks to Ms Rosita Sheen, Clerk to the Castle Acre Parish Council and Ms Mary Anne Garry

use and value
Cley-next-the-Sea [pictures]

The Survey has been the beneficiary of an account and documents giving the background, and details of the current status, of the allotments at Cley from the Trustees of the Trust that administers the site, the Miss H D Knott Will Trust. They show that there were agreements between the landowning families and parishioners as early as 1882. (Some of the tenants named in those agreements were still renting allotments as late as november 1884 (Joint Trustee's letter of 8 november 2005)). Prior to that there were 52 acres of Poor's Allotments awarded at the 1812 Inclosure, according to White's *Trade Directory* of 1845; the same source makes no allusion to garden allotments in the parish at that time.

Having acquired the Cley Hall and estate in 1839 the nonconformist Cozens-Hardy dynasty suffered financial hardship through the agricultural depression of the 1880s and onwards. The then-occupant of Cley Hall, Clement Williams Cozens-Hardy was a Liberal and of a philanthropic nature, much involved in promoting education through the Cley School Board and the Norfolk County Council of which he was one of the original members. He also advocated the provision of allotments (Cannadine, p189) and served on the first Corporation Allotments Committee through the harsh years of economic depression. A 1906 Ordnance Survey map confirms their existence at the current location at that time.

Clement's younger brother, Herbert, became Liberal Member of Parliament for North Norfolk after the Third Reform Act 1895 through the voting power of the agricultural labourer. Herbert was 'much concerned with the depressed state of agriculture ...[and] a classic example of the country gentleman in politics, even though that breed was well in retreat by then, both at Westminster and in Norfolk' (Carradine, p191). Focusing his attention on matters Norfolk, he asked questions about allotments in Norfolk (Carradine, p192).

The Cozens-Hardy family suffered a devastating blow when they lost sons in World War 1. The estate fell to daughters, the younger of whom transferred the Cley lands to the Knott family. Much of the land has been sold off since then.

In 1998 tenants wrote to Miss Knott, appealing for their plots to be spared from the sale of the thirty acres of allotment lands then existing. Most of that land was let to a few farmers but the garden allotment tenants argued:

'Some of us have had our allotments for generations, others for only a few years. All have worked hard improving the land, it is the working of the land and reaping the benefit in what it produces that is so important to us. For some it is the most important and rewarding occupation of our lives'.

A site of five acres for garden allotments was spared and the Parish Council made an agreement with the Trustees.

In december 2005 the Norfolk Recorders received a letter from one of the Joint Trustees of the Trust, providing documents and an account of an inspection made in august 2005 by Trustees, managing agents and Cley Parish Council to address problems – they were legion – on the site. Most were due to Parish Council failure of duty to maintain or enforce the regulations. The account presents a picture of dilapidation and dereliction of fences and gates and of resulting trespass and vandalism by humans and animals and the dumping of waste – old furniture, gas canisters, all manner of horrible and dangerous detritus; and of failure to cultivate and care, of misuse of the site for garages and parked cars, of transferred tenancies and even a shed in which a former tenant lived.

A sad end for a worthy vision but not without hope. The parties to the inspection came to a comprehensive agreement which would see the facilities and protections of the site improved by the Parish Council and an attempt by the tenants to form an allotments association, to encourage through a produce show and competition (trophies to be supplied by the Trustees) a new spirit of commitment to allotment gardening in Cley. A recent letter from the Trustee (28 may 2006) reports that 'significant progress is being made at the allotments and all parties are working to improve conditions...a number of new allotment holders have taken plots'. The photographs of the site taken at this time confirm that *remarkable* progress has been made in a short space of time, and that the allotments are thriving and an asset to community and tenants alike.

(1)   David Carradine *Aspects of Aristocracy: grandeur and decline in modern Britain* (Yale UP, 1994), generously supplied along with other documents by John Ebdon, Joint Trustee of the Miss H D Knott Will Trust.

Thanks to Mr John Ebdon, Joint Trustee of the Miss H D Knott Will Trust

Costessey

When the Costessey Estate was sold in 1918 the Sale Particulars revealed 33 lots of cottages, singly, in pairs or triples and with varying pieces of land attached from the smallest at 0.160 acres to the largest at 1.754 acres. Most of the pieces approximated to the quarter- or half-acre. Additionally were described 'cottages with land' of 5.274 acres, a 'cottage and smallholding' at 6.554 acres and another a 'cottage and fruit and kitchen gardens' of 22.238 acres. The picture it offered of this Estate was of tenant workers having some independence and a stake in the agricultural life of the county.

The Costessey Estate also offered three lots of allotments for sale:

(i)   48.2376 acres marked to the east of Long Lane at Bawburgh, shown on the map appended to the Particulars as 'NCC Allotments'. A note shows that this land was let to the Norfolk County Council for fourteen years from 14 october 1911 at £36-3s-9d per year;

(ii) 23.347acres to the east of Harts Lane on the Main Road, let to Bawburgh Parish Council on a yearly tenancy at £32 per year;

(iii) allotment gardens of 2.605 acres at Costessey (not marked on the map). They were on the edge of the village bounded to the south by the Green Hills and let to Mr C Cannell on a yearly tenancy of £68 per year, due to expire in 1919.

Later records including Ordnance Survey maps do not show Bawburgh as having allotments and the Survey records that they were lost.

OS maps of 1929 and 1938 (the Special Emergency edition) show allotments in Costessey:

(1)   a site to the south of Town House Lane (now Road);

(2)   a site between Folgate Lane and Sidney Road, above the

Vicarage (from the description this may be (ii) above);

(1) but not (2) was still shown on a 1946 map.

The Survey has generated some valuable background to the history of Costessey allotments.

Under the 1860 Inclosure Award the poor of Costessey were granted two parcels of land:

(a)   four acres for Exercise and Recreation;

(b)   ten acres 'for the Labouring Poor' with a commercial rent of £8 per year placed on it.

These sites border West End Road.

In a letter Costessey Parish Council identified (a) as ' "The Old Cricket Ground" and woodland to the east of the present allotment site' and (b) as 'all the allotments…in the main allotment area and Plots A–G…at the rear of properties in the West End' (letter of 26 april 2005). It is immediately apparent that these allotments were unmentioned in the Sale Particulars (so perhaps (i)–(iii) represented a private arrangement between Estate owner and tenants) and are curiously absent from O/S maps. According to the Parish Council, at the start of the twentieth century the allotments 'fell into disuse…and were allowed to lie fallow, possibly because of a combination of the high water table and the non-replacement of soil meant that they were non-viable'.

The Parish Council states that the ten-acre site, (b), is divided into two:

(b.1) Plots 1–34, about ten rods (a quarter-acre) each;

(b.2) Plots A–G, of various sizes.

They continue:
'Much work has recently been carried out by the British Trust for Conservation Volunteers (BCTV) and more is planned for May and June this year [2005]. After completion of this work, the fencing along the north side of the main allotment area will have been replaced as will the wooden bridge in the main allotment path and barriers will have been placed along this path wherever ditches abut it. A new metal gate has also replaced the broken five-bar gate to allotment plots A–G. Regular clearing-up and

grass-cutting along the main allotment path is carried out by arrangement with the Norwich Youth Offending Team whenever possible.

'Plots 7–17 are not currently let since they are being used for a conservation project run by the Wensum Valley Project. Plots 11 and 12 have been converted to a wildflower meadow and it is hoped to expand this to other plots with possible access from adjoining woodland to the east and eventually no access from the main allotment area. Whether this will come to fruitition is not yet known, but any plots not required will be returned to allotment usage. With the exception of the above plots, Plot 6 and Plot F (both inaccessible) and Plot 21 (too near the south fence and used as a footpath from the Old Cricket Ground), all the remaining plots are currently let with one of them split into half-plots. There are also ten people on the current waiting list for plots.'

From their beginnings until the present, the allotments have offered a rich and varied programme of possibilities for local people. Their provision and maintenance by a number of sources, private and public, has enabled local people to use local land for their own projects and interests, adapted over time to local conditions and needs.

Thanks to Mr Philip Leach, Clerk's Assistant, Costessey Parish Council

Dereham and District Allotment and Leisure Garden Association [pictures]

Before the Agricultural Revolution *'arable lands in East Anglia were mainly champaign (or open fields) in which the strips of the copyhold tenants lay, scattered and hedgeless, marked only by dole-stones – there is one mentioned by Etling Green – ditches or by meres...so that the whole looked like some vast allotment patch'.*

Boston and E Puddy
Dereham (1954)

Dereham is at the centre of a thriving community of allotments which together form the Dereham and District Allotments and Gardeners Association, one of very few associations in Norfolk and active in expressing and representing its members' interests. The group comprises, in Dereham, the following sites:

- Cemetery Road
- Dumpfield
- Cherry Lane 1 and 2
- Southend
- Toftwood
- Moorgate
- St Nicholas' Church

and in the surrounding area:

- Scarning
- Westfield
- North Elmham

In Dereham all but St Nicholas' Church site are owned and let by the Town Council: it is let privately by the Diocese. The village sites are run by their Parish Councils. Formerly there were allotments owned by the railway, as was usual, and let to their employees but these disappeared with the railway.

In 1251 Bishop Hugh de Northwold surveyed his manor and itemized

▪ pastures and woods and commons;

▪ landowners and those 'new enfeoffed', including those who had either a <u>place</u> [possibly a small enclosed pasture], or <u>messuage</u> [a strip in an open field which had been in grass and was enclosed for a variable length of time]. The survey listed

- 'Ralph, son of Vincent, holds a <u>pightle</u> of land by his messuage for half a penny';

- 'Richard Starling holds a certain piece of land for half a penny at the feast of St Michael' [apparently the farming year began at Michaelmas for his tenants, just as allotment tenancies are recorded as having done (Oulton, Little Plumstead)];

- 'William Ede holds a <u>dickstede</u> for one penny at the feast of St Michael' (Ben Norton, *The Story of Dereham* (Phillimore, 1994)).

Some enclosure had taken place in 688. In the Dooms (or laws) of Inclosure:

'If ceorl have…gedole land to tyne [divided strips to fence] and some have fenced their strips and some have not and stray cattle eat their common acres let those who own the gap compensate those who have fenced their strip' (Seebohm *English Village Community*, p110).

Systematic enclosure took place in 1626 and 1676 but the number of enclosures increased in the eighteenth century so that by the time parliamentary enclosure came in the Acts of 1812 only commons remained. There were no allotments for the poor provided for in the Act. A massive workhouse had been built to the north of the town at Gressenhall in 1777.

Toftwood appears to have been the first to take advantage of the 1812 enclosure:

'In 1815, under the award for Dereham, Toftwood Common was one of those enclosed, commoners whose common-rights were extinguished were compensated by an allotment of land. The common was divided into so many allotments that they were too small to be of agricultural value to their owners. Each was more suited for a garden allotment or the building of a small house or bungalow and in due course Toftwood became a suburb – without sewerage' (Boston and Puddy, p225).

The Ordnance Survey map for 1928 shows 5.633 acres of Toftwood Common as allotments, on the site now occupied by the Fred Nicholson School.

Although Zachary Clark's 1811 gazeteer of Norfolk charities and Brougham Poor Law survey of 1843 referred only to charities for the poor for Toftwood, both involved small pieces of land which were rented. Goodwin in 1659 left 'about two acres of land…for the use of the poor for ever' and this produced £2-5s in rent. Brougham reckoned Goodwin's bequest at three acres, producing £9-10s by the later date. Clark also recorded a 1763 Terrier for a cottage 'and piece of land of 30 rods [0.190 acre] for poor persons' but this 'has not been noticed since'. Brougham's record shows an 'allotment of 1 acre 2 roods', small enough to count as a single plot, bringing £3 per year.

In about 1992 a housing development utilized allotment land but the allotments were then replaced with land bought from a local farmer to create the present site of 2.27 acres which provides 41 plots of which 38 were taken by 29 tenants in 2005.

Dereham – Cemetery Road/Dumpfield Notes made by the current Secretary of the D&DALG Association show that Cemetery Road allotments, adjoining the waterworks, were the first to be created on the outskirts of the town. The waterworks was built in 1870; the Ordnance Survey map for 1882 shows the site already marked 'allotment gardens'. By 1906 maps the; site had been complemented by Dumpfield.

O/S 1906 and 1928 show a number of allotment sites in the centre of Dereham.

- There are two sites attached to Elvin Road, one to the north-west of 1.303 acres and another to the south which had gone for housing development by 1928.

- A site to the west of London Road, attached to the Agricultural Implement Manufactury is probably the Baxter Row site (which the Notes allude to as lost) next to the National School (presumably now the Northgate High School).

- There were sites on railway land. The Great Eastern Railway brought a line to Dereham in 1846. The 1906 map shows a site just south of the station, in a triangle of land between branching lines which by 1928 had been encroached upon by a turntable and engine shed; and another to the west of the station and sitting on the north side of the Lynn branchline, of 4.287 acres. There is also mention of railway allotments at **Scarning** (now a separate parish) which would have been available to railway workers.

- Dereham was formerly a town of plant nurseries. O/S 1906 shows that there were two further sites attached to Nursery Buildings to the east of the station and track where now stands an industrial estate. The first of these of 2.490 acres had been taken for building development by 1928 but the second, of 2.5530 acres, remained.

The Notes mention the loss of Baxter Row allotments in the same paragraph as that of Lynn Hill, ?Stod Lane and **Southend**. Another site, Larner's Drift, is recorded as having been sold some years before 2002 for £23 000-00 which money was not used by the Town Council for allotment improvements but left in a kitty. So much was learned by

Colin Nickerson of the Eastern Region NSALG when in 2002–3 the Town Council threatened to take Cemetery Road. But there remain to Dereham not only the Cemetery Road and Dumpfield sites, and Southend and Toftwood, but the **Cherry Lane/1** and **/2** adjoining sites, of 5.313 acres and 2.638 acres respectively, and Scarning at 1.1719 acres. Judging by the housing surrounding Cherry Lane these were created post-World War 2.

Additionally there is a small and picturesque site of some six plots on land belonging to St Nicholas' Church in the heart of the town, and administered by the Parochial Church Council.

The Scarning site is one of possibly three that have existed there. An 1882 O/S map showed a site of ten garden plots on ground adjoining White Lodge. As we noted, Scarning also had railway allotments, of 5.706 acres, shown on O/S 1928 as west of Scarning Fen and south of the railway line and these were held until the 1980s. The 1906 and 1928 O/S maps show Grove House on the Scarning Road with an allotment site attached of 2.447 acres; the modern Town Council-administered site, also next to a large (probably nineteenth century) house is of 1.719 acres which may make it identical to the Scarning Road/Grove House site but diminished. The Survey completed for the Norfolk Recorders by the Town Council records two sites, the one of 1.719 acres and a site owed to private tenancy from the Scarning United Charities. Whether this is separate from or identical to other sites mentioned here cannot be discovered.

Westfield The parish of Whinburgh and Westfield recorded in the Survey that there was a site of approximately twelve plots, situated at the hamlet of Westfield which was administered by the Westfield Fuel Charity. Attached to a useful letter from the Trust were papers of the 1810 Inclosure Act with very helpful maps and from the Charity Commission, dated 1965. These documents allow us to know the history of the two sites allotted at the enclosure award of 29 september 1812, one known as **Lolly Moor** and the other **Vinegar Hill**. Both, but the first especially, are on waste and soggy waste at that; and so they were intended as fuel allotments.

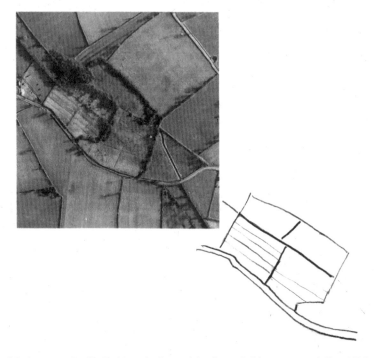

Aerial photograph of Lolly Moor in the parish of Westfield, now a Norfolk Wildlife Trust site. Lines marked on the diagram indicate drains; parallel lines, from field walking are not drains and may indicate strips. (Thanks to Norfolk Archeological Unit, Gressenhall).

Lolly Moor, of 5.330 acres remains an intact site today, thought always to be a fuel allotment from which the poor gleaned wood. In 1843 Brougham noted that the allotment produced £30-10s in rent and so was an instrument for raising cash to be spent on fuel, later distributed as fuel to the poor. An O/S map of 1906 showed the site as allotments and an aerial photograph of 1964 shows ditches and drains as well as lines that look suspiciously like garden strips, and which inspection confirms are not drains. Later on the land was leased for shooting rights and in 1978 the Norfolk Wildlife Trust, 'very caring tenants' started to lease the land, on which there is public access. They warn that the land remains boggy but 'supports a wide diversity of habitat', including marsh marigolds and orchids. The NWT conclude, 'the meadow flowers make a spectacular show'.

The same O/S 1906 map shows a pightle opposite the Primitive Methodist Church of the hamlet of Westfield of 3.291 acres, marked as allotments.

The Vinegar Hill allotments, administered by the Fuel Charity, are of 1.840 acres and in a curious dog-leg shape with a narrow band of land running beside some cottages to the lane, opening into two large fields behind the cottages. The land was cultivated 'until quite recently' (written in march 2005) when the tenants died: the plots are now rented to two, one of whom grazes her horse on her portion and the other is used for beehives. The strip at the side of the cottages is still used by the people whose cottage adjoins for producing vegetables, and a spectacular show it is.

Norwich allotment fairs – 2001 (top) and 2005 (bottom). (Thanks to Norwich City Council for 2001 pictures.)

Recent changes and additions in Norfolk – Hellesdon (top) moved to a new location in 2001, Aldborough (middle) was created at the millennium and Stalham before (2004) and after (2006). (Thanks to Clive Grint and Steve Taylor of Hellesdon Parish Council)

North Elmham The papers that were received in response to the Survey from the Parish Council inform us that their allotment land was bequeathed in perpetuity to the village as a charitable trust by the 1940 will of Annie Mary Smith, but that the site was established 'many years before 1939–45 War – have personal knowledge of this'. The land was of thirty acres in total of which a small portion contained 27 allotments plots, the rest being leased as arable land. At the time of the Survey, the plots had diminished to four, held by one man and his wife who produced vegetables on them for many years.

Attendance at the 2004 Annual General Meeting of the D&DALG Association revealed a thriving allotment scene for the town and environs. The dispute over Cemetery Road had been resolved in the Association's favour and the relationship with Dereham Town Council mended. Security measures and boundary issues would be improved by the Council: some sites reported invasions by local youngsters or residents exercising dogs. Take up of plots was good, with few vacancies on most sites. It had been a good year for produce, despite the incursions of pigeons and pheasants. The Association was clearly very supportive of its members. There were representatives from each site reporting to the Committee and the Committee itself saw the sites, not least to judge the winner of the Best Allotment Competition. There were prizes for produce, impressively won for a gigantic marrow by the young son of a tenant. The Association represents a thriving community that augurs well for its future.

Thanks to Ms Alice Urqhart and Ms Susan Lake, Secretary
to the D&DALG Association

Docking

Allotments in Docking were created at the enclosure of the commons in 1861 when four acres were allocated to the poor for recreation and four acres for sixteen garden plots, according to White's Trade Directory of 1864. From the same source they were still there in 1883.

The lords of the manor in Docking were the Hares who 'took possession of the Manor of Southmere and an estate in Docking in 1743…[In White's Trade Directory of 1854 it was stated]…The Rev H J Hare owns all Southmere, now called Summerfield Manor, and about one-half of the parish of Docking'. A map of 1937 shows the Manor and its lands including a field marked 'Allotment Gardens'. of (by estimate from the Ordnance Survey map for the area) approximately 49 acres, at the very southern edge of the estate on the west side of Docking and bordering the railway (all based on *Land Use of Norfolk*).

The Survey was rewarded with a full account from the parish record of the existing site. The first mention of allotments is in the Minute Book in 1919 when the Parish Council rented land from the lords of the manor, the Hare family. In 1932 and 1936 the rents paid to the landlord were £103-9s-6d and £78-1s-3d respectively, which, if rents were comparable with other sites in Norfolk for that time, suggests that a large amount of land was let. In 1949 the Allotment Register records a total of 69 acres. By 1993 the site had shrunk to 47.5 acres, Major Hare having 'taken over all the larger tenants as direct tenants to himself'. The Parish Council account goes on, 'Around 1940s, 1950s and onwards many tenants acquired more than one plot, exchanged plots and virtually became smallholders. Pigs and poultry were kept and sugarbeet, barley and wheat were grown. When I took over as Clerk in 1985 the largest tenancy was 9.5 acres!' The Clerk of the Council has indicated where this large acreage was and it, too, bordered the railway line.

The present-day allotment site is 3.5 acres, having fourteen garden plots, including 1.75 acres let to a farmer.

Thanks to the Clerk to Docking Parish Council

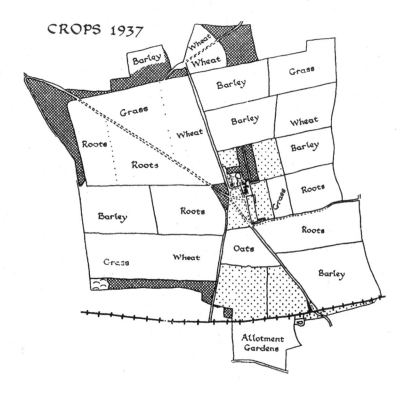

CROPS 1937

Summerfield Estate, Docking, with allotments next to the railway line (from Dudley, p150).

Great Snoring [pictures]

The allotments at Great Snoring are on land rented from the Walsingham Estate between The Street and Dildash Lane. The site totals some six acres and originally there were 32 plots, subsequently reduced to 23 of which 15 are vacant. Part of the site was levelled, fenced and grassed over to form an amenity (dog free) area for the enjoyment of the villagers known as Gurney's Ground.

The village archivists hold allotment records including:

- Register of Allotments and Unlet Allotments 1896–1907
- Allotment Rent Accounts 1895–1933
- Allotment Accounts 1933 1984
- Agreements for letting allotments 1895–1935.

The local guide (*Memoirs of Great Snoring in the 30s* by Revd. Harold Smith) on sale in the church describes the allotment site in the 1930s:

> '*Beyond it are the allotments –separated by narrow grass strips- on which many men work so hard and depend so much. Some are completely cultivated, and all dug by hand, with a planned rotation of vegetables to sustain a family through the year. On others there are hens, or even pigs. But all with a view to enriching a basic diet with eggs and bacon. Some allotments are constantly attended – tidy as if prepared for inspection. But some, not so, in Summer you'll see the allotment fence down to the main gate is covered with wild hops – but no one knows how to make 'wild' beer.'*

Aerial photo of Great Snoring, taken from the Church tower about 10 years ago.

Allotment rules permit geese.

Bob Wilkinson
Thanks to Great Snoring Parish Council

Gresham [pictures]

On 1 april 1895 Gresham Parish Council first considered the provision of land for people living in the Parish and it was agreed to find 10.75 acres at a suitable place and at a convenient rate. At the following meeting two sites were identified and it was agreed to apply to the agent for the local estate (Windham Estate) to rent these pieces of land for 'allotment purposes'. This approach was rejected by the agent who also declined to suggest alternative sites. In july the Parish Council considered using compulsory powers but this was later abandoned seemingly because 'of the expenses attending this procedure'. The Parish Minutes, make no further mention of allotments until 1907 but in the meantime **George Edwards** had been co-opted onto the Council and by 1904 had become Chairman.

In december 1907 it was resolved that in view of the powers contained in the new Allotments Act the Council should renew their plans and notices were printed and application forms issued. In february application was made to local landowner, Captain Batt, as follows:

> *Dear Sir,*
> *I am directed by the Parish Council of Gresham to inform you that they have received applications from the inhabitants of Gresham for 55 acres of land under the Small Holdings and Allotments Act 1907 and to ask you as the principal Owner of Land in this Parish may be pleased to let to the Parish Council that quantity of land suitable for this purpose for a term of 35 years.*
>
> *I shall be glad to receive your reply by the end of the present month, as my Council meets next on Monday, March 2nd.*
>
> *Yours Obedtly*
> *James Kemp*
> *Clerk*

The Parish had received seven applications for what were clearly smallholdings but were consistently referred to as 'allotments' in the Council's Minutes illustrating one of the many difficulties in determining different forms of land ownership as described in old documents and maps. The applications were listed as follows:

William Loades	*5 acres*
? Tyrrell	*5 acres*
Thomas Painter	*5 acres with Cottage, Cartshed, Stable &c*
Andrew Kent	*5 acres, Cottage, Stable, Cartshed, &c*
Geo Wm Thaxter	*20 acres, Cottage, Stable, Pighouse, &c*
Chas Farrow	*5 acres, Cottage, Stable, Pighouse &c*
Albert E Field	*10 acres, Cottage, Stable &c*

Captain Batt replied stating that he was willing to do all that he could to supply the land required but it took much negotiation which involved the Norfolk County Council, the Small Holdings Commissioners and the appointment of an Arbitrator.

Finally in 1910 the Parish Council of Gresham agreed with Captain Batt for the hire of field No. 77 on the Ordnance Map of the Parish of Gresham containing by Ordnance Survey 12.476 acres and a field No 204 containing 9.568 acres as follows:

1. The land to be available for possession at Michaelmas 1910.

2. The Council to pay the tenant right according to the valuation made in the manner customary to the County of Norfolk to be subsequently ascertained.

3. The Lessor to clear the existing drains.

4. The land is (to be) demised to the Parish Council for the term of fourteen years, the rent to be fixed on or before August 1st 1910.

5. The Parish Council to pay the Lessor's Solicitors scale charged in respect of the lease and the Lessor's costs of negotiation for the lease.

6. The rent to be fixed by Mr F Horner of Norwich whose charges shall be paid by the Parish Council.

7. The Parish Council are only to let to residents in the Parish.

8. No applicant who is already in occupation of land to be granted more than will bring his total occupation up to five acres.

Bob Wilkinson
Based on Gresham Parish Council records, with thanks

Harleston [pictures]

It seems probable that allotments first appeared in Harleston in the early 1840s. In June 1843, the same year in which the Poor Law Commissioners' Report appeared, the Harleston Farmers' Club discussed a question much debated throughout the nineteenth century, the condition of the labourer and how his position might be improved, prompted by the question, "Was the agricultural labourer in the position he ought to be?".

The questioner contrasted the situation of the agricultural worker in days of yore with those of 1843: 'He attributed [this state of affairs] mainly to the maladministration of the Poor Laws … He showed how the tie between master and man had been severed, destroying the parental feeling of the former and making it the business of the latter to extort from the common fund; and that nothing but voluntary acts of kindness, especially in sickness and extremity, could restore right feeling'(from *A History of Agriculture in the Parish of Redenhall with Harleston*, by Norman Ward, 1961, p71).

The speaker addressed specific remedies: he advocated education as the "essential base of all improvement" as well as "good examples on the part of the masters", and in this he was supported by many present.

The issue was of such weight that it was the subject of a further meeting at the end of which a resolution was passed, with this final recommendation:

"This meeting deplores that the condition of the agricultural labourer has not kept pace with the general improvement of society. It considers education the best means of meliorating it, such education as raises the standard of morality and not merely promotes mental cultivation amongst the peasantry. It strongly recommends cottage allotments; contract in preference to day work; and attention to the division and ventilation of cottages, especially in the sleeping apartments. It believes that such means, supported by good example and kindness, particularly in sickness, cannot fail to encourage and confirm all those kindly feelings between the employer and the employed, which are so essential to the welfare and comfort of both"(ibid, p72).

The practice flourished and so an 1895 map of Harleston, produced for the sale of the estate of Henry Lombard Hudson, Esq shows Lot 17 as allotments, on a site north of the railway line and to the west of Station Hill (see colour plate). The 1905 Ordnance Survey map of Harleston shows that the site, called Beck View, later abutted Station Hill, having grown from about 7 acres to 10.81 acres. The spread of allotments through the second half of the nineteenth century was aided by the development of railways; it was usual for some of the railway land to be allocated to railway workers, either attached to their cottages, or in the case of allotments at the margins of the track or embankment, as at Aylsham, Melton Constable, Dereham and Thetford. But this appears not to have happened at Harleston, perhaps because the Beck View allotments were already expanded and adjacent to the station. The vestiges of these plots remain. The 1905 O/S map shows a further site, called Jay's Green, off School Lane of 1.6 acres. In living memory there was a third site near the Cherry Tree Public House. The following account tells of the recent history and demise of the site. Charlie Keeble, who is now 85, remembers having an allotment in Harleston in 1937. The plot was opposite the Cherry Tree Pub and at the time it was owned by Mrs Pemberton who had the Dovehouse Farm down Shotford Road – opposite the Dove House. She was apparently very keen that local people should benefit from the allotments, and had a water supply installed to the site. Charlie had two allotments for which he paid ten shillings each year. On one he grew just potatoes which he sold and on the other greens, carrots, sprouts, beans, swede, potatoes and peas. He remembers that one year he was able to buy his son Keith a new two-wheeled bike with the proceeds from selling potatoes. After the War Charlie again took up his plot and one day he was working on the allotment when Frank Capstone, a local farmer, asked him if he would sell his plot for £10. Charlie refused and Mr Capstone said, 'Well, you will have to get off soon as Mrs Pemberton has died and her son wants to sell off the plots'.

Aerial photo of allotments in Harleston opposite the Cherry Tree public house.

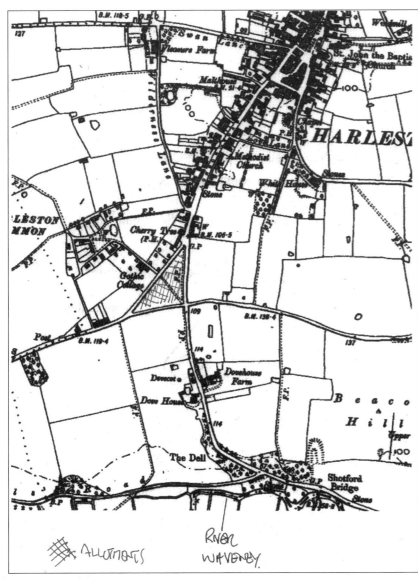

Map of Harleston with the pightle (cross-hatched) to show the allotments pictured (Thanks to David Neville).

The allotments in Harleston were used until towards the end of the twentieth century. A long-term resident of the town, Mr Sid Taylor a former Chair of Harleston Town Council and later Head of South Norfolk District Council, had an allotment at Beck View from 1954 until 1970. He remembers that the allotments were sought-after, there always being a waiting-list until the 1960s when interest waned. Tenants paid 8s per year for a rood, or quarter-acre, plot. The site had the benefit of a well with a pump, and had no rules or restrictions on what could be grown; neither was there an association. Most grew traditional vegetables – potatoes, carrots, parsnips, peas, runner beans, shallots and onions – as well as roses, for which the local firm of Whartons had made Harleston famous.

Both the Beck View and Jay's Green allotment sites were used for housing development in the 1980s, a fate not peculiar to Harleston, leaving one vestigial allotment.

Thanks to David Neville, Curator of Harleston Museum,
for research, documents and pictures

Litcham [pictures]

Allotments in Litcham were created by an agreement, drafted in 1833, between "the Trustees of the Town Land, the Minister, Churchwardens and Overseers of the Parish of Litcham … and the undermentioned inhabitants, labours and cottagers", to which were appended three names and eight crosses (PD459/111 in the Norfolk Record Office, supplied by Stella Evans 21.3.05, researcher for the FACHRS).

The agreement details the conditions under which tenants held their plots. They were to hold one rood of land, which should be cultivated by spade "for growing potatoes, onions and other vegetables". Tenants are instructed, "no second crop of potatoes be grown without the land being well manured after the rate of at least 12lb per acre" and "half the land only to be sown with potatoes in any one year". To the two who "shall cultivate their land in the cleanest and most fruitful manner …a premium or reward be given …assessed by the Minister and Churchwardens on view and "inspection of the crops and ground".

In 1834 when the Poor Law Commissioners reported,

> "Granted to…their heirs and assigns two closes of arable land in Litcham adjoining each other and containing 6A 2R 34P bounded by lands of William Collison Esq on the south and west and which had been allotted as aforesaid upon the same Trusts as were declared in the Indenture of 1709.

> "This land is now divided into 31 garden plots and let to poor persons belonging to the parish who are selected as likely to make a good use of them.

> "We recommended that, in future, in the distinction of these charities a decided preference should be given to those who should be of industrious habits and good character and especially to such as should not receive parochial relief according to the particular directions of Mrs Glover."

In 1834 the origin of the award was given as an Unknown Donor. But the description of the allotment lands provides clues which enable a trace to be made through earlier documents, indicating the lands' provenance.

The Indenture of 20 february 1709 is recorded in a MS Brown Book amongst the Litcham Church papers, as the expression of the charitable donation of Matthew Willamont the elder, blacksmith, who conveyed for the sum of £30 five acres of land to twelve local gentlemen and artisans to be held in Trust "for the use and advantage of the poor" of Litcham, "the rents and profits to be distributed on Christmas Day".

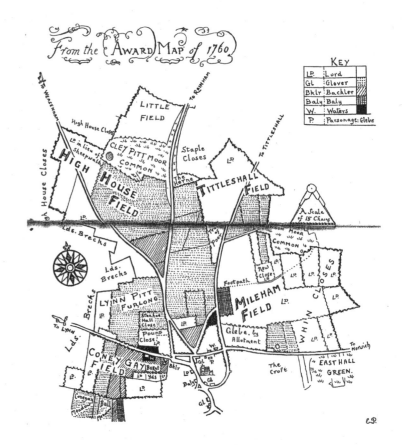

In a history of Litcham (*E I Puddy Litcham: the short history of a mid-Norfolk village (pub.Dereham, 1957)*), it is noted that the land consisted of "two pieces each of 3A at Tittleshall Stile furlong, half an acre in East Hall Hill furlong, another one-and-a-half acres from the same and one acre in Rowland furlong at the south end of Dow's Bush furlong"; the historian concluded, from the piecemeal nature of the award, that the old system of small strips in the common fields was extant in 1709.

The **Litcham Enclosure Award 1760** consolidated charity lands from a number of benefactors including Willamont's five acres and provided more compact holdings of 6A 2R 34P 'up the Tittleshall Road'. A 1760 Award map (above) shows this as a sector to the north-east of Litcham on the west side of Tittleshall Road, part of land owned by 'Ld', the Lord (of the Manor), Sir Armine Wodehouse.

Until 1760 some 550 acres were subject to common rights:

- some half-year open and some half-year closed lands (408 acres belonging to the Lord, Mrs Glover and five others, from description well beyond the village bounds and too far to walk for the villagers to find it useful);

- the North Ling, or Heath;

- Claypit Moor, Granson Moor and Easthall Green (all shown as common on the 1760 map);

- South Common.

A second **Award of 1770** adjusted for a grievance held: the North Common was exclusively for the use of the Lord in exchange for one acre or £10 each to 42 householders with commons rights, except fifty acres for turbary.

A third **Award of 1854** enclosed Claypit Moor, Granson Moor and Easthall Green, leaving the 50 acres of turbary on North Ling and South Common.

In **1811 Zachary Clark**, a Quaker philanthropist, published the results of his researches into charitable foundations in every parish in Norfolk, so that beneficiaries could be sure that they were receiving their due. He listed five charities for Litcham, including:

> "Two rods of land, vested in Trustees, let at £7 4s per acre which sum is paid to the poor every Christmas except 2s 8d for quit rent (one acre being copyhold).

He adds,

> "*Observation:* the returns state that it is not known from whom this land came but by the Terrier of 1806 it appears that it was an allotment under an Inclosure Act and contains 6A 2R 32P."

By the quantity of land involved it is clear that the piece of land is the one "up the Tittleshall Road" which did seem to have been neglected by the 1760 and 1770 Enclosure Awards. The **1806 Terrier** was another piece of tidying. Clark was concerned to indicate where monies might be available to the poor, so does not tell us which lands were re-allocated for the generation of income.

However, by 1834 the Poor Law Commissioners were describing the 'Unknown Donor's', originally Willamont the Elder's land, as divided into 31 garden plots. The Tithe Map for Litcham of 1842 shows a piece of commons situated where the earlier Tittleshall allotments were. This was all the land they had for cultivation since old Litcham was burnt in 1636 and the rebuilt cottages had almost no garden. Puddy finishes the tale:

> "In consequence of the need the Lord of the Manor allowed Mr Francis, tenant of High House Farm, who was one of the Trustees of the Poor, to enclose two or three acres of the South Common nearest the village as garden allotments for the poor. The first occupants were allowed them rent-free as the land was in very rough condition but later occupants paid rent without demur to the Trustees of the Unknown Donor's Charity, until the task transferred to Parish Councils. An 1815 map shows that the land was formerly occupied by a pound and stocks."

The South Common of Litcham is now a nature reserve. The allotments are still there, at the crossroads, on two sites nearest the village formerly occupied by the pound and stocks, and they are still administered by the Parish Council.

P.S. Norfolk Recorders heard from Litcham Allotment and Leisure Gardeners' Association (letter from Secretary 23 february 2007) that Charity Trustees had been approached by a landowner who wished to purchase the allotments in order to extend his property. The Association was formed in order to fight against this proposal and to rejuvenate the site.

Little Melton

As in other parishes neighbouring Norwich, market gardening was a significant part of agricultural life in Little Melton. According to the Little Melton Community Trust's book *Little Melton: the story of a Norfolk village* (published 2003), '...market gardening increasingly flourished here from the late nineteenth century. In 1891 as many as fifteen men were employed in this business and numbers grew as time progressed. John Watson Sparkes cultivated two acres near Grey Cottage as a Violet Nursery for nearly fifty years from the 1880s, employing many local people, and the Little Melton Light Railway was built where was once intensive market gardening. Glass houses stood here until the 1960s growing grapes and other exotic fruits, while earlier, in the late nineteenth century, the little known 'love apples' were a special delicacy. This is the old word for tomatoes...The sixty acres on the Greenacres estate, erected in the year 2000, were built on land once used for market gardening'.

Allotments in Little Melton evidently predated World War 1 since, soon after the close of the War, 'Application for the rental of allotments outstripped the supply, so these were sub-divided from half-acres or quarter-acres into ten or twenty rods apiece.

'In 1921 Mr F Allcock was allotted ten rods on appeal, he explaining

"that he had nowhere to empty the night soil, as he has no garden adjoining his house convenient for that purpose".

'By 1922 Mr W J Bailey...had vacated his rental of three acres of parish land, which was sub-divided as follows:

Mr Kinch 1 acre at £2 per annum;

Russell Lofty to hire a half-acre at 15s-0d per annum;

G Woodgett three-quarters of an acre at £1-2s-6d per annum;

Albert Eden, A Woods...[and]... F Allcock... a quarter-acre at 7s-6d per annum'(p36).

In 1931 drainage pipes were laid across the land.

In 1938 the record shows that the Poors' Land Charity Trust Committee was 'responsible for the allocation and upkeep of allotments' (p39).

Allotments were still in place in 1961 when 'Mr Jakes was…seen carrying a gun…and was told to stop this at once'(p42). There are no later references to the site.

Little Plumstead

Little Plumstead is the parish which now includes Great Plumstead; since World War 2 it has become the larger of the two settlements. It is in the gently rolling countryside just to the east of Norwich, bordering Thorpe-St-Andrew. It is sliced by the northbound railwayline that connects the city with North Walsham and the north coast and bounded to the south by the Norwich to Great Yarmouth line.

the records
A plethora of materials was made available by the Parish, including the Allotments Account Book 1938–64; three hefty Minute Books dated 4 december 1894–29 march 1935, 25 february 1935–25 november 1968 and 25 november 1968–27 april 1976; and the Allotments Register from 8 july 1898 to the 1950 Audit.

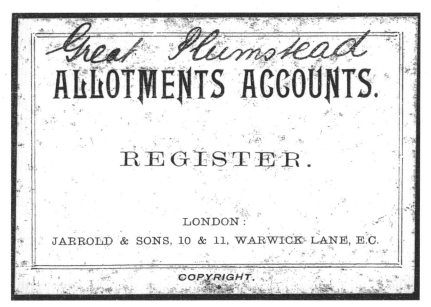

Thanks to Little Plumstead Parish Council.

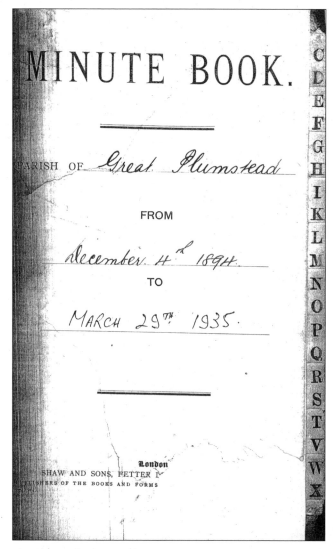

Thanks to Little Plumstead Parish Council.

A letter was read from Mr. Hansell in answer to the one sent by the Council as to the Allotments, saying that Lord Rosebery could not see his way to pay the local rates besides giving 25% reduction in the rent.
It was proposed by Mr. R. Smith & seconded by Mr. S Vincent that the allotments now held by the Rev Howard be taken over by the Parish Council on the terms offered by Lord Rosebery. viz. 30/- per acre. Landlords pay ~~rates~~ tithe & Taxes & the tenant pay local rates. carried unanimously & the clerk was instructed to write to the Rev. Howard to notify the same. and to Mr. Hansell as to when this takes effect

The Minute for 3 february 1896 for Little Plumstead Parish Council records when the allotments came into local authority responsibility. (Thanks to Little Plumstead Parish Council).

allotments history

The parish record gives us only one site for garden allotments, the one alluded to in the Minute of 9 september 1895 when the Reverend John T Howard offered to pass the management of the allotments to the Parish Council (see above) and the one still found to the south of Middle Lane in Great Plumstead. It has undergone some changes. Originally it was the land of Lord Rosebery of the Postwick Estate who leased it to the Parish Council until the Estate was sold to Mr Ernest

William Smith Bartlett, of Surrey. Via a mortgage from Norfolk County Council in 1945 the Parish bought the site and came into full possession in 1970. The Parish Council has used some of the seven acres as a bowls club and recreation ground for the village and some land has been sold for development, leaving approximately one acre for allotments.

The first tenancy agreements, thirty in all, were signed at Michaelmas 1896. There were 28 plots of one rood (a quarter-acre) and two plots of twenty poles (one-eighth of an acre). Now there are seventeen plots on the acre.

By inference, the allotments having been the charge of the Reverend Howard before the Parish Council came into existence, they predate 1895; and tenants were given notice prior to the new agreements being created in 1896. Very probably the Rev Howard was one of the Guardians of the Poor and the garden allotments a means of alleviating the difficulties of the poor people of the parish: in pre-World War 1 Minutes there are references to payments to the Guardians and as late as 1920 the Poor Rate charged on the allotments increased, and so the rents also were increased. When exactly they would have come into existence as garden allotments can only be a matter of speculation. The villages benefited from parcels of land described in the Norfolk section of the 1843 Report on the Poor Law by Brougham: Great Plumstead had a Fuel Allotment of 29A 3R 5P (referred to in parish Minutes) and Church Land of 5 acres; and Little Plumstead had a charitable donation of 2A OR 18P from the Hobart family, presumably the Town Lands referred to in Council Minutes; and there was a Poor's Allotment by the Inclosure Act of 1800 of three fields amounting to 34A 1R 22P. Brougham itemizes the income the parish received from letting these lands; he makes no suggestion, which he was wont to do, that even a part of them was used by the poor for grazing or cultivation. In view of the fact that the land used for garden allotments belonged to Lord Rosebery it may be that the scheme was a later one instigated by him (he had created one such in the neighbouring village of Postwick, according to White's Trade Directory of 1945). No connection can be made through documents and the earliest Ordnance Survey map showing the garden allotment site is dated 1919. On the 1929 and 1946 O/S maps the Poor's Allotments fields (based on their size) to the west of the settlement are marked 'allotments'.

The allotments share many of the features of other sites in Norfolk whose history has been traced (see **Oulton**) but there is one element that emerges from the Minutes which appears to be special to the Plumsteads and which may reflect a continuity with their status as a benefit to the poor: in the years up to the 1930s they were used by the Parish Council as an instrument of welfare. Rather as the Guardians of the Poor used to examine the status of the applicants for dole, the councillors ensured that plots were distributed to those with greatest need:

- firstly, those who were householders, and hence with families – in 1897 the "first married applicants on the list" were given priority; in 1907 non-householders who applied for allotments were denied; in 1913 and in 1920 householders were favoured over other applicants;

- secondly, that there was an even distribution across families – in 1910, 1913 and 1922 applications were refused because two or three members of the same family already held tenancies.

Parish Council meetings were held infrequently in the early days, and most of their business concerned those aspects of parish life to which the distribution of money (namely the charitable funds) or other benefits (the allotments and later on housing) was attached. After WW1 the allotments take up less time as other matters encroach: Plumstead was unlucky in being beset by a number of nuisances until rural areas acquired proper amenities– a disused gravel pit that was foul and unsafe, the smell from sewage discharged from the nearby mental hospital and smoke from uncollected refuse from the Thorpe End Garden Village that was burned – apart from the run-of-the-mill problems of roads, lighting and so on. After 1929 the allotments and their management caused some difficulties due to their uncultivated or poor or even "disgraceful" condition. This is a chorus which recurs during the years of WW2 and then in the 1960s and early 1970s, in the first case because people had been taken into service and in the second because of waning interest, seen throughout Norfolk and the rest of the country in those decades.

World War 1

The First War caused scarcely a ripple on the pond that was Parish Council business. In 1916 the Council was asked to consider anyone in the parish over the age of 41 as suitable for National Service but reported that it 'believed they were engaged on work of National importance'. Anyone younger than 41 was answerable to the Military Authorities. At the same meeting the Council read out a letter from the Norfolk Agricultural Committee about the full use of cottage gardens and allotments, but deferred the business until a later meeting, which never came. In 1918 a Food Production Department letter was 'ordered to be laid on the table, it being felt that everything was being done that could reasonably be done'. Certainly all the allotments were in use, and the tenancies maintained.

World War 2

The Second War was heralded in 1938 by the appointment of Air Wardens to the parish. The government was quicker off the mark when it came to ensuring food supplies for the nation than had been the case for the First War and in October 1939 the Council received a request from the Norfolk War Agricultural Committee Executive to 'see that all allotments under their jurisdiction are cultivated in a proper husbandlike manner'. The Clerk was instructed to inform all allotment-holders that they would be required to make the fullest use of their allotments.

In april 1940 the Council was asked if allotments could be spared 'for the children to cultivate', under supervision, and a tenant agreed to let half of his plot be used by them. 'Mr Jones very kindly offered to use his gyrotilla to break up the land, thus saving the children the hard labour of digging.'

By june 1940 the Sprowston War Agricultural Committee complained that some tenants had failed to cultivate their plots and the Council responded summarily by immediately terminating the agreements of seven of the tenants, with two others receiving notice. George Rushbrook, a tenant, and two Councillors, Mr Evan Jones (a market gardener) and Mr Henry Thomas Key (a farmer), collaborated to clear the 'trees and undergrowth' of one plot and the plots were distributed between them, remaining in multiple-tenancy until after the War when there was a renewal of interest in allotments.

In September 1941 the Ministry of Agriculture and Fisheries agitated about the use of 'derelict gardens and waste land'. A piece of land owned by Mrs Pleasants at Little Plumstead was inspected and reported to be 'useless'. The Council also read out and answered the questions on a circular sent by the Norfolk Home Food Front.

Once the War was over, in the 1950s, some tenancies were taken up, although George Rushbrook continued to hold 2.25 acres which, in a Minute of 1954, it is revealed, he cropped as sugar beet. As we have seen, the demand for allotments declined through the 1960s along with the condition of the plots. Although attempts were made in 1961 to provide water for the site, it was thought to be impractical. In 1962 a tenant allowed his fowls to run rampant over other plots in defiance of the Council's requests to fence them in, until finally he was threatened with notice to quit. But in 1967 and 1968 there were again complaints to the Council about 'the unsatisfactory condition of uncultivated allotments'. A set of tenancy agreements for the years 1975–80 reveals that only eight plots were in use and that, as time progresses, they were increasingly divided into smaller lots, between 150 and 240 square yards. One tenant was given notice to quit because of complaints about the condition of his plot which was affecting neighbours, and the moment was seized to divide it into six. An interesting feature of that period was the increasing involvement of women, which typically for the present has persisted.

the tenants

For most of their history the Plumstead allotments have been fully occupied and with a waiting list. The Plumsteads have their share of tenants who managed to hold their tenancies for a remarkably long time:

- Jonathan High 1896–1935, 39 years to be succeeded by his widow, who kept the plot until 1938;

- Samuel Vincent 1896–1923, 27 years;

- Richard Smith 1896–1925, 29 years;

- Ernest Tite 1896–1922, 26 years;

- Ernest Gamble 1896–1941, 45 years;

remembering that the date at which the allotments were created is unknown. Of the original tenants, most whose tenancies dated from 1896 were only there for between 5–11 years, suggesting that the site may well have gone back much earlier. During the 1920s, despite a high turnover in tenancies, some did hold much longer tenancies, and there are a few whose tenancies persist until the record dies sometime in the 1950s and were of considerable length:

- Grantley Rushbrook 1913–end, as long as (ala) 37 years;

- Fred Maidstone 1914–end, ala 36 years;

- George Rushbrook 1919–end, ala 31 years.

Troubles struck periodically. As early as 1896 an allotment became vacant because a tenant 'left the parish', an event recorded in the early 1900s until 1914 on seven occasions. Generally in those early years the turnover was high: although we cannot know how long the original tenants had held their plots, of the second and subsequent cohorts until WW1 presumably enforced absences for its own reasons most, fifteen in total, are of 1–5 years' duration and many others, seven in total, of 6–12 years' duration. In 1908 there were at one time six vacant plots. 1912 was a year in which tenants fell into arrears and there were difficulties in collecting rents. A second period of high turnover occurred in the early 1920s when six 1–5 year and two 6–12 year tenancies occurred but it was a time of increasing stability. Some plots fell into dilapidation. In 1929 an Allotments Committee was formed, which has persisted throughout the period covered by the Minutes, to inspect the site regularly. In march 1930 the Council resolved 'in view of the present depression in agriculture the Rural District Council be urged to insist that, as far as possible, an economic rent be charged on all RDC cottages so that no undue burden be placed on the main body of Ratepayers'. It would be easy to interpret these tumultuous times as due to the agricultural depression and the inter-war depression, when the able-bodied with mouths to feed looked elsewhere for work. A

Table for the population of the Plumsteads (based on available Trade Directories, with 1845 and 1864 as baselines) bears out the suggestion.

Year	Population of Great Plumstead	Population of Little Plumstead
1861	342	319
1881	334	329
1901	347	303
1911	327	350
1921	335	362

At the time represented by these numbers the tenancy of the allotments was by villagers from Great and Little Plumstead, Witton and Thorpe-St-Andrew, and so changes in the populations of any of these settlements had an effect. Before WW2 all but three of the tenants came from Great Plumstead; after 1947 all were from Great Plumstead, presumably because of the distance of the site from Little Plumstead and boundary changes. In 1973 the Minutes record Mr Frost as stating that 'more and more interest was being shown in allotments and [he] enquired if allotment land at Little Plumstead could be made available for Little Plumstead residents'. Mr Frost repeated his request at the Annual Meetings of 1974 and 1975, and in 1976 he was still applying for a plot.

Some other patterns of allotment holdings that are seen in other parts of Norfolk are found in the Plumstead records. As we have seen, tenants were often succeeded by their widows. There were three women from the original tenancy of 1896 who may have been widows but others held allotments independently as well: Laura Lond became a tenant in 1905; Hannah Webb took a plot in 1920, to be succeeded by Francis Webb. It was commonplace for sons to take on the family plot, too, and for two or three members of the same (presumably extended) family to be cultivating plots at the same time. Thus the same surnames recur throughout the record: George, Sutton, Maidstone, Brister, Harmer, Nichols, High, Tite, Vincent, Jermy. As with other parts of rural Norfolk, the continuity of families living in the same place and continuing with family traditions is strong.

One final touch of colour can be added to this picture: the Trade Directories throw some light on the trades, if not of tenants themselves, of members of their families. As you would expect, there are no tenants represented amongst the tradespeople of Little Plumstead, although family members abound. In Great Plumstead we find:

- Henry Brister, shopkeeper in 1904. Both Henry Brister Senior and Junior were amongst the original tenants;

- Robert George, another original, was a wheelwright;

- a Samuel Vincent, from 1896, was a farmer in 1904. In 1908 a Samuel Vincent was described as a hawker;

- Ernest Tite, also from 1896, was Clerk to the Parish Council. He worked his allotment until 1922, but was still Clerk in 1933;

Samuel Ellis Jermy was a blacksmith in 1908, which he remained until at least 1917 when he was awarded a tenancy. And as we have seen, during WW2 two of the Parish Councillors, both agriculturalists, acquired allotment land.

Despite their proximity and accessibility to Norwich, Great Plumstead and Little Plumstead in the early years of the twentieth century display the characteristics of many small communities in Norfolk in having an agricultural base combined with a number of trades that made them all but self-sufficient. To meet the demands of self-sufficiency if not survival the garden allotments must have been a vital part of the whole.

Thanks to Mr Ian Bishop, Clerk to the Parish Council

Methwold

Methwold has a site of ninety-five plots which 'range from singles to multiples of singles, details of which change from time to time' (letter from Lt Cdr Brian Newton MBE, Clerk to the Trustees of the Thomas Batchcroft Trust, dated 26 may 2006). The site is 25A 2R 20P (approximately 10.25 hectares) on the edge of the village.

A Charity Commission document of 22 march 1894 lists the charities which made up the Trust. The charities can be traced back to the early nineteenth century, where they are listed on a board in Methwold church and include '26 acres 22 perches of arable land lying near the Cock in Methwold – this was allotted by the Award of the Commissioners of the Inclosure Act bearing the date 6 march 1807 in lieu of lands formerly purchased of John Butters ' and ' two acres of pasture land lying in Foulden – this land was purchased of William Chapman with certain monies left by Dr Batchcroft, formerly of Caius College, Cambridge for that purpose'. These were poor's allotments, monies arising from rents from the lands being paid to the poor of the parish twice-yearly.

Happily the Parish reports that, however the allotment plots are combined, 'usually we manage to maintain a "full house"'.

Thanks to Lt Cdr Brian Newton MBC, Clerk to the Trustees of the Thomas Batchcroft Trust

Norwich [pictures]

The tradition of gardens and nurseries, and of tenanted land, in and around Norwich goes back to its mediaeval past. Cathedral accounts show that the gardens were a vital component of life within the precinct: 'Wedged in amongst this motley array of buildings were gardens of all shapes, sizes and functions…' and letting between officials of the Cathedral was commonplace (Noble, p4). Early maps of Norwich show that much of the land within the city boundary was open land. Since much of the city is protected by the sinuous River Wensum, meadowland and marsh bordered the Cathedral Close and Castle. To this day there is open, if functional land, to the east and to the west. Chapelfield Gardens is named after the field adjacent to the chapel that can be seen on the earliest map of any accuracy, that of Thomas Cleer made in 1696 (Frostick, p21). Just before that date, in 1662, Thomas Fuller wrote words that were to be endlessly quoted: 'Norwich is (as you please) either a city in an orchard, or an orchard in a city, so equally are houses and trees blended in it' (*The Worthies of England*).

The natural historian, philosopher and physician to Queen Elizabeth I, Sir Thomas Browne, renewed a lease on 7 december 1681 from the Dean and Chapter for a piece of land in the Cathedral precinct: 'A meadow I use in this city, beset about with sallows'. Sir Thomas tenanted the land from at least 1669. The meadow was on the south side of a causeway leading to the ferry, presumably Pull's Ferry which connected Cathedral land to the county beyond on the east side of the city.

The Norfolk historian the Reverend Francis Blomefield mapped Norwich in 1776. Within the city's edge and to the north-west of the city, bordering the south side of the river, was a piece of **dole** land called Dasy's Dole. Dasy's Dole is shown on 1783 map of T Smith (Frostick p58) but by 1789 Anthony Hochstetter shows much of that piece of land built upon and the remaining small portion has become an orchard (Frostick, p60). An illustration of the north-east approaches to Norwich of about the same period gives us a clue to the formality and orderliness, and the variety of species, cultivated at the city's edge. Public gardens created in the eighteenth and nineteenth century developed the culture of open green spaces for which Norwich was famous throughout Europe: 'From early morn till late at even in the summer months of the eighteenth century these gardens were thronged with the pleasure-seekers of county and city' (Knights, p8). By 1910, when the city had long since overflowed its original boundary and become much more built upon, gardeners were still the third largest working group in Norwich, 574 in total – but a long way behind boot and shoemakers who numbered 4931.

Through the nineteenth century Norwich continued to flourish and expand – towards its end the Corporation acquired 184 acres of Mousehold Heath which were within its boundary from the Cathedral, on condition that the Corporation used '…all lawful measures to prevent the continuance of trespasses, nuisances and unlawful acts and to hold the Heath for the advantage of lawful recreation' (Meeres, p172). Since Mousehold Heath was and still is used for allotments, the Cathedral appears to have anticipated a requirement that had been fully met by the then-Corporation.

Garden allotments in Norwich first date from 1840 (Archer, p24), their location unknown. A map of 1873 of Thorpe which was then part of the city shows the Railway Station and workshops close to cottages with long gardens on the Great Yarmouth Turnpike Road, and another set of cottages having separate plots. They are on land bordering the track of the Great Eastern Railway, and must be on railway ground.

The beautiful first edition Ordnance Survey map for Norwich, on which every tree and feature was marked, dates from 1883. It shows a set of twenty or so allotments, bordering the river, to the north-east of the Carrow Works and nearby another few, three or four, behind some cottages that lie between the Malthouse on Carrow Road and the Gothic Works. Another set of twenty-six allotments are shown within the grounds of the Great Hospital, part of Cathedral land, behind St Helen's Terrace fronting Bishopgate and their eastern boundary is the river. Intriguingly in mediaeval times gardens were let by the Cathedral sacrist who had tenants for the Carnary gardens next to the charnel-house, a garden near St Helen's Church called St Helen's garden,and a small lawned garden (Noble, p4); and they are in the exact position of gardens marked on George Cole's 1807 map (Frostick, p63–65). They can still be identified on a later land-use map which post-dates the 1929 O/S Norwich map (because of streets and housing that have appeared since earlier maps) but is not as late as maps of 1945.

By some quirk of legislation, responsibility for sanitary measures having been left with the local authorities since the Act of 1887, it seems to have fallen to the committee in charge of 'housing for the working class' to deal with allotments, too. By the early 1900s maps are supplemented by Corporation records.

Because Norwich is the only town in Norfolk of a size to represent the coming of industry to the county, later details of Norwich allotments are integrated with the main text.

Thanks to Norwich City Council Allotment Officers Martin Warren and Carrie Bewick

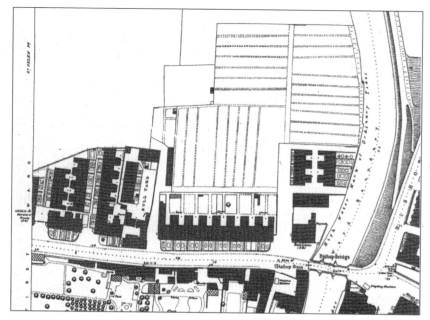

1885 Ordnance Survey (1st edition) map of Norwich showing the grounds of the Great Hospital behind St. Helen's Terrace, marked in strips.

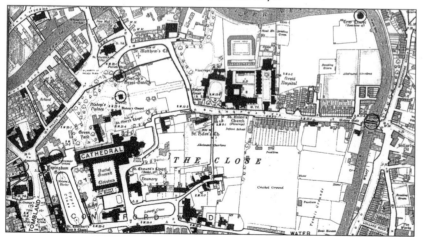

Map of Norwich prior to 1929, showing allotment gardens marked on the same piece of ground as on the 1885 O/S map, behind St. Helens Gardens.

Oulton with Irmingland

The parish of Oulton with Irmingland incorporates the hamlet of Oulton Street. It is south-west of the Blickling Estate, now the property of the National Trust, and north-east of the Heydon Estate; according to White's Trade Directory, much Oulton land was the property of the Bulwer family. As we shall see, both estates negotiated that their land be used as allotments. The settlement of Oulton, incorporating Oulton Hall and the Church of St Peter and St Paul is set in undulating, woody and watery land; Oulton Street is as flat as the proverbial pancake – an airfield was attached in World War 2 – and features a noncomformist church and the railway crossing of Bluestone Station, on the M&GNR.

Parish records go back to 1888. The Parish Council Minute Books date from 16 april 1912, but there is as well a Parish Council Accounts and Allotments Rent Book which dates from 3 may 1895 to 1953; a separate Allotments Account Book; and the Register of Allotments, starting on 18 december 1888 and kept up to date until 2002. In 1888 Oulton was administered by the Aylsham Sanitary Authority until the 1895 Local Authorities Act brought the Parish Council into being. Such a complete record from the inception of Parish Councils until the present is a rare treat.

allotments history

There is a vestigial allotment on an original site off the Aylsham Road that runs through Oulton Street of 0.777 acres; it is currently let as a field allotment, for grazing a horse.

In 1888 the main acreage of allotments, known as the Blickling Allotments, was of 12 acres 24 poles. It was divided into sixteen plots of varying sizes: five were of one acre, and two half-acre plots were let as one, one was of 3 rods 16 poles, eight were half-acre (or slightly more) plots, and just one plot was a quarter-acre. By 1908 the Blickling Allotments were shown as 11 acres 24 poles; it appears that they were located on two sites, of 4 and some odd acres on Aylsham Lane, which were formerly used by cottagers living nearby, and the remainder found down a loke off Oulton Street. From january 1912 until 1919 another site of 12 acres 2 rods, called the Heydon Allotments, was administered by the Parish Council. This was divided into three four-acre plots and one half-acre plot. The Council was informed in october 1918 by the Heydon Estate that the allotment land was to be sold, and the Council tried through the County Agent to acquire the land, only to be told that 'during the War my Committee have no powers to purchase land for smallholdings or allotments'. Despite other attempts to secure the land for allotments, the Heydon Estate wrote to confirm that the sale would go through on 11 october 1919 , Michaelmas, and notice was sent to the tenants. The purchaser emerged as George Overton, one of the plot-holders.

The Blickling Allotments were worked intact until 1933 when 4 acres 3 rods 24 poles were given up by Harry Peckham who had accumulated land as plots had been vacated by other cottagers. He had been one of the original plot-holders of the parish, having worked his land a remarkable 45 years until he was succeeded on one of his acres by his wife Blanche in 1934. When no applicants came forward for the remaining acreage and the Parish Council was forced to give notice to the Blickling Land Agent, Mr C R Birkbeck, the Council was dismayed to be told that since all the allotment holdings were served by the one contract, they would have to give notice to all the tenants. Such was the urgency that a special meeting was held, on 5 october 1932. The Minutes record that such an outcome would 'be a hardship to the Street holders'. The Council wrote to Birkbeck the following day: 'Allotment holders off the Street allotments consider they would be hardly treated if compelled to give them up…there are nine tenants'. After a protracted and tough negotiation which took the form of reminders to the Blickling Estate that the drainage in the loke had not been improved despite repeated reminders throughout 1932 so that the loke was under standing water, and requests for a reduction in rents on the allotments, a new agreement was drawn up in 1934 between the Estate, Parish Council and tenants allocating 6 acres on Oulton Street and 1 acre on Aylsham Lane, and the Estate would waive tithes providing the allotments were 'kept in a neater condition'. Face was thus saved on both sides. Although there were fewer tenants at that time, the size of plots is remarkably consistent, with five one-acre plots, three half-acre plots and one three-quarter-acre plot being taken up.

Feb 13th 1917

A Meeting of the Parish Council was held on the above Date at Mr Seaman's at 8 oc in the evening W H Bolton in the Chair Messrs: Seaman, English Campbell & Sparrow —

The Chairman read the minutes of the last Meeting & then said they were called together to discuss a letter from the Norfolk War Agricultural Committee in which it was suggested the Parish Council shd form a Committee or Form themselves into a Committee to see that all Gardens & Allotts shd be thoroughly Cultivated, a discussion followed & it was decided to after going thro: the Gardens & Allotts of the Parish that a few might want assistance but that all cd be cultivated in the Parish without outside help; a list of those, wives whose Husbands were at the front, men, who were too old &c to cultivate their land, was taken & individual Member of the Council agreed to see these people so that arrangements may be made for all —

With regard to the question whether we had a War Food Society in the Parish & if not, wd we organise one; it was decided we had not one & did not think it wd make any difference as everyone was doing as much as possible already

Walter H Bolton
Chairman.

March 28th 1917

A Meeting of the Parish Council was held on the above date at Mr Seaman's at 7.30 PM W H Bolton in the Chair Messrs: Seaman Late Farrow Campbell English & Sparrow

The Minutes of the last meeting were read. A discussion followed with regard to the Gardens it was decided that all the gardens wd be cultivated, the Chairman then read the correspondence recd from Mr Cox with regard to the seed Potatoes it was settled who shd do the carting when they came & they were to be weighed & divided out in proportion etc . With regard to National Voluntary Service the Meeting was of opinion that the Labourers shd not Volunteer as they were wanted on the land where they were, & if they volunteered they might be sent somewhere else to do exactly the same work —

G. R. Seaman
Chairman

Oulton with Irmingland Parish Council Minutes for 13 february 1917 and 28 march 1917 (Thanks to the Parish Council).

In 1948 the Parish Council paid rent to the National Trust, not the Blickling Estate. Although the record becomes less detailed over time, it is not until 1967/8 that the acreage of the allotment site is shown as 5 acres 3 rods (5.750 acres), when there was presumably a single tenant as the Parish Council was receiving a field rent. The Parish Clerk wrote that in 1987 'the land was bought from Broadland District Council…[having been sold]…in 1946 to Saint Faith's Rural District Council [the precursor of Broadland] by the National Trust for £50.

The land was acquired from BDC on the understanding that it would only be used for recreational purposes and without development potential unless the Parish Council wanted to build a new village hall, in which case the land could be used for that purpose'. The Clerk recorded the size of the site as 0.777 acres, located on the Aylsham Road; this suggests that the Oulton Street site continued to be rented from the National Trust after 1948 but was lost at some time between then and 1967/8. From 1999 to 2001 two plots were worked within the field but the whole site reverted to field in 2002.

parish council responsibilities

In the first days of the Parish Council it deals with little else than allotment matters; it is as if it were set up almost entirely for that purpose. Too much water and the clearing of ditches, requests for the landlord to supply and then maintain a gate to the Street site, very occasional complaints about a neighbour's behaviour are familiar motifs. The Parish Council took over the running of Bell's Charity, from which money was distributed regularly to poor widows, and was concerned with the welfare of its parishioners; and it negotiated for council housing. Between the Wars there was a dire need for council housing and the Council agitated long and hard on behalf of needy families. Following a special meeting to discuss the housing for agricultural workers, in may 1927 the Minutes itemize extreme examples: one family of eight was living in a 'two up, two down'; two families, one of four living in a 'one up, one down', had notice to quit. Two of the three names cited belong to former allotments tenants, suggesting that the plot was a key part of their survival in hard times. Roads maintenance and the nagging of those responsible was also a recurrent theme. From the beginning of WW2 allotments business hardly intrudes into the parish record and after 1951 it vanishes altogether.

allotments and the two wars

On 13 february 1917 the Parish Council was called together to discuss a letter from the Norfolk War Agricultural Committee (NWAC) in which it was suggested that they should form a committee to ensure that all garden allotments were thoroughly cultivated. The Council thought about each of the gardens and allotments and decided that 'a few might want assistance' and it drew up a list of 'wives whose husbands were at the Front' and 'men who were too old to cultivate their land'. Still the parish would not need outside help and individual members of the Council agreed to see these people so that arrangements to help them could be made. The Council also considered whether or not the parish needed to create a War Food Society. It decided that the NWAC should be told that 'it would not make any difference as everyone was doing as much as possible already'.

On 28 march 1917 a further meeting to discuss wartime measures initiated by the NWAC agreed that all gardens should be cultivated, and made plans for carting and distributing seed potatoes. With regard to the National Volunteering Service; 'the Meeting was of the opinion that the labourers should not volunteer as they were wanted on the land where they were and if they volunteered they might be sent somewhere else to do exactly the same work'.

The impact of WW2 on Council work was greater. On 17 october 1941 the legendary request from Aylsham RDC that iron railings and other non-functional iron be sacrificed to the war effort came, and plans were made for air raid shelters, sand bags, Home Guards, promises of help. A letter from the Ministry of Agriculture came for the meeting of 8 november 1940, asking if more land for allotments was needed, but at that time the parish had all the land it required, and the matter was not referred to again.

tenants

In the most general terms, the tenanting of the Oulton and Street allotments follows a pattern seen elsewhere in rural areas where privately-owned land attached to homes is still available: it was greatest when the allotments were formed, the number of tenants dipped from WW1 and then remained the same until the end of WW2 and then it dived from the end of the 1950s and 1960s, reviving fractionally in the 1990s, until remaining interest in garden allotmenteering seems to have been lost. This pattern is typical of a hamlet in rural Norfolk, where people have gardens large enough for their aspirations, or where they may have acquired one of the original estate or farm cottages still blessed with its quarter-acre.

At the original 1888 allocation there were sixteen tenants. Comparing the tenant numbers with information gleaned from Trade Directories, White's 1864 volume gives the population of Oulton as 357; this early figure for a period when Norfolk farming was experiencing a boom serves as a baseline with which to interpret the following Table (based on available Kelly's Directories):

Year	Population of Oulton	Number of tenants	% of population
1891	372	16	4.3
1901			
1904	360	14	3.9
1911	331	10	3.0
1921	349	8	2.3
1931	318	7	2.2

Currently in rural Norfolk the percentage of population renting an allotment is about 1.0% (from the North Norfolk District Council use of land for leisure survey 2005). What this Table cannot tell us but which the Oulton Minutes make explicit is that from the early days of the allotments' history until after WW2 there was never a shortage of tenants; if anything, people were waiting to take up plots as they became vacant even if, as time went on, it was to aggregate land.

Aggregation was another, typical feature of the allotments in their heyday, so that some individuals had large acreages. From the first 1888, even distribution where the largest holding was one acre, by 1911 one individual had two acres and by 1914 another, Henry Peckham of the Aylsham Road site, held 4 acres 1 rod 16 poles, while of the four holdings on the Heydon site (until 1919) three were of four acres. This arrangement persisted until the 1934 agreements came in, when the largest plots, as we have seen, reverted to the single acre, before the post-WW2 collapse of interest meant that the site was retained as a field allotment.

The number of tenants over time reveals not only a general trend until the present day but speaks of other events, short and medium-term. The most poignant of these were the two world wars, and the intervening general economic slump. As we have seen, even the tiny population of Oulton suffered dips in numbers through the agricultural depression that Norfolk reflected from the beginning of the nineteenth century. Without having identified individuals this interpretation remains somewhat speculative but where turnover of tenants has been so stable it takes little imagination to see the small duration of some of the tenancies during the World War 1 period as a reflection of the loss of the parish's sons: of the ten available tenancies in 1914 four changed hands before 1918. A similar pattern emerges for World War 2. In 1939 Oulton had eight tenancies, increased to ten in 1940/1 and then reduced to nine in 1944. Over the period 1939–46, excepting those who had held allotments for decades or (in the case of Blanche Peckham who succeeded her spouse on one plot after Henry Peckham, presumably, went to the great allotment in the sky after 45 years of tending his four-plus acres; and Mrs J Wells who only held her half-acre for two seasons), the cessation of two tenancies could be attributed to losses in the War. At no other periods are the tenancies so brief.

Another, typical theme can be detected from the Allotments Register: the tendency for widows to take over their husbands' plots. In 1888 James Poll held a tenancy, to be succeeded by Sophia Poll, who held the plot until 1905. Blanche Peckham is one case in 1934 and another is Maria Wells (not the same person as Mrs J Wells) who succeeded Thomas Wells in 1924. Since the other major Parish Council function at its inception was to administer Bell's Charity for poor widows which it regularly did, the attraction of an allotment holding in helping to maintain independence or simply just body and soul is obvious.

Unusual, however, is the case of Mrs Alice Maria Wells whom Kelly's Directories for 1916 and 1933 describe as a beer retailer, not the same thing as the local hostelry, the Pitman Arms, was in different hands. She took on an acre plot in 1928 and held it until 1940. Did she grow barley on her land, or was it to help feed herself?

What also is true of the Oulton allotments is that plots were kept in families, or perhaps other family members joined the patriarch in taking up allotments. Oulton families were clans; the directories giving details of local tradespeople and officers reveal that. The same surnames, if not individuals, occur again and again, some of them still familiar local Norfolk names: Bartle, Pask, Rounce, Bullock, Poll, Overton, Lake and Lakey, Leary, Clements. William Lynes held his plots amounting to just over one acre from 1910 to 1939, and Charles Lynes took on his own plot from 1932 to 1953. William Bullock Senior was one of the original tenants in 1888, to be joined by William Bullock Junior in 1890 (ceasing in 1916, likely one of the WW1 fatalities), Harry Bullock in 1910, and Joseph Willie Bullock and George Bullock, on separate plots, both in 1924.

A feature which commands respect of these pioneer allotmenteers is the duration of their tenancies: Walter Jeary 1888–1937, 49 years; Henry Peckham 1888–1933, 45 years; William Webster 1901–1951, 50 years. Later on two to three decades is more common: William Lynes 1910–1939, 29 years; Herbert Golding 1937–1960, 24 years; J H Ampleford 1940–1960, 21 years.

Both of these characteristics of the Oulton allotments, the longevity of the tenancies and the closeness of family ties, speak of a feature of Norfolk allotments that can be observed elsewhere: the constancy of the population within a location, and this is a feature that has been noted in other arenas. For some families it would not be too much to speak of a tradition of tenanting allotments, and of a way of life which persisted for several generations and which even persists today (Burnham Market records show that some of the same families are allotment holders as were the original tenants at the end of the nineteenth century). What their way of life might have been may be glimpsed by expanding the horizon from the parish records to the trades directories (and even more from the censuses, it will be admitted):

- John Bartle, presumably the same who held a half-acre from 1888 to 1906, was a gamekeeper;

- Henry Keeler tenanted a quarter-acre from 1888 to Christmas 1891, and was the parish clerk. (In 1904 both George Keeler and Thomas Keeler were farmers.);

- Henry Kiddell held an allotment from 16 august 1889 for one year; he, as wheelwright, grocer and beerhouse keeper in 1864, would have been the relative of George Kiddell who held an allotment from 1915

to 1932, and George Kiddell may have been one of the Kiddell Brothers, who were blacksmiths, wheelwrights and wagon builders in 1904, noted in 1908 as agricultural implement makers and agents, wheelwrights and wagon builders. Great oaks from little acorns grow;

- Robert Fairbairn held a tenancy from december 1901 to 1916; in 1904 a Robert Fairbairn was sub-postmaster, draper and grocer;

- James and Sophia Poll's tenancy was from 1888 to 1905. A Mrs Jane Poll was a farmer in 1900;

- Charles Carman took on an acre in 1900; in 1908 and 1916 a Charles Carman was described as a farmer;

- Mrs Alice Maria Wells' trade as beerkeeper has already been described;

- William Alfred Pask took an allotment from 1932 to 1936. He was a grocer and looked after the Post Office;

- George Overton, who was first a tenant and then owner of the Heydon Allotments, was a coal deliverer.

Not all agricultural labourers, certainly. This arrangement of combining allotments with a variety of trades, some of them in the large category, may be a reflection of a pattern that was found elsewhere in Norfolk and for an example the village of Hevingham, just the Norwich side of Aylsham, will serve. Kelly registers wheat, roots, barley and hay as the main crops grown in the area. Given Oulton's isolation in the days when carting was the main mode of travel (the roads were not metalled until after WW2), garden plots would have been an important source of food for the village and the larger plots of income for those, small farmers and tradespeople, who made a living however they could. Unquestionably a somewhat isolated and a hard way of life, it nonetheless needed to be sustainable. The list of trades to be found amongst a population of three hundred and some (which would have included the owner of Oulton Hall, also local JP and Chair of the Parish Council, the church incumbent, and a schoolteacher to run the charitably-donated Free School), the list of trades offered, skills mastered and resources available in a small community is impressive.

Thanks to Mrs J H Rogers, Clerk to the Parish Council

Potter Heigham

Potter Heigham on the Broads illustrates how significant was the change brought in by the 1894 Local Authorities Act.

'At the first Parish Council meeting in 1894 a resolution was passed to purchase land for allotments in the village. There was a general demand from the family men. In those days most of the working men were land workers on low incomes and they wanted the opportunity to use their skills to supplement their income. The only way they could do that was on a plot of land.

'Their demand was considered to be a genuine need and in due course land was made available and divided into plots of various size from one acre downward according to demand. The scheme progressed until it consisted of about thirty acres of land in the parish' (George, p6).

The Survey generated indentures for parcels of land. The first of these was in 1896 between the Parish Council and Samuel Pollard, a shopkeeper of Potter Heigham, for the field of 12.514 acres called Pollard's Field. 'Their main choice of crop was soft fruit as they could cultivate and manage that by hand and with the help of their families at peak periods. Also at that time the railway was in operation and there was a market for fruit in the towns up the line.

'Many of the cottages in those days had a pigsty at the bottom of the garden in order to fatten a pig or two for the house. Often they would kill one and sell the rest to cover the cost of feeding. Pig manure is fine stuff for fruit so the two enterprises worked well together at the time. The lease of Pollard's Field was renewed in 1904 and 1907 and in 1909, through a mortgage agreed with Norfolk County Council, the parish bought the land.

'The schoolmaster at the time was Mr Goldsmith and he took a great interest in this enterprise. He got the growers together in discussion and the result was Potter Heigham Fruit Co-op, on which he served as secretary. In that capacity he found buyers for the produce and also arranged transport from the field to the destination. A smallholder in the village would be engaged with his horse and wagon to pick up the fruit from the grower and drop off empty containers, then deliver his load to the railway station. The Co-op had its own named containers of which there are still a few about. School rules were more flexible in those days and when the fruit was ready to harvest the schoolmaster would close the school and give the children two weeks off, which was deducted from their summer holiday. That worked out very well, it allowed the children to help with the family fruit picking and also enabled them to earn some pocket money as there was work for all' (George, p6). The M&GN Joint Railway abuted the field, with a station at Potter Heigham, and ran to North Walsham and Yarmouth.

Fruit-growing became a family custom, according to Ron George, the author of this tale. 'My family has always grown raspberries as a side line since the Fruit Co-op was formed many years ago…In those days the varieties of raspberries were everyday phrases. Names like Norfolk Giant, a late variety, Lloyd George a very popular but not long-living maincrop, and Red Cross, a fair early good cropper. They are all in the past now like the apples that were grown locally such as Beauty of Bath, Gladstone, New Queen, Old Queen and Doctor Harvey and in most cottage gardens stood a Victoria Plum tree while the top name in blackcurrants had to be Baldwin.

'Popular varieties of potatoes were Majestic, Duke of York, King Edward and during the war [World War 2] emerged a new variety called Home Guard. They all had their own attractive flavour according to the land in which they were grown but have been replaced by modern-style heavy croppers.

'One old favourite that is still very popular today in spite of many new varieties is the Bramley Apple' (George, p17).

'The whole system worked very well for all concerned until the farmers became envious of their men's achievement and planted acres of fruit themselves. As so often happens, this glutted the market' (George, p6).

By 1920 a further field of 8.463 acres off Green Lane was rented from Norfolk County Council. It was made up of fourteen plots: one of 2.320 acres; one of one acre; five of three-quarters of an acre; two of a half-acre; five of a quarter-acre. The indenture for this site was renewed in 1949.

A map of 1938 shows a second site of 11.430 acres adjoining Pollards Field as a single large space, whereas Pollards Field, itself 12.514 acres, is divided into strips: one of 1.75 acres; two of 1.50 acres; four of one acre; seven of a half-acre; one of a quarter-acre. The closure of railways, of course, put an end to commercial fruit-growing on allotments and smallholdings at Potter Heigham, and many other villages around the county, once and for all. Now the railway line is the route for the A149 road. Nonetheless Potter Heigham still retains two sites, Pollards Field on which there are eight agricultural tenancies and Green Lane which is occupied by a further eight agricultural tenancies and sixteen garden allotments, ranging between five to twenty rods.

Thanks to Mr Michael Farnsworth

Reepham [pictures]

Reepham was amongst the first settlements in the county to establish garden allotments, in 1830 following Swing Riots.

'In mid-november two or three hundred people from Cawston, Salle and other of the surrounding villages came to Reepham demanding wages of 2s 6d...Unfortunately or otherwise a detachment of cavalry had arrived in the town a short time before them. The magistrates, with the constables and the military stopped the crowd at the entrance to the town, where they were addressed at great length by the Reverend John Bedingfield Collyer on "the dangers and follies of their tumultuous proceedings" and how they were liable to the "penalties of the law". Whether because of the exhortations of Mr Collyer or from the presence of the soldiers, the people went quietly away' (Piercy, p39).

Nonetheless, within days there were incidents of machine-wrecking in adjoining parishes. 'On 23 november a threshing machine was destroyed at Themelthorpe, two days later one was destroyed at Kerdiston and another at Whitwell' (Piercy, p40). Rioters gathered in Reepham on 26 november 1830 and attacked the local magistrate, '...Sir Jacob Astley...[who]...was greeted with such a volley of sticks and stones from the assembled townsfolk that he fell from his horse and was forced to make a sharp and undignified exit...(Lee, p32)...In later incidents firemen on their way to a fire in Reepham were attacked by a crowd while at Heydon the village fire engine was wheeled out for another blaze, only to be discovered to have been sabotaged' (Lee, pp33–4). Agricultural machinery was destroyed at Cawston and Foulsham and the paper mill at Lyng was attacked (Piercy, p49).

The crowd was pacified by measures delivered on 1 december 1830 by the Reverend Collyer from an upstairs window of the Kings Arms, where he and local landowners and farmers had met to agree emergency measures: 'There was to be a minimum wage...and a new payment structure designed to ensure that every labourer had the opportunity to earn fourteen shillings a week [the average was then nine shillings and sixpence per week, according to James Kent, a contemporary writer]; there was to be a new subscription fund aimed at providing blankets and other necessaries for the poor; and...the employers would see to it that threshing machines were no longer used in the district' (Lee, p34–5).

At these words the market-place became quiet and the crowd left, their grievances met.

The *Norfolk Chronicle* for 20 november 1830 records:

> 'Having often advocated the plan of letting small portions of land to industrious cottagers, we feel much pleasure in stating that it has been acted upon at Reepham, by Messrs Birchams who last Michaelmas divided and let eleven acres of land, which has proved a great accommodation and comfort to 33 poor families. Also at Heydon by Mr Richardson (author of the district farm plan) who has let a field of nearly seven acres to fourteen industrious men of that parish. Men, women and children, to the amount of about forty, are employed in digging their several portions of half an acre each with an alacrity and cheerfulness that is quite gratifying. The seed has been purchased for them and the money is to be repaid after the crops of wheat and potatoes are got in.'

Bircham estate records do not reveal where on his many acres the allotment land was located, and neither are there references to them in White's Trade Directory for 1845.

Despite their increasing popularity throughout the nineteenth century, allotments in Reepham disappear, perhaps literally; there is no record of them on tithe maps of 1846. The earliest Ordnance Survey map of 1886 is similarly empty, but the O/S map of 1906 shows two sites, one of 1.956 acres behind Newland Villas, on Ollands Road and another of 1.462 acres at right-angles to and between Ollands Road and Station Road, just below the junction of the latter with the Kerdiston Road and north of the Cattle Sale Yard. Both plots were owned by a member of the Eglington family.

The first of these, but not the second, is recalled by Mr Wesley Piercy, a resident of Reepham since 1917; the land was finally taken for building in the late 1980s. Mr Frank Bibby tells us that the Ollands Road site also went under the developer in about 1985. They are among a number of sites that existed within living memory. Reepham, like Aylsham and Haveringland, was a town where fruit, including soft fruit, was grown in fields adjoining Crown Meadow and Broomhill. Allotment holding and smallholding, as on land on Station Road now occupied by the new Rectory which was used for market gardening and pigs (according to Miss Judy Wilkin), would have contributed with farming to agricultural practice and the national table. There are still apple orchards towards Kerdiston. Mr Micky Downes also recalls that Mr Cyril Eglington, another of the same family, let allotments on yet another piece of land next to Robins Lane, again lost to houses in the 1980s. Mr Piercy has a further recollection of Parish Council-owned allotments behind Sunbarn Close on the land now occupied by the Fire Station but these were lost in the 1970s, presumably when it was built. Miss Judy Wilkin identified a site by Reepham railway station, which was in use in the 1980s and is still vacant; and another at Hackford, believed to be next to the railway line; and at Ede's Mill, in Whitwell.

Reepham in wartime responded to the 'dig for victory' campaign by creating allotments on at least two sites, big ones: one was on a field opposite the primary school in Whitwell Road, and the other on the school playing field itself which was just for the schoolchildren.

With the recent resurgence of interest, for the existing 6 plots off the Norwich Road there is a waiting list of in excess of 12 people and expected waiting-time has already reached 12 years for some.

Thanks to all these local people for helping to add another piece of the allotments history jigsaw

Salthouse

Salthouse lies a few miles to the east of **Cley-next-the-Sea** on the north Norfolk coast. Where Cley nestles between the sea and the river, its church sentinel to the Wiveton postern across the estuary-that-was in the days of Hanseatic League trading, Salthouse straddles the littoral between sea and the low hills with heathland at its back. That stretch of coast is best-known for the saline marshes built out of accumulated mud and tidal seepage which support its distinctive folds of grasses and samphire. Since 1650 the sea was excluded by a vast shingle bank built by the Dutch and renewed between 1851–55 following a devastating storm in 1845. The replacement bank had all but vanished by the second edition Ordnance Survey map of 1904. This map shows that the coast between road and sea was sectored east-west by the New Cut drain and by roughly north-south drains, so dividing the whole area into parcels. The entire area is marked as smallholdings. Most but not all the drainage channels are present on the Inclosure Award map of 1853 (*Salthouse*, p67) so that the parcels of land are larger with the exception of a quadrant abutting the road and against the Beach Road. This is divided into smaller, numbered plots most of which from the inscriptions were held freehold and a few copyhold. There were also two big plots of five acres each 'for the labouring poor of Salthouse' (p71). A Terrier of unknown date but clearly post-enclosure refers to the ten acres as allotments 'now occupied by about 27 tenants and are part of land reclaimed from the sea by raising a Bank'. Rents were collected by Allotment Wardens and contributed to the 'Poor Rate Fund' (p73). (An 1854 Rate Book assessment for poor relief shows virtually all householders, including trades, having land attached to their properties – the people of Salthouse needed to make use of every piece of land available, it seems.) It is remarkable that land could be productive so soon after being inundated. The Bank gave way again in 1862, making the existence of smallholdings in 1904 rather surprising.

Today as reported by a resident and allotment holder, allotments are on the heath, which was enclosed in 1781 with common rights, on an exposed and windy but productive part of the hills. At the time of writing water is about to be laid on.

Terrington St Clement [pictures]

According to their own record the allotments at Terrington-St-Clement were created in 1816, making them amongst the earliest in Norfolk established specifically as cultivable plots for which there is a certain record.

Terrington is in the Fenland, and hence its commons were part of an intercommoning arrangement with adjacent parishes:

"At the end of the thirteenth century the vills of Walton, Walpole, Terrington and Walsoken seem to constitute a unity among themselves … The foundation of this seems to lie in the possession of a common marsh and it is made the more secure by common payments and works to keep out the sea…The leet of the marsh mentioned in the late thirteenth century by the Ely jurors was no new thing. It can be traced back through the twelfth century and it appears to have been based upon an economic foundation" (D C Douglas *The Social Structure of Medieval East Anglia* (1927) pp196–8. Map of *Parish Boundaries in Norfolk Marshland*, showing especially Terrington-St-Clement, in H C Darby *The Mediaeval Fenland* (David & Charles, 1940), p69 refers, below).

Since Terrington's allotments are even today below sea level, the importance of sharing and maintaining land in Fenland must be an entrenched principle.

The parish history informs that between 1760 and 1818 Acts of Parliament permitted five million acres of common land to be enclosed: 'Some villagers lived in tied cottages with probably an eighth of an acre of land but most people did not have enough land on which to support their large families'.

Unusually Bryant's Map of 1826 shows the first allotment site, now called Churchgateway, as 'Garden'. There is no reference to the site in Zachary Clark's directory of charities in Norfolk (1811) or in Brougham's 1843 report to the Commissioners. White's *Trade Directory* of 1845 describes how:

'... the Reverend Ambrose Goode and other gentlemen desirous of bettering the conditions of the poor parishioners induced one of the principal landowners [the Bentinck family] to let to the overseers 22a2r30p to be relet at modest rents in lots of 2–4 roods [half to one acre]. This experiment produced such beneficial effects by reducing the poor rates and improving the habits and consequently the circumstances of any of the more troublesome parishioners that the former opponents became strenuous advocates of the plan and a few years afterwards the overseers took over land of about 22 acres and relet in the same manner with the same beneficial results.'

From the same source for 1883 we learn that on the 22 acres there were 62 allotments, let at 12s-3d per rood. Today there are three sites:

- Tower Road, 12.03 acres having 45 plots – traditional vegetable growers produce hardy crops requiring large amounts of land and little attention – maize, broad beans, potatoes, beetroot, onions.

- Churchgateway, 22.29acres with 84 plots. Currently there are some six tenants, mostly local farmers renting large amounts of land and growing single crops for commercial use (willow slips to produce small bushes which are for decoration, for example for conference halls, mostly sent down to London; wheat; daffodils. The practice of Terrington produce finding its way to London goes back to the days when there was a railway loopline, abolished by Beaching with dozens of local jobs, which would send six trainloads of strawberries per day during the summer, as well as tomatoes grown in glass houses). One remaining tenant works his plot for vegetables. The plot resembles a large strip, with a shed on it. The site has a road up the centre provided by the Council. In both cases the Council provides no water for the sites – tenants rely on rain. The soil is black Fenland loam and of excellent quality and yield.

- Sandygate Lane, 6.76 acres on land reclaimed beyond the Roman Bank post-1790 – originally the revenue from this site was used for a fuel charity. In 2000 the land was converted into a local amenity, the Millennium Wood.

There are always problems to deal with on allotments. Unusually, in this case there are no complaints about vandals and there is no protective fencing for the sites. The farmers' wheat encourages a pest weed, blackgrass, which invades other plots and there is ravaging by pheasants and pigeons.

The allotments of Terrington-St-Clements are spoken of with pride as a valuable tradition of many years; they are well-supported and managed.

Thanks to Mr Brian Howling, Terrington-St-Clement Parish Councillor

Thompson

In the nineteenth and twentieth centuries Thompson, Merton and Tottington were estate villages owned by Lord Walsingham. This state of affairs came to an abrupt end in 1942 when the Ministry of Defence commandeered many square miles of land – '8 500 acres, one hundred houses, twelve farms, timber, sand and gravel pits', according to a letter (dated 1 march 2005) received from Lord Walsingham in response to the Survey questionnaire – on the pretext of the War effort and in 1950 compulsorily purchased the land to provide army training grounds.

Neither Merton nor Tottington have ever had allotments, as Lord Walsingham writes, 'all houses having vegetable gardens prior to World War 2'. In Thompson, similarly, houses built for estate workers in the nineteenth century had land attached: 'Thompson is a well-spread traditional village and historically cottagers had their own vegetable gardens…[the cottages] have half-acre gardens. In 1921…rents…were under 2s-6d a week and agricultural wages twenty-five shillings or so. I remember when I first worked at sixteen in 1941 I earned twenty-one shillings as a boy (and it was the first time I had handled a one-pound note)'.

A field in Thompson – 'at the Danish end of Thompson' – became the allotment site, probably through the agency of Lord Walsingham's father after World War 2 when council houses were no longer built with land attached. The field was next to Philly Abel's council house. When an employee of the estate and allotment tenant who had bought his house but had no space on his land he was permitted to build his garage on a corner of the allotment field, 'and later used it as a forge (now abandoned)'.

'But generally council house tenants and other residents do not grow their own veg these days and…[although]… Breckland District Council Planning Department recently recommended the field should be developed to provide the housing the Deputy PM is looking for…there is no intention to withdraw it as long as [the tenant] wants it' The field 'is still rented by [Philly Abel's] son from the Walsingham Estate'.

Thanks to Lord Walsingham

Toft Monks

According to the Parish Allotment Register and Rent Book 1906-58, the allotment site off Burnthouse Lane in Toft Monks now consists of 1.25 acres. The Register and Cash Books show that the rents produced £13 per year throughout the whole period 1906-60. The land is part of the Town Estate and is administered by Trustees appointed by the Parish Council as a charity which on 29 september 1959 was 'returned to the Vicar of Toft Monks'. The Town Estate Charity is recorded by Brougham's 1843 *Report* where it consisted of '11 acres 3 roods 3 poles and a house' producing £29-16s annually to support the Parish Rates. By the time of White's Trade Directory of 1864 the rent was £44-19s per year ' for Church rates, and coals'.

There are a number of patterns emerging in the tenancy records which are common to other parishes.

- Some of the tenants held their plots for long periods of time: Frederick Brock 1906–1931, 25 years; George Long 1906–25, 19 years; Charles Turner 1906–26, 20 years; Sidney George Snowling 1926–60, at least 34 years; John R Read ?1931–1946, 15 years (the 1930s record is unclear); George Meen 1946–1960, at least 14 years.

- A widow, Jemima Curtis, succeeded her husband James Curtis in 1917. Between them they held four acres from 1906–1926.

- During the same period Henry Curtis held one acre; more than one member of an extended family working plots on the village site is common in Norfolk at that time. Unusually there is no evidence of plots being held by successive generations.

- None of the plots was vacant throughout the period of the record.

- Although the site offered ten plots, from the time of the record in 1906 until 1927 there were only five or six tenants, when it dropped to four. From 1936 to 1946 there were three, from then until the end of the record there were just two tenants and it became untenanted in c.1984. Now it is let for grazing. Toft Monks is unusual for the twentieth century in seeing simply a steady decline in the number of tenants rather than the fluctuations reflecting world events of elsewhere in Norfolk.

The holdings were mostly of one acre, with one individual holding four acres at the outset of the record. In 1908 a tenant (Frederick Brock) of 1 acre 2 roods 29 poles acquired a further acre, until 1923 when reverted to the original holding. In 1925 Stephen J Grimson increased his holding from one to two acres, reverting to the single acre just a year later. These are the only two hints that world events might have influenced holdings in Toft Monks (cf **Oulton** and **Little Plumstead**).

Otherwise from 1926 Sidney George Snowley steadily enlarged his four-acre tenancy until between 1941 and the end of the record in 1960 he held nine acres, leaving 2 roods 29 poles for John R Read.

The later tenancies are notably and increasingly held by Aldeby and Haddiscoe people, suggesting that Toft Monks saw a declining population in the latter half of the century, who used the land commercially.

Thanks to Toft Monks Parish Council

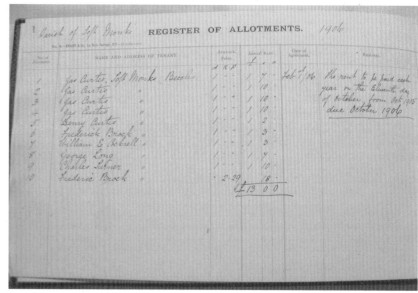

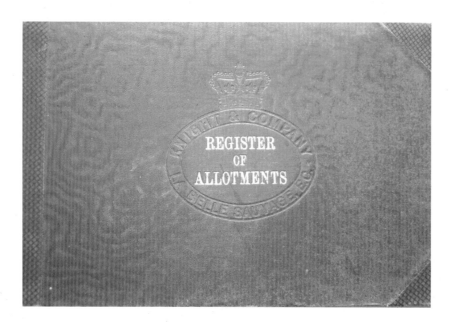

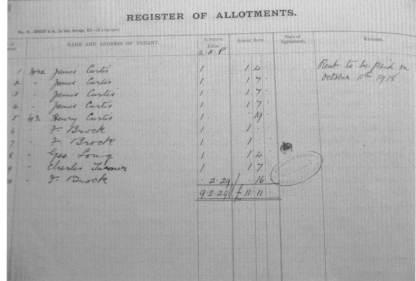

Topcroft

By the 1807 Inclosure Act for Topcroft 79 acres 6 poles of the commons were apportioned. None was left for public use. Of the thirty-six awards made, only one was substantial, four were of five or six acres and eleven of one or two acres, leaving fifteen acres or thereabouts to be divided between seventeen people – not surprising that by 1840 when the Tithe apportionment was made, the records show that very few – five only – of the same surnames appear in that list. The conclusion must be that the great majority of those awarded land sold up within a generation. But it is surprising that none of the largest landholders (including two esquires) are mentioned in the Tithe Apportionment, and that it is the smaller, 1–2 acre holdings that seem to produce the entrepreneurs. One of the smallest local-boys-made-big held 3 rods 36 perches – nearly an acre, it has to be admitted – and another a mere 2 rods 16 perches, slightly more than a half-acre. As far as it was possible to match inclosure awards to field names, the very big holdings of 1840 were of pasture, not arable or woodland, although some of those listed as larger landholders do appear to have acquired arable land.

There is no suggestion or evidence that the very small awards were used as garden plots, showing that the existence of small amounts of land following enclosure does not presuppose garden allotments but, interestingly, the small plots had been consolidated into the holdings of relatively few people within a relatively short space of time.

Topcroft Village: a book for the new millennium
(The Topcroft Millennium Book Group, 1999)

use and value
Trowse [pictures]

Trowse Parish Council administers two allotment sites at Trowse Newton:
- Trowse Allotments (formerly known as the Dell) on the east side of White Horse Lane has 54 plots. This site, originally of 3 acres 2 rods 16 poles, was acquired through Deeds created between the Council and J P Colman Ltd on 12 december 1921;

- Block Hill allotments has twenty plots.

Another Deed between the Council and Russell J Colman dated 8 october 1921 puts 5 acres 2 rods 31 poles in three parcels of land at its disposal:
- one piece known as Top Piece allotments;

- the Café Allotments (originally 6 rods and extended by a further 5 rods in 1938);

- a third piece, consisting of two sections, 'New Allotments' (also known as Hospital Allotments) and Block Hill allotments, of which the existing site is the successor. Neither Top Piece nor the Café Allotments still exist, the latter having been taken for police housing in 1968. The A47 Norwich Southern by-pass claimed parts of the Block Hill/New Allotments in 1992.

Trowse Newton was transformed when Jeremiah James Colman (1830–98) moved the family mustard mill from Stoke Holy Cross to Carrow between 1856 and 1862. Railways first ran from Norwich in 1844. In the last quarter of the nineteenth century Colman acquired land neighbouring Carrow. From the Harvey Estate in 1869 he bought twenty-four railway cottages in Thorpe, next to the station; in 1874 he leased dwellings, the Harvey Arms public house, a blacksmith's shop (NRO/BR61/3/50/1–25 and NROBR61/3/50/26–38), eventually buying these properties in 1897. In the same year he bought Wortley Estate land which formerly had been a market garden and buildings in The Street and White Horse Lane and in Whitlingham Lane, called Staithe Pasture.

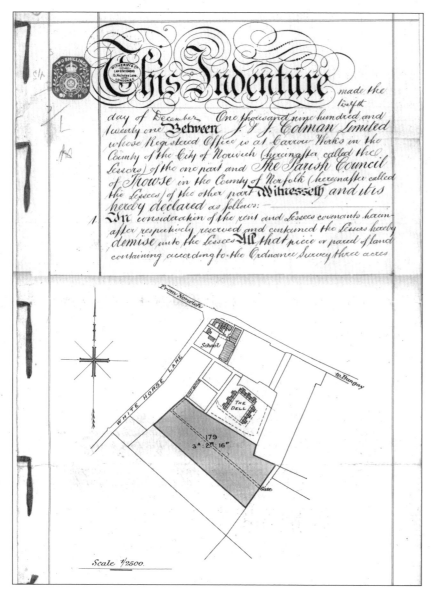

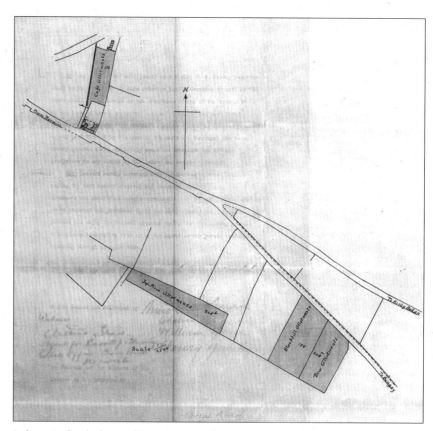

Indentures for the lease of four pieces of allotment land in Trowse between Russel J Colman and the Parish Council, dated 8 october 1921 (Thanks to Trowse Parish Council).

Indentures for the lease of four pieces of allotment land in Trowse between J and J Colman and the Parish Council, dated 12 december 1921 (Thanks to Trowse Parish Council).

Colman was both entrepreneur and dedicated nonconformist; he became a Baptist Deacon in 1861, and he held public office as Mayor of Norwich and a Liberal MP for many years. At Carrow Colman introduced the ideals of the Port Sunlight, Rowntree and Bournville models in a modest way to the environs of Norwich. Trowse Newton resembled the first planted villages of the industrial eighteenth century, like Saltaire:

'The firm [J and J Colman Ltd] pioneered what would now be viewed as aspects of social welfare including workers' houses, a school in 1857, a hot meals service in 1868 – vegetable stew and a pint of coffee for 4d – and a dispensary in 1864. Carrow Fire Brigade was created in 1887, Lakenham Cricket Ground was acquired by the firm in 1878 (NRO resume of records transferred to the Port Sunlight Archive in 2000).

Colman's strict nonconformism entailed that his workers became teetotal and so a café was provided for socializing to which, as we have seen, in due course were attached garden allotments. Colman had been a keen horticulturalist since his youth and often held Norwich Horticultural Society meetings in his gardens. A natural extension of this enthusiasm was the encouragement of gardens and, eventually, allotments for his workpeople. One of them wrote to thank him:

'Sir, Pardon the Liberty but let me as A Cottageher [sic] in Thorpe Hamlet thank you and through you Mrs Colman for the support by your purse And the Encouragement by your presence of our Flower Show for the mingling together of the Rich among the poor on such days I Believe have A great Effect upon them for the better it take away A great deal of the soreness that there is Among the poor I wish there were more of such Meetings why not one in Every Parish we should understand each other better the poor would be all the Better for it we all have Windows I believe we all love flowers some more than others no doubt I believe the sight of flowers Awaken many serious thoughts if I can meausure others corn by my own bushel the truth is I have great faith in flowers they keep us out of mischief they teach us to study the good and the great God for sure he is to be seen in

the Beautifull flowers of this Earth if we learn to look at them Aright hoping that your example may be A Presedent for all future Mayors towards our flower shows I subscribe myself one of your prize winners and have the good fortune to be one of your Workmen' (Colman, p51).

Described as a friend to the working class, Colman viewed allotments as 'one practical scheme' for helping them. 'As far back as 1857 he had endeavoured to do something in the direction of encouraging gardening, and in later years he or his Firm tried to do more to develop the system of allotments for he was, to quote his own words, "fully convinced of their value and the need of a wider extension of the benefit they bring". In his election address of 1885, he said, 'On the question of the land, I think some measures are desirable beyond the promotion of Cheap Transfer and Abolition of the Laws of Primogeniture and Entail. I agree with the principles of the Bills for the Extension of Allotments [resulting in the 1887 Allotments for the Labouring Classes Act] and for the Enfranchisement of Copyholds and Leaseholds, and while I am not in favour of any revolutionary enactments, I think that in the directions indicated by these Bills, legislation may do much to facilitate the acquisition of Real Estate by a much larger proportion of the population than now enjoy it' (Colman, p356).

The 1887 Act specified the details by which allotments could be run, including that buildings were allowed if toolhouse, shed, greenhouse, fowl house or pigsty. So supportive was he that he built pigsties for the Dell Loke allotments in Trowse Newton, a unique provision for Norfolk (Survey). The pigsties were – still are, though not used for pigs – substantial clinker-built sheds, tarred and tiled to be durable. They contributed to the natural growing cycle in which consumption of waste organic matter and replenishment of the nutrients in the soil are crucial elements. And they were a source of food, like the customary pig for annual slaughter.

Nowadays the only direct manuring by animals permitted at the Trowse allotments is by chickens, and lorry-loads of manure are delivered to tenants by agreement with a local farmer. Recent Parish Council records reveal that the allotments have had their problems, as they all do: a boundary dispute between neighbours; letters to tenants between 1986 and 1990 about the state of the allotments, rubbish having accumulated; incursions through road-building; devastation by rabbits; and on the day of a visit, fences down from outside one site, and chickens taken by human predators. As far as records tell, the plots have always been in demand, with greater uptake recently by young people, especially women, due to a new housing development at Crown Point. There is no association for tenants, but Trowse Newton is close enough to the city for them to join the Norwich Bluebell Road Association for the benefits of buying seed and equipment.

Allotments are well-cultivated with a great variety of produce, members help each other out and are well supported by an enthusiastic Council. The view from the allotments is a provocative mixture of new and old, surrounded as they are by fields and water-meadows and the benefits of Colman's vision on the one hand but with a vista across the River Yare to housing developments at Lakenham and the A47 slip-road surmounted by the concrete and pebble-dash slab that is County Hall commanding acres of glittering vehicles parked around it. Just so with Trowse allotments: a mix of experience and trial, tried and tested and experiment, tradition and innovation – just what allotments do best.

Thanks to Ms Nicky Barnes, Parish Councillor for Trowse

West Winch

West Winch acquired allotments in October 1844 when the Labourers' Friend Society was formed to have 'full power to hire land' (Regulation V) and 'to see that allotments of land are properly cultivated according to the rules quoted below in full laid down by the Committee' (Regulation VI). According to White's *Trade Directory* of 1845 the 'excellent plan' was proposed by Mr James Wake, a Registrar, 'for the purpose of hiring land and letting it out to the poor, on the *allotment system*'. Accordingly both manorial (presumably in the gift of Lord W H H Cholmondeley of Houghton Hall, the Society's President) and glebe allotments were created. A map of 1861 shows the former (Site 1) sandwiched between closes that front Main Road of West Winch and Watering Lane (Eller, p216ff).

The Ordnance Survey map of 1929 confirms the existence of Site 1 and gives its acreage as 5.996 acres. It shows a further Site 2 of 3.015 acres, also to the west of Main Road north of the Methodist Chapel and south of Long Lane. Another, Site 3 was shown in a 1928 Ordnance Survey map to be 10.286 acres but by 1929 was 9.893 acres; it was also to the west of Main Road opposite the Corn Mill. There were many fields of smallholdings in the vicinity of the Corn Mill, on the east side of Main Road.

The Survey response states that allotments, which would have been Site 1 from the location, were discontinued 'about forty to fifty years ago...and the land had a school built on it'. The inference is that Sites 2 and 3 were re-used before that point, possibly when land was lost through the straightening of the River Nar.

West Winch Labourers' Friend Society
In October 1844, 'through the Christian and active benevolence of the Right Hon., the Lord W.H.H.Cholmondley, Lord of the Manor of West Winch, in the County of Norfolk, a Society was formed for the benefit of the labourers and poor of the aforesaid parish of West Winch.

The 'Rules and Regulations' of the society were as follows

i   This society shall be called the West Winch Labourers' Society.

ii   The object of this society shall be to benefit the labouring classes, to ensure their self respect, and to make them useful members of society.

iii   The society shall consist of a president, vice presidents, an acting committee, visitors and a treasurer.

iv   Friends subscribing five shillings a year, or three pounds and upwards at once, without being entitled on account of such payment to any benefit or advantage from the society, will become honorary members.

v   The management of this society shall be in a committee, composed of seven, three of whom shall have powers to act. The president, vice presidents, acting committee, visitors and treasurers shall have full power to hire land, and to direct the expenditure of all moneys for the purpose of the said society.

vi   The visitors shall have full power to see that the allotments of land are properly cultivated according to the rules laid down by the committee; and, if required, instruct the members as to the mode of cultivation.

vii   Hiring members not to dig clay, nor cut the fences without an order from the visitors, or acting committee; nor to injure their neighbour's land, by carting at improper seasons.

viii   The treasurer to receive all moneys, and to pay such sums as the committee shall direct.

ix   Premiums to be given to the oldest men and women of the parish at the annual meeting of the society, if the funds will admit of them.

Contemporary comments on the 'Allotment System':

'It may safely be assumed that a practice which diminishes the poverty of the labouring class, and promotes their good conduct, cannot but be beneficial to the community at large.' – Committee of the House of Commons, 1843.

'The impression on my mind,' observed the late Sir R.Peel, Sept. 1844, *'is in favour of allotting to the respectable labourer on a farm, such a small portion of land as would afford occupation to the <u>vacant hours</u> of himself and his family, and give him an interest in the soil'*

Bob Wilkinson

glossary

agricultural associations can be thought of as one of the subterfuges of the landowner to subvert the poor rate. The aim of the association was to encourage the independence of the agricultural labourer by rewarding "good conduct and industrious habits" among **cottagers**, servants and labourers.

Anne Digby writes in *Pauper Palaces* (Routledge, 1978),

"The first of these associations in Norfolk was the Launditch Society,

formed in 1831. Prizes included those for independence. For example, in 1835 second-class prizes were awarded to 'James Futter of **North Elmham**, James Boldero of Gressenhall and Charles Craves of Worthing for supporting a family of five children under 12 years of age without ever receiving any relief from the parish, the former three sovereigns and the latter two sovereigns each".

A poster advertising the Forehoe Association (representing a Hundred – see poster over) lays out a panoply of prizes, substantial for the day, which encouraged loyalty and sobriety amongst farm servants and tradesmen: for saving in a Savings Bank; for supporting "the greatest number of children under 12 years of age, born in wedlock..." – cautious caveat – "...without receiving or having received any parish relief except in sickness"; and to the **cottager** for the "greatest number of potatoes in his own garden", the "greatest weight of onions in his own garden or allotment, on the least quantity of land (not less than half a rod)", and so on. Knitting stockings, socks and gloves, making beeswax and honey and brewing malt beer also qualified for reward.

allotment the modern term for a piece of rented ground used for growing vegetables, fruit and flowers, sometimes for keeping fowl or animals, usually for personal use when it is a garden allotment. Even so allotments exist where produce is sold. On some O/S maps and their derivatives sites are marked as 'garden allotments' and 'allotments' to distinguish the former from **field gardens** or **smallholdings**.

allotment field another term for **field garden**.

allotment gardens another term for **garden allotment**.

bce before common era (equivalent to BC)

close 'small enclosed fields not included in open or common field system. Usually near village and farmstead'(Holowell, glossary). Appear frequently on maps, eg Norwich 1776, Castle Rising.

common garden another term for garden allotment.

commons 'Most commons are not, as is often supposed, free to the public at large but only to certain people who have the right to take from them certain natural resources which include grazing for stock, and fuel, either wood or peat. Rights of common are private rights and the soil of commons has private owners who may not obstruct these rights, and the loss can even continue today' (Hales, p70).

---

cottagers

The model cottage with its garden of, usually, a quarter- or half-acre was the provision for favoured labourers of the landowning proprietor. In 1797 Thomas Bernard gave An *Account of a Cottage Garden near Tadcaster*. The garden described therein had 'fifteen apple trees, a greengage and three plums, gooseberry and currant bushes, vegetables and beehives...[he] got forty bushels of potatoes from his ground'. Arthur Young's *General View of the Agriculture of the County of Norfolk* (1804) includes a description, illustration and plans of cottages built by Mr Robinson at Carbrooke, north-east of Watton. Young claims that 'it is a new practice in west Norfolk to let cottages on leases or hires, a practice that ran counter to the trend of hiring and firing for task'. He lamented the absence of cottages at Snetterton and the neighbouring parishes, declaring that the poor people in west Norfolk 'are very neat in their well-cultivated gardens; the land fully cropt and in high order and the hedges neatly clipt; but their gardens are much too small; they deserve additions'. In 1863–4 the *Norfolk News* surveyed the *Cottage Homes of England*, describing the cottages on several Norfolk estates. At Holkham, away from the trophy cottages at the gate, conditions were 'wretched' and 'unfit to live in'. Mr Brampton Gurdon of the Cranworth Estate received a favourable verdict, as did some of the homes on Lord Walsingham's Estates (Susanna Wade-Martins/2, p63). When the railway companies began work in Norfolk in the 1850s, where they built cottages for road-crossings or station staff they, too, were accommodated with a quarter-acre garden.

1839.

THE HUNDRED OF
FOREHOE ASSOCIATION

For Promoting and Rewarding Good Conduct, and Encouraging Industrious Habits amongst Cottagers, Labourers, and Servants, both Agricultural and Domestic.

PRESENT MEMBERS.

THOSE MARKED THUS * ARE OF THE COMMITTEE.

*Right Honorable Lord Wodehouse, President.
*John Mitchell, Esq., Vice-President.

The Rt. Hon. and Rev. Lord Bayning
The Hon. & Rev. Armine Wodehouse
*The Hon. & Rev. William Wodehouse
John Weyland, Esq.
Mr. Culyer
— Neave
— Press (Wymondham)
— Read
— Gray
G. D. Graver, Esq.
*Rev. J. S. Cann,
Captain Ives
— Stephen Gooch
J. T. Graver Browne, Esq.

*Mr. Thomas Atkins
— John Hipkin
— Robert Liddelow
— Thomas Sutton
— Cadywold
Rev. W. Smith, (Honingham)
E. Press, Esq.
Rev. D. Jones
*W. R. Clarke, Esq.
Mr. Brunsell
— J. G. Howlett
— John Coleman
— Thomas Bayes
— Hurnard
*— F. G. Taylor

W. Daniel, Esq.
*Mr. Francis Reynolds
— Rowing
— Thomas Banham
*Mr. Farrer, (Treasurer)
— John Cann
*Rev. C. B. Cooper, (Secretary)
Rev. F. de Soyres
Mr. Ellis
— Robert Cann
— G. Hart
— Rix
*Rev. M. B. Darby, (Secretary)
Mr. Robert Britton
— Robert Clarke

Charles S. Onley, Esq.
W. Herring, Esq.
Mr. J. Leeder
— J. Curman
— John Howlett
— G. Weston
— Joseph Carpenter
— W. Atkins
— J. R. Nettleship
— J. T. Tallent
— D. Alexander, Jun.
P. C. Gilman, Esq.
Mr. Priest
— Matthew Cooper
Mrs. Elizabeth Fisher

Mr. Culley
Rev. Edward Marsham
Mr. Philip Pitts
Rev. J. H. Browne
Mr. John Matthews
Miss Burroughes
Rev. H. Francillin
S. H. I. N. Gilman, Esq.
Mr. W. H. Tipple
— J. H. Tipple
Mr. Clamroch
Mr. Turner
— James Davey
— John Leatherdale
— Sparkhall

Mr. Parker
— Besson
— William Spruce
W. R. Cann, Esq.
Mr. S. T. Postle
— Thomas Cann
— John Palmer
— Thomas Tice
— William Sutton
— Joseph Muskett
Miss Morse
E. P. Clarke, Esq.
Rev. Thomas Mann

Subscriptions become due on the 1st. of October; and all Subscribers, who do not signify to the Secretaries in writing, previous to that day, their intention of withdrawing from the Association, will be considered Subscribers for the current year. The Members of the Committee are severally authorized to receive Subscriptions.

The following REWARDS and PREMIUMS are offered by the ASSOCIATION; and will be adjudged at a Meeting of the Committee, to be held at Wymondham, on Tuesday, October 22nd, at Eleven o'Clock; and distributed at the Annual Meeting, which will be held at the same place, at Two o'Clock, on Thursday, October 24th, 1839, when the Members of the Association will dine together, and an early application for Tickets is requested.

AGRICULTURAL SERVANTS.

1. To the SINGLE MAN … *Two sovereigns*
3. To the next … *Two sovereigns*
3. To the SINGLE WOMAN … *One sovereign*
4. To the next … *One sovereign*
5. To the LAD, or YOUTH … *Ten shillings*
6. To the next … *One sovereign*
7. To the GIRL … *Ten shillings*
8. To the next … *Ten shillings*

TRADESMEN'S SERVANTS.

17. To the SINGLE MAN … *Two sovereigns*
18. To the SINGLE WOMAN … *One sovereign*
19. To the LAD … *Two sovereigns*
12. To the LABOURER … *Thirty shillings*
13. To the next … *Two sovereigns*
15. To the SHEPHERD … *Thirty shillings*
16. To the next … *One sovereign*

AGRICULTURAL AND TRADESMEN'S SERVANTS.

25. To the FARM SERVANT or TRADESMAN'S SERVANT … *Three sovereigns*
26. To the FARMING LABOURER or JOURNEYMAN TRADESMAN … *Fifty shillings*
27. To the next … *Thirty shillings*
28. To the next … *Twenty sovereigns*
29. To the next … *One sovereign*
30. To the next … *Twelve shillings & sixpence*
31. To the next … *Seven shillings & sixpence*

COTTAGERS.

33. To the COTTAGER … *One sovereign*
34. To the next … *Fifteen shillings*
35. To the next … *Fifteen shillings*
36. To the COTTAGER … *One sovereign*
37. To the next … *Ten shillings*
38. To the COTTAGER … *One sovereign*
39. To the next … *One sovereign*
40. To the COTTAGER … *Fifteen shillings*
41. To the next … *Ten shillings*
42. To the next … *Ten shillings*
43. To the next … *Five shillings*

44. To the POOR WOMAN or GIRL … *One sovereign*
45. To the next … *Ten shillings*

46. To the COTTAGER … *Fifteen shillings*
47. To the next … *Fifteen shillings*
48. To the next … *Ten shillings*

PLOUGHING.

49. To the PLOUGHMAN … *One sovereign*
50. To the next … *Fifteen shillings*
51. To the next … *Ten shillings*
52. To the next … *Five shillings*
53. To the PLOUGH LAD or YOUTH … *One sovereign*
54. To the next … *Fifteen shillings*
55. To the next … *Ten shillings*
56. To the next … *Five shillings*

57. To the PLOUGHMAN … *Two sovereigns*
58. To the next … *One sovereign*
59. To the next … *Fifteen shillings*
60. To the next … *Ten shillings*
61. To the PLOUGH LAD or YOUTH … *Thirty shillings*
62. To the next … *One sovereign*
63. To the next … *Fifteen shillings*
64. To the next … *Ten shillings*

GENERAL NOTICES.—All Claimants for Prizes must be Inhabitants of, or employed in, the Hundred of Forehoe; and the Association reserves to its Committee, the power of determining all questions that may at respecting the merits or qualifications of Claimants, and of refusing to award any Premium it may think proper. Printed Forms of Certificates may be had of the Secretaries, or of any other Member of the Association. Claimants must send their Certificates, (filled up) to either of the Secretaries during the week previous to the Annual Meeting.

[PHILO, PRINTER, WYMONDHAM.]

Thanks to Dr Paul Cattermore, Wymondham Abbey Archive.

Whenever folk work in isolation and need occupation and a source of fresh food the practice was adopted and so pubs and inns also had large gardens in some cases. Even as late as the 1970s the village policeman's house was attached to land, as at Cawston: a condition of tenure was that the plot would be well-cultivated, a means of keeping the local bobby on call if needed by the local people!(anecdote from Christopher Hulse).

Estate cottages abound throughout Norfolk, usually in the livery of clunch, brick or flint according to the local geology and the design of the landowner's estate house. Some serve as lodges at the gates to the house. To this day many retain their gardens, cultivated traditionally. In other cases the garden has been adapted to modern practices, including a holistic approach that incorporates organic and natural methods of pest-control and nurture.

Cottages in Salle, on the estate of Sir John White, with traditional quarter acre gardens.

Also in Salle, but no longer an estate garden, the attached and extended garden is laid to a divided mix of leisure, traditional fruit and vegetables, and a wood and wildlife area.

Thanks to Naomi Horrocks and Paul Levy.

dibbling

Four seeds in a hole:
One for the rook and one for the crow
And one to rot and one to grow.

A dibbler resembled a three-pronged fork.

'I learnt the proper way to dibble from a very old man, Charlie Sharman. I was quite young at the time. Old Charlie must have first used the dibbles in the field round about a hundred years ago. One of the last times he used them – I recollect him telling me – was to dibble winter beans. All of us round here used to grow about a quarter of an acre of corn on our allotments; and I used to dibble my corn as most of the others did. Just after the First World War when times were very bad I used to go around dibbling corn and so on in other people's allotments, just to earn a shilling or two'.

So spake Joe Thompson, born 1901, speaking in about 1964 to George Eward Evans. Dibbling was described by two Elizabethan farmers, the Essex man Thomas Tusser who wrote *Five Pointes of Good Husbandry* (1573) and Sir Hugh Plat in *The Arte of Setting Corn* (1600). He described the practice as having originated with the accident of a 'silly wench' who dropped wheat seed in holes intended for carrots. The practice appears to have begun in the thirteenth century and to have persisted through the nineteenth century, at least in Suffolk and Norfolk, until the beginning of the twentieth (Susanna Wade-Martins/2, p70), despite the introduction of Jethro Tull's mechanical drills for corn some century and a half earlier. In 1821 a farmer described conducting an experiment by comparing yields from fields in one of which seed had been drilled and in the other dibbled; evidently dibbling favoured some types of corn. It was a more efficient way of sowing since it was less wasteful and there is also the suggestion that the cost of labour was so low in Norfolk that it was cheaper to use dibbling teams (which consisted of men followed by three women or children who had abandoned school for the purpose in order to drop the seed into the hole) than a team of horses and men for drilling. In the 1840s a team would cost approximately 7s 6d per acre. Peas, beans and corn were all planted in this way.

'When you were dibbling in the field you didn't need anything to guide you: you just followed the flag, that's the furrow. But where the land was flat you had no guide so I put down the string. Then I used to dibble round and round this line making two rows each time. I went round just like a horseman did when he was a-ploughing a *stetch*, walking backwards and putting my feet down exactly as the old man had taught me. I then used to cover up by raking the land over.'

By the end of the nineteenth century and for the most part dibbling was used not on farms but on the allotments but by the time of the interview most of the large allotments had reverted to farmland because the 'old boys' were too elderly and their children had moved away from the isolation of cottage or hamlet existence and the dibbler was used only as a general purpose tool on the allotment.

dole

If thou of fortune be bereft
And of thine earthly store are left
Two loaves; sell one, and with the dole
Buy hyacinths and feed the soul.

William Shakespeare

dole (1) or **dolestone** is the marker, the boundary stone that indicates the site and limit of individual holdings. David Yaxley (*A researcher's glossary* (Lark's Press, 2003)) found allusions to doles of this sort in a 1445 reference to the Vicar of Paston who '... hath pullid uppe the doolis'. E P Thompson located a fearful *Exhortation to be spoken to such Parishes where they use their Perambulation in Rogation Week:*

"Accursed be he, said Almighty God by Moses, who removeth his neighbour's doles and marks: they do much provoke the wrath of God upon themselves, which use to grind up the doles and marks, which of ancient time were laid for the division of **meers** and **balks** in the fields, to bring the owners to their right. They do wickedly, which do turn up the ancient terries of the fields, that old men beforetimes with great pains did tread out; whereby the lords' records (which be the tenants' evidence) be perverted and translated sometimes to the disheriting of the right owner, to the oppression of the poor fatherless or the poor widow … So witnesseth Solomon. The Lord will destroy the house of the proud man: but he will stablish the borders of the widow". **dollver** is used on an enclosure map of 1665 of Common Fen in Downham Market and Wimboltsham, labelling each strip as a dollver or doll. It is thought that the term refers to the stones that marked each strip.

Basil Cozens-Hardy (*Norfolk Archaeology* 31/166-7, 1957) may provide the link between the first meaning and the second:

'A dole was a piece of bruery or waste land owned in severalty and physically defined, if not by banks, then by dole stones or other boundary marks' and he alludes to a dole marked out by banks at Brampton, with its accompanying Dole Cottages.

dole meadows (2) can be found on many maps. For example, a 1766 map of Norwich by Samuel King and another of 1783 by T Smith (Frostick, p58) shows a piece of land within the city boundary, close to the meanders of the River Wensum in the north-east which is named Dasy's Dole. A map of Cawston, probably made at the time of enclosure in 1800, shows lands attached to the manor house which include a field labelled 'Dole' and a nearby Dole House (presumably named for the field and not the function) and another field, Mayes's Dole. The Tithe Apportionment map of Shimpling, as late as 1871 also shows a Dole Meadow (Paul Cattermole *Shimpling*, (2000)).

A dole meadow was a common meadow divided into portions between claimants to the use of the land. These might be allocated by the drawing of lots or rolling dice on a certain day. In Forncett-St-Mary, according to Blomefield's history of 1750, there was a Corn Dole whereby the land thus allotted was used to grow corn. In other places the crop would be hay. At Upton Fen, north of Upton Great Broad and at Borough Common, near Martham, the old peat diggings were allocated by dole. The origin of this meaning is the anglo-saxon *doelan*, to divide or deal out and can be found as dools, duels (hence the Duelling Stone at Cawston does not refer to an incident that took place in the Civil War), deals, dales.

A **dole** (3) can also be a piece of land given charitably, the rent of which buys bread, commonly, which is doled out to the needy, usually at Christmas. It was often the prerogative of the landowner or the church to make such gifts. Four acres at Tharston buys bread for the poor. At Lowestoft from the sixteenth century part of the herring catch (a tithe) called Christ's Dole was provided by the fishermen for the church. Such doles resemble fuel or poors' allotments.

dole (4) had become a charitable distribution of relief for the poor by the nineteenth century: writing about Norwich Dole Charities in his social study (1910), C B Hawkins argued for the abolition of "the old system of parish doles and all the begging, cringing and imposture which they inevitably bring with them … [they] achieve absolutely no permanent good whatsoever and simply add to the problem of underemployment".

It is a hop, skip and a jump from this arrangement to that of a ubiquitous welfare state and 'going on the dole'.

But the last word can be that of Francis Bacon writing in 1625 (*Essays: of riches*):

'I cannot call riches better than the baggage of virtue; the Roman word is better – *impedimenta*; for as the baggage is to any army, so is riches to virtue – it cannot be spared nor left behind, but it hindereth the march; yea, and the care of it sometimes loseth or disturbeth the victory. Of great riches there is no real use, except it be in the distribution; the rest is but conceit; so saith Solomon, "Where much is, there are many to consume it; and what hath the owner but the sight of it with his eyes?" The personal fruition in any man cannot reach to feel great riches: there is a custody of them, or a power of dole…'

enclosure

In Norfolk behold the despair
of tillage too much to be borne
by drovers from fair to fair
and others destroying the corn,
by custom and covetous pates,
by gaps and by opening gates.

The flocks of the Lords of the soil
do yearly the winter corn wrong;
the same in a manner they spoil
wth feeding so low and so long;
and therefore that champion field
doth seldom good winter' corn yield.

from CommonFields
or the history and policy of the laws relating to commons
and enclosures in England
Thomas Edward Scrutton (1886)

Enclosure is the creation of a physical boundary around a piece of land. The boundary might be a ditch, a hedge, a wall.

Making barriers in the landscape …

- enabled land use to be controlled and, even in the act of making the barrier, altered its ecology and hence agricultural potential. It drove agricultural progress and improvement, especially in the eighteenth and nineteenth centuries when the term designated a recognized movement arising from enclosure;

- laid a claim to land and modelled social relations within the landscape. In this guise there were three types of enclosure:

  - **informal**, a matter of land-grabbing. This might be as creeping defiance, called **encroachment** as when mediaeval cottagers ate into the roadside; or by the powerful asserting their strength;

  - **formal**, of which there are two modes:

  - **private agreement** between landowners. One might buy adjacent plots to enlarge an estate, called **engrossment**. Many early enclosures of commonlands, pastures and manorial wastes were by private agreement, but few records remain;

  - **parliamentary Act**, historically first **private**, later **General Act**. Private Acts of Parliament were largely concerned with the drainage and enclosure of marshes. Enclosure Commissioners were authorized to issue awards without submitting them to Parliament for approval. Under General Act manorial wastes and lands subject to indefinite rights of common were excluded but included in later general acts that were passed annually. After 1845 Commissioners were empowered to authorize enclosures only on condition that land was set aside for allotment use. This was the first enshrinement of the basic concept of the present allotment movement.

enclosure allotment a parcel of land large or small allotted to an individual on Parliamentary Enclosure of a common or open field. Sometimes, if rarely, the allotment made at Parliamentary Enclosure was for garden allotments (**Litcham, Swaffham**).

farming to halves see *share cropping.*

farmers clubs and associations
Richard Noverre Bacon, Farm Manager for Earl Leicester of Holkham, presented his prize-winning *Report on the Agriculture of Norfolk* to the Royal Agricultural Society in 1844, in which he described the five farmers' clubs in Norfolk. Farmers' clubs were formed in the rest of England at the beginning of the nineteenth century in order to discuss and disseminate ideas and innovation in, for example, agricultural practice at a time of great change, when 'improvements', including mechanization, were afoot and when adverse climate put a brake on production and turned farmers' minds to new stratagems to maintain their income.

Bacon identified the five clubs as follows:

- Harleston, founded 1838 "and one of the earliest in the country";

- Watton, founded 1839;

- Stoke Ferry, founded 1840;
- Blofield, founded 1840;
- North Walsham, founded 1841.

Each club had a "good library and an Autumn Root Show for prizes".

In 1844, Bacon informs us, the chief topic was manuring, an ancient and fundamental issue for the farmer but this included "artificial", ie chemical, manures. These included guano, bone dust, nitrate of soda, gypsum, urate and sulphates of ammonia and soda.

Bacon characterized the clubs:

"Farmers' Clubs furnish the link which by uniting speculative theory and practical knowledge with just so much of sociableness as secures the free interchange of thought and opinion, reconciles the anomalies which at first appear to exist. The members read in companionship, speculate in companionship, experimentalize in companionship; and in the Reports of the five Norfolk Clubs, we have examples of the manner in which different classes of minds will produce each its peculiar good. The **Harleston**, as the first founded, is the most cautious and practical [which did not in june 1843 prevent the Club from strongly recommending cottage allotments, as the Report of the Harleston Farmers' Club shows] ; the Watton, convened in a district of more advanced cultivation, is more decided; the Stoke Ferry follows in the same track; the North Walsham is the boldest in experiment; the Blofield the most scientific. But all conduce to the same end, the extension of knowledge – the diffusion of liberal opinion and unfettered discussion – and the dispersion of those prejudices which formerly lay like a mist over the land, and concealed the extent of that fertility which science would seem to render inexhaustible".

Optimistic times.

Bacon also described two agricultural associations in Norfolk. The West Norfolk Agricultural Society founded in 1834 whose President was the Earl of Leicester was a reconstitution of the earlier Norfolk Association. The East Norfolk Agricultural Association was founded in 1842 by Lord Wodehouse Lord Lieutenant of the County. The Societies' objects were "mutual instruction and improvement" in both arable and stock farming. Their membership was low and their impact at that time appears to have been limited (Ward p60).

field gardens They 'were enshrined in law by the General Enclosure Act 1845 which required parishes to allot field gardens at enclosure and to appoint Allotment Wardens who would be a mixture of parochial authorities and elected members' (Ashby, p13). The term was taken over by the Act since prior to 1845 it referred to garden allotments on sites not adjoining the settlement. In Norfolk plots on these sites may have been of the standard, quarter-acre or multiples (**Potter Heigham**).

fuel allotments Awarded at enclosure, these were parts of the **wastes** allocated to former commoners on which they were allowed to forage for fuel. An example is Lolly Moor in **Westfield**.

garden allotment see *allotment*.

guinea gardens 'named after the yearly rent, were set up for the middle classes in Birmingham, Coventry and Sheffield from the eighteenth century for recreation as well as food production' (Clifford and King, p9).

lammas lands Lammas Day is 1 august, and is the day by which the harvest has been gathered. Once the hay was in peasants had the customary right to use the common meadow and when their turn came round or they drew an entitling lot in the shape of a specially marked apple or piece of wood they could grow a crop on part of the meadows themselves (see *dole*).

leisure gardens
Combining the words 'leisure' and 'garden' is for some a tautology and for others an oxymoron. In the context of allotments it is a technical term, for distinguishing the purpose of renting a piece of land of allotment size from that of growing produce.

A leisure, or pleasure, garden is a rented plot in an urban area on which flowers are grown, for the pleasure of growing them and for their enjoyment once grown. Often the dilapidated garden shed has been foresworn for a summer-house to enhance the garden and from which it can be admired. The idea was promoted with enthusiasm by the Thorpe Report of 1969 , a government commission which investigated the role of traditional allotments and recommended ways of improving urban spaces and urban lives; Thorpe had travelled throughout Europe and was impressed with the commitment of flat-dwellers in Germany and Holland who often had to travel some miles to their plots in order to tend them and refresh themselves through contact with nature; they had become a form of weekend retreat, almost a second home, in many cases. Thorpe was influenced especially by the danish designer Carl Theodor Sorenson who, in 1948, planted a garden colony of fifty hedged ovals as "gardens … like small green oases where the individual's leisure life can blossom within a community".

But there are english precedents. A Leisure Gardens Unit was established at Birmingham University in the mid-1970s, following the discovery of the Edgbaston *guinea gardens*. An International Leisure Gardens Federation Congress was held there in 1976. More recent discoveries include a group of gardens, each surrounded by a privet hedge, in Warwick and seven sites of more than a hundred plots in west Cambridge were occupied between 1830 and 1925. They were created on building land enclosed in 1802 by act of parliament which had remained vacant; the colleges were landlords and from 1830 allowed their servants to use the plots rent-free; and later the privilege was extended to artisans and tradespeople who, in view of their status, paid rent. When the 1897 Allotments Act was passed, tenants were given rights to their plots ; the colleges gradually reclaimed the land for building.

What chiefly distinguished the leisure garden from the allotment is the emphasis on flowers and cultivation for pleasure, rather than a practical purpose. As with all matters linked to allotments there is blurring: in Cambridge the gardens were occupied by members of florists' societies for developing cultivars; and fruit, as well as flowers, were grown by some (Brown and Osborne, pp95–108).

mere a strip of unploughed turf.

parish gardens Yet another name for **allotments**, used in the 'Town and Gown' rent book for Foulsham ?1820–45.

pightle A word now associated with lanes, as in Pightle Way in Reepham, where formerly there were allotments. The sage of Reepham, Bernard Frankland, understood a pightle to be a small triangular piece of land, impractical for ploughing. The aerial photo of **Harleston** shows a pightle.

poor's allotments A term first recorded in an enclosure Act of 1806 for Wiltshire, when the *waste* and *commons* would have become inaccessible to the commoners. These lands would have been an important source of fuel, either as sticks to be gathered, furze to be grown and cut, or dug if turves of peat. To compensate for this loss land might be allotted to replace the resource but much more likely was land managed by the parish and rented out, the income used to provide, usually, fuel as coal or often bread for the poor on prescribed days of the year.

potato clamps or *pies* 'In years gone by, when cottages had good sized gardens in which families could grow most if not all of their vegetables, they very rarely had enough frost-proof shed room to store all their potatoes as well as everything else in the winter so they would store their main crop potatoes in a clamp in the garden which, if constructed well, kept potatoes in good condition until they were needed for use. In fact I have known apples stored in the same way…The potatoes would be built into a cone-shaped heap…preferably sheltered from the east wind…the heap would be covered with straw to keep out the light which would send the potatoes green. [This could be prevented by storing some apples with the potatoes.] The straw would then be held in place with a few spadefuls of soil…except for a small area at the very top which was left for a ventilator…In those days potato clamps were part of the garden scene during the winter months' (George, p32). The same device was used, still is, to store beet or swede or carrots in fields.

potato grounds or ***lands*** 'The use of roadside verges as waste grounds of potential usefulness was not lost on one reformer who wished to see "in newly-enclosed parishes where the public roads have been awarded sixty feet wide about one-third might be apportioned to the use of the poor" (Rockcliffe, pp213–4). Here a poor man could graze a cow, cut hay and plant potatoes' (Richardson, p170). Farm workers might use a corner of a field that the plough could not reach if the farmer was amenable, sometimes in exchange for goods in kind. They might be strategically placed to deter predators, like rabbits. One generous landowner in Booton still allows his gardener to dig a patch of potatoes in an unused corner of his land, and when the gardener dug up his crop he did the same for the landowner and would not be paid for the labour. The essential difference between a potato ground and allotment is that the former is temporary.

share cropping or ***farming*** the practice of renting land to farm where at least part of the rent is in kind, this was commonplace up to the eighteenth century and persisted in some arrangements involving potato grounds.

smallholding the practice of renting a piece of land of a few acres for commercial purposes. When the produce from allotments could legally be sold (to 1922), the distinction between an allotment and a smallholding was one of size; technically (from 1908) a smallholding is not more than five acres. Currently smallholdings are becoming fashionable as a new 'back to the land' wave occurs (*Guardian* supplement 6 august 2005), sometimes linked to farmers' markets or to outlets that specialize in local and often organic food.

At the start of the twentieth century Hevingham was a village in which the practice of combining a number of trades, most of them connected with the land, made subsistence in relative isolation possible. Between the Wars Hevingham people were known as 'little-doers', because they combined being farmers with other occupations:

'Most of the people in Hevingham got a living, "little-doers" we called them. There were farmers, bakers, butchers, broomtiers, carpenters and wheelwrights, grocers, shoemakers and blacksmiths' (Benton, p165).

If they were farmers, like the author's father, they had often started if not continued in a small way, with a few acres, perhaps rented as a smallholding from Norfolk County Council (Benton, p14). The pattern was to keep chickens, a cow for milk and butter, a sow and perhaps breeding ponies. They would grow vegetables, turnips, potatoes and carrots, for sale.

'Being a smaller farm than the one we left, my father had to farm more intensively and he started a round in Norwich with chickens and vegetables every Saturday...My mother usually went with him, and I can well remember sitting between my parents with a rug over our knees, and on a not too comfortable seat. We jogged along about nine miles into Norwich. The main Cromer road used to be full of horses and carts of all descriptions as Hevingham was nearly all smallholders and broomtiers. I have seen as many as twenty carts come past our farm, loaded with potatoes and carrots, and in lots of cases brooms' (Benton, p15).

Benton's father and he himself invested most of their land in growing blackcurrants, for which there was a particularly heavy demand from 1914 and through the inter-War years (p97, pp138–9). Although Benton made no mention of it Hevingham's allotment site of seventeen acres and 34 plots dates back to 1922.

spade husbandry

'Oh, the incredible profit by digging of ground! For though it is confessed that the plough beats the spade out of distance for speed...yet what the spade wants in the quantity of ground it manureth, it recompenseth with the plenty of the fruit it yieldeth...'Tis incredible how many poor people in London live thereon so that in some seasons gardens feed more poor people than the field' (Thomas Fuller, *The Worthies of England* 1662).

From 1770s onwards philanthropic landowners sought ways of alleviating the distress of the agricultural poor; this was one such remedy. In a pamphlet of 1837 *Some account of employment of spade husbandry, with remarks on the utility of that practice when agricultural labour is superabundant*, John Yelloly FRS set out details of the system.

Instead of ploughing land, farmers should employ men – more than would be needed to work the land conventionally – to cultivate with spades or forks. It involved digging to a depth far greater than the plough could reach. The benefits for the farmer were that land could be brought into production that the plough would not manage; and with an extraordinary seven-year rotation more of it would yield, with better yields than otherwise. In the medium term it was anticipated that the poor-rate would be reduced, so that the farmer's profit stayed in his pocket.

Around 1844 a detailed pamphlet was produced by James Henry Kent MRCSL *Remarks on the injuriousness of the Consolidation of Small Farms and the Benefits of Small Occupations and Allotments: with some observations on the past and present state of the Agricultural Labourers.* Based on the experience of his own village of Stanton in north Suffolk where in October 1842 44 acres of land had been allotted to about 95 parishioners. Advocating the combination of allotments and spade husbandry, he set out a detailed programme for the system and enumerated sixteen benefits.

spong or **spang** a long narrow strip of land separating two fields. When not required as a green lane it could be cultivated by the agricultural labourer for his own use. In the parish of Howe in Norfolk where cottages have a piece of land attached, one property 'still possesses a spong – a long narrow strip of land on which the occupants were originally intended to subsist' (from the Clerk to the Parish Meeting 25 february 2004).

surveyors' allotments 'Before tarmac was used roads were built and repaired from local material. Most villages had their own supply in the form of a stone, sand or even clay pit…They were known as Surveyors' Allotments as the Road Surveyor for the area had access to the material…When men were out of work the best they could hope for was two or three days a week digging or cutting material out of these pits ready for carting out. The number of days work they were awarded varied according to the size of their dependent family. Alternatively they were detailed to hoe mud off the roads in the winter months.

'The Surveyor would then hire someone from the village with a horse and cart to haul the material and tip it where it was needed to repair the potholes. The roadman would then repair the road with his hand tools. He would also keep the grips and roadside ditches clear to drain the roads and in summer mow the verges back all round the village' (George, p36).

terrier register of land, indicating its ownership.

town garden yet another name for **allotment**. In march 1909 the diary of William Cullen describes his acquisition of one in Bury St Edmunds and of his pleasure in it (Percival, p240).

verges Still an important feature of some roads and lanes in Norfolk, they were sometimes used as **potato grounds.** 'In south-east Norfolk 'narrow' or 'street' commons and greens are visible remnants of a linear network of grazing verges' (Clifford and King, p420). They persist as green lanes throughout the county and were a feature of Fenland intercommoning (Birtles/3, pp177–9).

wastes associated with **commons**, the wastes of a parish were the marginal uncultivable lands, including fens, marshes and heaths.

yard small piece of land, allotment.

references

Authors named in bold make up the **bibliography.**

ANDREWS, Sophie *The allotment handbook* **(eco-logic books 2001)**

ARCHER, John E/1 *Social unrest and popular protest in England 1780–1840* **(Cambridge University Press 2000)**
/2 *'By a flash and a scare': arson, animal maiming and poaching in East Anglia 1815–1870* **(Clarendon Press Oxford)**
/3 *The nineteenth century: half-an-acre and a row* **(Economic History Review, Vol.50, (1997) pp21–36)**

ASHBY, Arthur W *Allotments and Smallholding in Oxfordshire: a survey* (Oxford 1917)

BACON, F Essay: *of the greatness of kingdoms and estates* (Blackie 1905)

BACON, R N *Report on the agriculture of Norfolk*, presented to the Royal Agricultural Society in 1844. It won the annual prize. R N Bacon was the Farm Manager of Thomas Coke, the Earl of Leicester

BENNETT, Nell *All year round – an allotment diary* (Mullett Press 1992)

BENTON, E O *Man and boy in a norfolk village* (1981)

BIRTLES, Sara /1 *Common land, poor relief and enclosure: the use of manorial resources in fulfilling parish obligations 1601–1834* (Past and Present 165, november 1999)
/2 *The impact of commons registration: a Norfolk study* (Landscape History 83–98)
/3 *'A green space beyond self-interest': the evolution of common land in Norfolk c 750–2003* (unpublished doctoral thesis for Centre for East Anglian Studies University of East Anglia march 2003)

BOURNE, George *Change in the village* (Duckworth 1912)

BRIGGS, Asa *Go to it: working for victory, or the Home Front 1939–45* (Mitchell Beazley 2000)

BRITTAIN, Vera *Testament of Youth* (Victor Gollancz 1933)

BROWN, Jane *The pursuit of paradise* (Harper Collins 1999)

BROWN, Jane and OSBORNE, Audrey *We shall have very great pleasure: nineteenth century detached leisure gardens in west Cambridge* (The Garden, Journal of the Royal Horticultural Society spring 2003).

BUCHAN, Ursula *By the Grace of God* (The Garden (journal of the Royal Horticultural Society) Vol 130 part 12 (2005), pp888–893)

BURCHARDT, Jeremy *The Allotment Movement in England 1793–1873* **(Royal Historical Society 2002)**

BURCHARDT, Jeremy and COOPER, Jacqueline (eds) *Breaking new ground: 19th century allotments from local sources* **(FACHRS Publications (forthcoming))**

CALDER, Angus *The People's War* (1969)

CAPP, Bernard *Separate domains? women and authority* in *The experience of authority in early modern England* (eds Paul Griffiths, Adam Fox and Steve Hinde (Macmillan 1996))

CARNALL, Luci *What is the meaning of having an allotment for under thirty-five year olds?* (unpublished MSc in Health Through Occupation, University of Brighton Faculty of Health, School of Health Professions, 3 october 2003)

CATTERMOLE, Paul *Shimpling* (1998)

CLIFFORD, Sue and KING, Angela *England in Particular: a celebration of the commonplace, the local, the vernacular and the distinctive* (Hodder & Stoughton for Common Ground, 2006)

COBBETT, William *Rural Rides* (London 1830, Penguin edition 1967)

COLLING, Angela *Earth and life: the dynamic earth Table 4.3* (Open University Press 1997)

CORBISHLEY, Gill *Ration Book Recipes* (English Heritage 1990)

CRADDOCK, Gerald *Dig for Victory* (NSALG Magazine 2006 Issue 1 pp19–20)

CROUCH, David *The art of allotments-culture and cultivation* (Five Leaves 2003)

CROUCH, David and RIVERS, Peter *Survey of allotments, community gardens and city farms: Urban Research Summary No 23* (University of Derby september 2006 (www.communities.gov.uk))

CROUCH, David & WARD, Colin *The Allottment: its landscape and culture* (Five Leaves 1997)

DEWEY, P E *British agriculture in the First World War* (Routledge & Kegan Paul 1989)

DIGBY, Anne Pauper Palaces (Routledge & Kegan Paul 1978)

DOWNHAM MARKET AND DISTRICT AMENITY SOCIETY *History of Downham Market* (Downham Market Society 1999)

EDWARDS, George, MP OBE *From Crow-scaring to Westminster – an autobiography* (Labour Publication Company Ltd 1922)

ELLER, George (ed) *Memorials, archaeological and ecclesiastical of the West Winch manors, from the earliest ages to the present period* (Kings Lynn 1861)

EVANS, George Ewart *The farm and the village* (Faber & Faber 1974)

EVANS, Nesta (ed) *Aspects of Diss History* (Diss Museum Trustees 1994)

FITTON, R S and WADSWORTH, A P *The Strutts and Arkwrights 1758–1830* (Manchester University Press 1958)

FOLEY, Caroline *Practical allotment gardening* (New Holland 2002)

FROSTICK, Raymond *Printed plans of Norwich 1558–1840* (self-publication 2002)

FRY, Mary Joan *Friends lend a hand in alleviating unemployment – the story of a social experiment extending over 20 years, 1926–1946* (Friends' Book Centre, 1947)

FULLER, Thomas *The worthies of England* (1662)

FURNER, Brian *Food crops from your garden* (Pan 1976)

GEORGE, Ron *The time of the bittern: reflections of life in a Norfolk village* (Desne Publishing 1994)

GIRARDET, Herbert *The gaia atlas of cities* (Gaia Books Ltd 1992)

GRIFFITHS, Mark *A century in photographs 1900–2000* (The Times 2000)

HAGGARD, H Rider /1 *A farmer's year, being his commonplace book for 1898* (Longman's Green & Co 1899) in LEIGHTON
/2 *Rural England* (Longman 1906, vol 2)

HAINES, Cicely/1 Letter to Norfolk Recorders 10 january 2006, attaching *Bluebell Model Allotments and Gardens Association: Norwich allotment provision and administration – some historical dates*
/2 *Bluebell Sheds – History 1924–2004, with maps, photos and scale drawings of the sheds and the site and Request sent to English Heritage for listed-building status for the sheds*

HALES, Jane *Norfolk places* (Boydell Press, 1975)

HALL, Sir Daniel *The future of our farming* (Countryman Vol XXIII No 2 1941 pp266–72)

HALL, George W *Food in wartime* (G Bell and Sons, 1914)

HALL, T H /1 *The law of allotments* (London 1886)
/2 *The Allotment Acts* (London, 1888)

HELLYER, A G L *Wartime gardening for home needs* (Collingridge, 1942)

HOLLAND, Michael (ed) *Swing unmasked – the agricultural riots of 1830–1832 and their wider implications* (FACHRS Publications 2005)

HOLOWELL, Steven *Enclosure Records* (Phillimore, 2000)

HOWARD, Ebenezer *Garden Cities of Tomorrow* (Faber & Faber 1902)

HOWKINS, Alun *Poor labouring men: rural radicalism in Norfolk 1870–1923* (Routledge & Kegan Paul 1985)

HURTWOOD, Lady Allen of *How allotments could be made an asset to the community* (1938)

HULME, Mike and BARROW, Elaine (eds) *Climates of the British Isles present, past and future, Table 13.7 and Appendix D1 and D2* (Routledge & Kegan Paul 1997)

HYPE, Michael *City fields, country gardens* (Five Leaves 1998)

KEBBEL, T E *The agricultural labourer* (Swan Sonnenschen 1907)

KNIGHTS, Mark *Highways and byways of old Norfolk* (Jarrold 1807)

JACKSON, Dr Andrew *National farm survey 1941–3 – land-use and tenure in England and Wales* (County War Agricultural Committee commission)

JESSOPP, Rev August *Arcady for better or worse* (Unwins 1887)

LEAPMAN, Michael *One man and his plot* (John Murray 1976)

LEE, Robert *Unquiet country: voices of the rural poor 1820–1880* (Windgather 2005)

LEIGHTON, Clare *A calendar of english husbandry* (Collins 1933)

LEIVERS, Clive *The provision of allotments by employers in Derbyshire* (paper for the FACHRS Conference on Communities in the Countryside 21.5.2005)

LISTER, Richard Percival *Allotments* (Silent Books 1991)

LLOYD PRITCHARD Muriel F *Norfolk Friends' Care of their Poor 1700–1850* (Journal of the Friends' Historical Society, 1947)

MARWICK, Arthur *The Home Front: the british and the Second World War* (Thames & Hudson *1976)*

MAY, Trevor *Agricultural and rural society in Great Britain 1846–1914* (Archive Series for Arnold 1973)

MEERES, Frank *A history of Norwich* (Phillimore 1998)

MILES, David *The tribes of Britain* (Weidenfeld & Nicholson, 2005)

MINISTRY OF RECONSTRUCTION (His Majesty's Stationery Office 1918)

MORRISON, Herbert *An Autobiography* (1960)

MORSON, Maurice *A city's finest* (1992)

MOZELLE, Boaz *Allotments, enclosure and proletarianization in early nineteenth century southern England* (Economic History Review XLVIII, 3(1995) pp482–500)

NATIONAL ALLOTMENTS SOCIETY *The model allotment* (National Allotments Journal No 33, Autumn 1937 pp12–15)

NATIONAL SOCIETY OF ALLOTMENT AND LEISURE GARDENERS *A brief history of the allotment movement* (NSALG Ltd, received june 2004)

NELSON, G K *Over the farmyard gate* (Alan Sutton 1995)

NOBLE, Claire *Norwich Cathedral Priory gardeners' accounts 1329–1530* in *Farming and gardening in late mediaeval Norfolk* (Norfolk Record Society LXI 1997)

NORTH NORFOLK DISTRICT COUNCIL *Open Space and Recreation Study* (final draft published 7 october 2005, researched and produced by Atkins)

OWELL-SMITH, S *Edwardian England 1901–14* (Oxford University Press 1964)

OPPERMAN, Chris *Allotment folk* (New Holland 2004)

PAINE, Thomas *Agrarian Justice, opposed to agrarian law and to agrarian monopoly; being a plan for meliorating the condition of man, etc.* (editor M Philip in *Rights of Man, Common Sense and other political writings* (Oxford 1995))

PERCIVAL, Elise *Arts and crafts influences in east anglian gardens: gardens and gardening in Norfolk and Suffolk*, chapter 5 *Gardens of the working class* (unpublished doctoral thesis, CEAS UEA 1999)

PERRONE, Jane *Allotment Keeper's Handbook* (Atlantic Books for Guardian Newspapers 2007)

PHILP, Mark *Paine* (Oxford University Press 1989)

PIERCY, Wesley *My town – essays on the history of Reepham* (The Reepham Society, 2007)

PIKE, Alastair and PIKE, Anne *The Home Front in Britain 1939–45* (Tressel Publications 1985)

POOLE, Steve /1 *MAFF* (NSALG Magazine 2005 Issue 2 pp15–16)
/2 *'Great War' gardeners* (NSALG Magazine 2002 Issue 1 pp27–8)
/3 *Victory Diggers* (NSALG Magazine 2002 Issue 2 p26)
/4 *Post-war discord* (NSALG Magazine 2003 Issue 1 pp28–9)
/5 *Hail Caesar* (NSALG Magazine 2006 Issue 1 pp16–17)
/6 *Landmark year* (NSALG Magazine 2006 Issue 2 pp16–17)
/7 *Common ground* (NSALG Magazine 2002 Issue 3 p22)
/8 *The Allotment Chronicles: a social history of allotment gardening* (Silver Link Book, Nostalgia Collection, 2006)

PORTER, Roy *English society in the eighteenth century* (1982)

QUAKER TAPESTRY SOUVENIR HANDBOOK (Quaker Tapestry Exhibition Charity, obtained 2006)

RAND, Michael *Close to the veg: a book of allotment tales* (Marlin Press 2005)

REYNOLDSON, Fiona *The First World War 1914–18, Book 2: War in Britain* (Heinemann Educational Books, 1988)

RICHARDSON, J *The local historian's enclosures* (1993)

RICHES, Naomi *Agricultural Revolution in Norfolk* (Frank Cass 1967)

ROCKCLIFFE, F *Poor-potatoes-enclosures* (Annals of Agriculture 35 (1800))

ROYAL HORTICULTURAL SOCIETY *The vegetable garden displayed* (9th impression, 1944), and many, many more titles covering the period 1917–1946

RUDÉ, George *Crowd in history* (Wilney 1995)

SERPELL, Michael Friend *A history of the Lophams* (Phillimore 1980)

SHAW, Anthony Batty *Sir Thomas Browne of Norwich* (Browne 300 Committee/Jarrold & Sons Ltd, 1982)

SHAW, G B *The land question* in *Everybody's political what's what* (Constable Co, 1945)

SHELTON, Robin *Allotted time: twelve months, two blokes, one shed, no idea* (Sedgwick Jackson 2006)

SPRINGALL, L Marion *Labouring life in norfolk villages 1834–1914* (George Allen & Unwin 1936)

STAGG, Frank Noel *Salthouse, the story of a Norfolk village* (2002)

STEADMAN. Rex *Vox Populi: the Norfolk newspaper press 1760–1900* (unpublished FLA thesis 1971)

STEINBECK, John *Once there was a war* (1958)

STOKES, Geoff *To sell or not to sell* (NSALG Magazine 2004 Issue 2 pp24–25)

SUDELL, Richard *Practical gardening and food production* (Odhams, 1940)

TATE, W E *Enclosure movement* (Walker & Co, 1967)

THE TIMES *Picture guide to gardens 1900–2000*

THOMPSON, E P/1 *The making of the english working class* (first edition 1963, Penguin 1991)
/2 *Customs in common* (New Press, New York 1993)

THOMPSON, Flora *Lark rise to Candleford* (1945, Reprint Society of Oxford University Press 1948)

THORPE, Harry *Report* on the *Departmental Committee of Inquiry into Allotments* (HMSO 1969)

TITCHMARSH, Alan *Allotment gardeners' handbook* (1993)

TUCKWELL, Rev W *Reminiscences of a radical parson* (Cassell 1905)

UNWIN, George *Samuel Oldknow and the Arkwrights* (Manchester University Press 1924)

WADE-MARTINS, Peter ed. *An Historical Map of Norfolk* (Norfolk Museums Service 1994)

WADE-MARTINS, Susanna /1 *Norfolk a changing countryside 1780–1914* (Phillimore, 1988)
/2 *Changing agriculture in Georgian and Victorian Norfolk* (Poppyland 2002)
/3 *The riots of 1830* in *An historical atlas of Norfolk* (ed Peter Wade-Martins) (Norfolk Museums Service, second edition 1994, pp126–7)
/4 *Farms and fields* (Batsford, 1995)

WARD, Norman *A History of Agriculture in the Parish of Redenhall with Harleston, South Norfolk*, an unpublished essay produced by Norman Ward for Culham College in 1961

WATTS, Richard – letters from Paston Parish Council dated 11 march, 28 march, 25 may and 25 may 1895

WILLIAMSON, Tom *Hedges and walls* (National Trust 2002)

WILT, Alan F *Food for war: agriculture and rearmament in Britain before the Second World War* (Oxford University Press 2001)

WINFREY, Sir Richard *Leaves from my life* (West Norfolk and Kings Lynn Newspaper Co Ltd 1936)

YELLOLY, John FRS *Some account of the employment of spade husbandry* (J Ridgway 1838)

YOUNG, Arthur *A General View of the Agriculture of the County of Norfolk drawn up for the consideration of the Board of Agriculture and Internal Improvement* (David & Charles reprinted 1969)